POLAND,
PAST AND PRESENT

POLAND, PAST AND PRESENT

A Select Bibliography of Works in English

by

Norman Davies

M.A. (Oxon.), M.A. (Sussex), F.R.Hist S.,
Doktor Nauk Humanistycznych (Cracow).
Lecturer in Polish History, SSEES, University of London;
Senior Associate Member,
St. Antony's College, Oxford.

ORIENTAL RESEARCH PARTNERS

Newtonville, 1977

ISBN (cloth) 0 - 89250 - 010 - 7
ISBN (paper) 0 - 89250 - 011 - 5

For a detailed catalogue of our Russian and Polish Biography
Series write to the Editor, Dr. P.H. Clendenning, Oriental
Research Partners, Box 158, Newtonville, Mass. USA 02160

PREFACE

This volume was born more from a historian's despair than from any spontaneous delight in bibliography. It was prompted by the pains of trying to teach Polish history with no proper reading guide either for my students or for myself. It has been compiled in a somewhat amateur fashion, and but for the advice of colleagues, would have contained even more errors and lacunae than those which no doubt have still escaped attention. It is presented in the belief that minor shortcomings cannot spoil the main purpose of opening up the subject to a wide audience for whom Polish history was hitherto remote and inaccessible.

The Bibliography is directed towards the great majority of historical students and scholars who have no knowledge of the Polish language. It is inevitable that work undertaken in western Europe and North America should predominate, but every effort has been made to include the fruits of scholarship in Poland wherever it is available in an international language. It is hoped that it will prove useful not only to historians seeking information on the Polish aspects of their specialist interests, but also to students and general readers in need of guidance on the broader trends.

My thanks are due to Professor Hugh Seton-Watson, who first encouraged me to undertake the project:

to Dr. P.H. Clendenning of ORP whose initiative raised it from the private to the commercial plane:

to Dr. John Screen, Mr. Paul Valois and Mrs. Janina Cunnelly, Librarians at SSEES:

to Mr. John Wall and Mr. Gregory Walker of the Bodleian Library:

to my colleagues, Dr. Paul Skwarczyński, Mr. Paul Falla, Mr. James Clayson, and especially Mr. David Morgan for valuable contributions:

to my stalwart assistants, Messrs David Lowis, Mirek Ostrynski, Michal Nalewajko and Marek Krason, and Richard and Elizabeth Davies, and particularly to Miss Barbara Komoniewska.

SSEES, London University, 1976

NORMAN DAVIES

CONTENTS

CONTENTS

CONTENTS

CONTENTS

INTRODUCTION

Despite Poland's central position in European history, serious study of the subject outside Poland has tended to be rather peripheral. In the main, historians have been content to import their knowledge of East Central Europe from German and Russian distributors without questioning the credentials under which it was marketed.

Nowadays, in a fast-changing Europe, traditional interpretations are bound to be questioned. The old *Machtgeschichte* is defunct. Prussia has ceased to exist. The attitudes of the USSR as inherited from Tsarist Russia are as obsolescent as the fiercely nationalist viewpoints which they have usually provoked in response. In this context, Polish history will have an increasingly important place in the re-integration of European history as a whole.

Until recently, the linguistic and technical obstacles facing Western scholars interested in the history of Poland were all but insuperable. Apart from the partial studies of German and Russian historians, the subject had fallen prey to a host of tendentious and eccentric interests - political, ideological, party, national and minority. Foreign historians only intervened at points of special concern - the Italians in Renaissance studies, for instance, the French in the Revolutionary period, the Anglo-Saxons hardly at all. No general bibliography was available to anyone unfamiliar with the Polish language.

Fortunately, the situation is gradually improving. The output of a large historiographical industry in Poland is increasingly presented in international languages. Excellent work is being undertaken in Germany, where the re-examination of past attitudes to Eastern Europe has of necessity been most rigorous. Above all in Great Britain and the USA a steady stream of academic monographs and articles is beginning to fill the gaps which have yawned for so long. It is the aim of this Bibliography to present a guide to this disparate but surprisingly copious material.

Bias, of course, continues to be a prominent feature of most writing on Polish history, and the compiler obviously cannot answer for the objective merit of the items included. Before judging a work, it goes without saying that the reader should look twice at the author, and at the date and place of publication.

The Bibliography is primarily concerned with works in English. Items in French, German or Italian have been included only when nothing comparable in English was available.

Both books and articles are included. The former have been collected from numerous catalogues and bibliographies, and notably from the holdings of the Library of the School of Slavonic and East European Studies in London, the latter from a survey of leading historical and Slavic journals published in Britain and North America. No systematic attempt was made to comb German, French or Italian periodicals, and any titles from such sources are confined to windfalls which come the way of a specialist working in the field.

No chronological limits were imposed. The various sections cover the whole of Polish history from the beginnings to the present day. Publication dates reach to December 1975, an 'addenda' section at the end covers works that have appeared up to Autumn, 1976.

In arrangement, practicality has been the touchstone. By organising the material into sections and sub-sections, few of which contain more than thirty items and most of which contain less than a dozen, it is intended that the titles relevant to any particular subject can be found at a glance; and by appending a cross-reference system at the end of each sub-section, it is hoped to overcome the injustices of classification. The 'guide' entries which precede each main section indicate the principal landmarks.

Selection is inevitably arbitrary, and omissions are bound to occur. Some of these are deliberate - such as that of historical novels or of wartime propaganda pamphlets. Others will only become apparent, to the compiler's mortification, in due course. At all events, the general reader should have more than enough to satisfy his curiosity, and the specialist an adequate basis from which to prime his further reading.

The description of items and the abbreviations follow a style devised by the publisher. Page references for articles and single volumes are usually included, except where there may be some doubt in titles not personally inspected.

The 'List of Abbreviations and Periodicals' is provided to check abbreviated titles in the text of the Bibliography, and to facilitate the task of finding periodicals in certain catalogues which list them under the place of publication. It has been supplemented by Appendix I, which lists all the main periodicals relevant to Polish history, regardless of language of publication. Two further appendices are designed to guide the reader over two more frightening obstacles, namely Polish terminology and Polish place names. Even in works written in English, historians are apt to use Polish terms with no simple English equivalent. The Glossary (Appendix II) lists some fifty terms of this sort which are frequently encountered. It is also quite difficult to find one's way round the maze of unfamiliar Polish place-names, many of them with changing applications and almost all with confusing foreign variants. The Gazeteer (Appendix III) lists the more common ones, divided into 1) Provinces and 2) Towns and Cities.

Readers who have no access to a major university or national library may find difficulty in tracing some of the specialised material. In such cases, application can be made at local libraries to obtain books and periodicals through the inter-library loan scheme. Readers in Poland should enquire about such facilities at the British Council Library, Aleje Jerósolimskie, 59, Warsaw.

ABBREVIATIONS

ABSEES   Soviet and East European Abstract Series   (Glasgow)
Acta Baltico-Slavica   (Białystok)
Acta Historiae Artium Academiae Scientarum Hungaricae   (Budapest)
AHRF   Annales Historiques de la Revolution Française   (Rheims, etc.)
AHY   Austrian History Yearbook   (Boulder, Colorado)
American Political Science Review   (Baltimore)
Am HR   American Historical Review   (New York)
Annales [:Economies, Sociétés, Civilisations]   (Paris)
Annali della Fondazione Italiana per la Storia Amministrativa   (Milan)
Annuaire de l'Institut de Philologie et d'Histoire Orientales et Slaves   (Brussels)
Antemurale   (Rome)
Antiquity   (Gloucester/Cambridge)
APH   Acta Poloniae Historica   (Warsaw)
Archiv für Reformationsgeschichte   (Leipzig/Gutersloh)
Armenian Review   (Boston)
Army Quarterly   (London)
AUAAS   Annals of the Ukrainian Academy of Arts and Sciences in the United States   (New York)
Bibliothèque d'Humanisme et Renaissance   (Paris/Geneva)
BIHR   Bulletin of the Institute of Historical Research   (London)
Bull. de la Société de l'Histoire du Protestantisme Français   (Paris)
Bulletin International de l'Académie Polonaise des Sciences et des Lettres   (Cracow)
Bull. Pol. Inst.   Bulletin of the Polish Institute of Arts and Sciences in America   (New York)

Cah.Hist.Mond.   Cahiers d'Histoire Mondiale   (Paris/Neuchatel)
Cahiers Pologne - Allemagne   (Paris)
Cambridge Econ. Hist of Europe
Canadian Journal of Economics and Political Science   (Kingston/Toronto)
Catholic Historical Review   (Washington)
Central European Federalist   (New York)
CHJ   Cambridge Historical Journal   (London)
CHP   Cambridge History of Poland,
C Med.H.   Cambridge Medieval History
CMH   Cambridge Modern History
Connoisseur   (London)
CR Acad. Polonaise   Comptes Rendus de L'Académie Polonaise des Sciences et des Lettres
CSP   Canadian Slavonic Papers   (Revue Canadienne des

Slavistes   (Ottawa)
CSS   Canadian (and American Slavic Studies   (Montreal/Pittsburgh)
Czasopismo   Prawno   -   historyczne   [Annales   d'Histoire   du
   Droit]   (Poznań)
East Europe   (New York)
Ec.HR   Economic   History   Review   (London   etc.,)
EEQ   East European Quarterly   (Boulder, Colorado)
EHR   English Historical Review   (London)
ESR   European Studies Review   (Lancaster)
Europa Orientale   (Milan)

Geografica Polonica   (Warsaw)
Geographical Magazine   (London)
Geography   (London)

Hist.J   Historical Journal   (Cambridge)
History   (London)
Hist.Z   Historische Zeitschrift   (Munich)
HSS   Harvard Slavic Studies   (Harvard)
HT   History Today   (London)
Humanisme et Renaissance   (Paris)

Jb f E d UdSSR   Jahrbuch für Geschichte der UdSSR und der volks-
   demokratischen Länder Europas   (Halle)
JCEA   Journal of Central European Affairs   (Boulder, Colorado)
J Cont. H   Journal of Contemporary History   (London)
JGO   Jahrbuch für Geschichte Osteuropas   (Breslau etc.)
JMH   Journal of Modern History   (Chicago)
Journal of Ecclesiastical History   (London)
Journal of the Royal Asiatic Society   (London)
JSS   Jewish Social Studies   (New York)

Kyrios   [:Vierteljahresschrift   für   Kirchen-und   Geistesgeschichte
   Osteuropas]   (Berlin)

La Cultura   (Milan)
Le Moyen Age   (Paris)
Les Temps Modernes   (Paris)
Lithuanian Quarterly (Lituanus)   (Chicago)

Mediaevalia et Humanistica   (Boulder, Colorado)
Mediaevalia Philosophica Polonorum   (Warsaw)
Mélanges d'Archéologie et d'Histoire publiées par l'Ecole Française de
   Rome   (Paris)
Miscellanea Mediaevalia   (Berlin)
MLR   Modern Languages Review   (London)
Monuments de la Société de l'Histoire et Archéologie de la Bretagne

National Geographic Magazine   (Washington)
NCMH   New Cambridge Modern History
Neues Archiv für sächsische Geschichte   (Dresden)
Nineteenth Century and After   (London)

Nuova Rivista Storica   (Milan)

Oriens   (Leiden)
Österreichische Osthefte   (Vienna)
Oxford Slavonic Papers   (Oxford)

PAN   Polska Akademia Nauk
Past and Present   (Oxford)
Petit Ouvrier de France et de Pologne   (Grenoble)
Polish Perspectives   (Warsaw)
Population   [Revue trimestrielle de l'Institut National d'Etudes
    Démographiques   (Paris)
Population Studies   (London)
PR   Polish Review   (New York)
Proceedings of the Huguenot Society   (London)
Publicationes Institutionis Philologicae et Slavicae Universitatis
    Debreceniensis   (Debrecen)
PWA   Polish Western Affairs   (Poznań)

Recueils de la Société Jean Bodin   (Brussels)
Rev.Hist.   Revue Historique   (Paris)
Rev. Hist. de Droit Fr[ançais] et Etr[anger]   (Paris)
Rev. Hist. Econ. Soc.   Revue d'Histoire Economique et Sociale   (Paris)
Review of Politics   (Notre Dame, Indiana)
Revue Belge de Philologie de d'Histoire   (Brussels
Revue des Etudes Juives   (Paris)
Revue des Etudes Slaves   (Paris)
Revue d'Histoire Moderne et Cont[emporaine]   (Paris)
Revue du Nord   (Lille)
Revue Int[ernationale] d'Histoire Militaire   (Paris)
Revue Int. d'Hist. pol. et const.   Revue Internationale d'Histoire
    Politique et Constitutionelle   (Paris)
RHD   Revue d'Histoire Diplomatique   (Paris)
Ricerche Religiose   (Rome)
Ricerche Slavistiche   (Rome)
Riv. Stor. Ital.   Rivista Storica Italiana   (Turin)
Russian Review   (New York)

Scand.   Econ.   Hist.   Rev.   Scandinavian   Economic   History
    Review   (Stockholm)
Schweizerische Zeitschrift für Geschichte   (Zurich)
SEER   Slavonic and East European Review   (London)
Sov. Jew.Aff.   Soviet Jewish Affairs   (London)
Soviet Studies   (Glasgow)
SR   (American) Slavic (and East European) Review   (Washington)
Standen en Landen [:Anciens Pays et Assemblées d'Etats: études
    publiées par la Section Belge de la Commission Internationale pour
    l'Histoire des Assemblées d'Etats]   (Louvain/Paris)
Studia Hist. Oecon.   Studia Historiae Oeconomicae   (Poznań)
Studies in the Renaissance   (Austin etc.)

ABBREVIATIONS

Survey   (London)

TLS   Times Literary Supplement   (London)
Transactions of the Unitarian Historical Society   (London)
TRHS   Transactions of the Royal Historical Society   (London)

Ukrainian Quarterly   (New York)
Ukrainian Review   (Munich)
University of Birmingham Historical Journal   (Birmingham)

Wiener Archiv [für Geschichte des Slawentums und Osteuropas]   (Graz
    etc.)
World Today   (London)

Zeitschrift für Schweizerische Geschichte   (Zurich)
Zeszyty Naukowc Katolickiego Uniwersytetu Lubelskiego   (Lublin)
Z. für Ost. Zeitschrift für Ostforschung   (Marburg/Lahn)

Abbreviations relating to languages:

(Cz) Czech; (Eng) English; (F) French; (G) German; (I) Italian; (L)
    Latin; (Lat) Latvian; (Lit) Lithuanian; (R) Russian; (Ukr) Ukrainian

A. BIBLIOGRAPHY

The inadequacy of existing bibliographies provides the main justification for the present volume.

The standard works, (**0004**) and (**0036**) assume a knowledge of Polish. Tazbir (**0009**) and Skirowska (**0050**) are confined to postwar scholarship in Poland. Zabielska (**0062**), though exhaustive, is unannotated and non-selective.

Crowther (**0013**) and Shapiro (**0047**) are excellent, but refer only incidentally to Poland. Meyer (**0038**) concentrates on works in German.

The American Bibliography . . . (**0002**), and a German counterpart (**0051**) specifically related to Polish studies, are both in the process of being brought up to date. But Lorentowicz (**0034**) for French scholarship is now nearly forty years old. Tamborra (**0125**) contains some useful bibliographical references to work in Italy.

In Great Britain, ABSEES (**0001**) with its annual biography, should provide a regular supplement for future publications.

The Monthly Catalogue (**0040**) frequently contains important bibliographical items on Poland and East Europe, as do the *Advance Bibliography of Contents* (Periodical) and the *Reference Services Review* (Appendix I).

0001   *ABSEES (Soviet and East European Abstract Series)* University of Glasgow. Vol. 1, no. 1, July 1970 -; (a quarterly publication); contains 'Soviet, East European and Slavonic Studies in Britain: a Bibliography: an annual publication within ABSEES,' compiled by VALOIS, PAUL, CROWTHER, PETER, (1971), vol. 3, no. 1, 1972; (1973) vol. 5, no. 1, 1974.

0002   *American Bibliography of Russian and East European Studies, (1956-)*, Bloomington (Indiana), 1957-.

0003.   BARDACH, J., *Introduction bibliographique de l'histoire du droit et d'ethnologie juridique* (D/12 - 'Pologne'), Bruxelles, 1965, Pp. 74.

0004   BAUMGART, J., GLUSZEK, S., ed., 'Bibliografia Historii polskiej za lata 1944-66', Wrocław-Kraków, 1952-68, (with continuations to 1972).

0005   BAXTER, J.H., *What to Read about Poland*, Edinburgh 1942, Pp. 20.

0006   BEGEY, MARIA AND MARINA, *La Polonia in Italia: Saggio Bibliografico, 1799-1948*, Turin, 1949, Pp. 295.

0007   BESTERMAN, THEO., *A World Bibliography of Bibliographia*, 4 vols, (4th edition), Lausanne, 1965. 'Poland': vol. III, pp. 4906-4936.

0008   BIRKENMAJER, A., *Etudes de l'histoire des sciences en Pologne*, Warsaw, 1972, Pp. 814.

0009   'Bibliographie sélective des travaux des historiens polonais parus dans les années 1945-1968', vol. 2 of *La Pologne au XIII Congrès International des Sciences Historiques à Moscou*, J. TAZBIR, ed., Warsaw, 1970, Pp. 303.

0010   *Bibliographie sur la Pologne Pays, Histoire, Civilisation*, (2nd edition), ('Histoire', pp. 73-117), M. MANTEUFFLOWA, ed., Warsaw, 1964.

0011   CHOJNACKI, W., KOWALIK, J., *Bibliografia niemiecka bibliografii dotyczących Polski 1900-58*, (German Bibliography of Bibliographies concerning Poland), Poznań, 1960.

0012   COLEMAN, MARION M., *Polish Literature in English Translations: a Bibliography*, Cheshire (Conn.), 1963, Pp. 180.

0013   CROWTHER, P.A., *A Bibliography of Works in English on Early Russian History to 1800*, Oxford, 1969, Pp. 236.

0014   DANILEWICZ, MARIA, *The Libraries of Poland*, St. Andrews, 1943, Pp. 63.

0015   DANILEWICZ, MARIA; NOWAK, JADWIGA, *Bibliography of Works by Polish Scholars and Scientists Published outside Poland in Languages other than Polish*, (Polish Society of Arts and Sciences Abroad), London 1964, Pp. 175.

0016   DANILEWICZ, M., JABLONSKA, B., ed., *Catalogue of Periodicals in Polish or Relating to Poland and other Slavonic Countries, Published outside Poland since 1 September 1939*, Polish Library, London, 1971, Pp. 126.

0017   DURKO, J., ed., *Bibliografia Warszawy, 1864-1903*, Warsaw, 1971, Pp. 1880.

0018   EPSTEIN, F., 'A Short Working Bibliography on the Slavs', *S.E.E.R.*, vol. 22, 1944, pp. 110-20.

0019   GÖMÖRI, G., 'Polish Studies - Literature, 1860 to the Present Day', *YWMLS* 1972, 1973, pp. 769-78.

0020   GRZYBOWSKI, K., *Poland in the Collections of the Library of Congress*, Washington, 1968, Pp. 26.

0021   HINDS, A.B., *Descriptive List of State Papers Foreign: Poland, 1586-1661*, Public Record Office, London, 1937, ff. i. + 47.

0022   HORAK, S., *Junior Slavica - Selected, Annotated Bibliography of Books in English on Russia and Eastern Europe*, New York, 1968, Pp. 244.

0023   HORECKY, P.L., ed., *East Central Europe - a Guide to Basic Publications*, (Part 5, Poland) Chicago, 1969, Pp. 956.

0024   HOSKINS, J.W., *Early and Rare Polonica of the 15th-17th Centuries in American Libraries*, Boston, 1973, Pp. 208.

0025   JONES, DAVID LEWIS, *Books in English on the Soviet Union, 1917-73: A Bibliography*, New York, 1974, Pp. 200.

0026   KANET, ROGER, *Soviet and East European Foreign Policy: A Bibliography of English and Russian Language Publications*, Oxford, 1974, Pp. 225; California 1975, Pp. 208.

0027   KERNER, R.J., *Slavic Europe - a Selected Bibliography in Western European Languages* (Part III 'The Poles'), Cambridge, Massachusetts, 1918, Pp. 402.

0028   KERNIG, C.D., ed.,*Marxism, Communism and Western Society: A Comparative Encyclopedia*, 8 vols. New York, 1973. Vol. VI, pp. 318-416, 'Polish Marxism' and bibliography.

0029   KUCZYŃSKA, A.; REMEROWA, K., *Libraries in Poland*, Warsaw, 1961, Pp. 108.

0030   KUKULSKI, L., 'Polish Studies - Literature, From the Beginning to 1860', *YWMLS* 1972, 1973, pp. 754-68.

0031   KUSIELIEWICZ, E., *Bibliography of English Works on East Central European History*, (typescript), New York, 1960.

0032   LACHS, J., *Marxist Philosophy: a Bibliographical Guide*, Chapel Hill, 1967, Pp. 166.

0033   LOBIES, JEAN-PIERRE, ed., *IBN, Index Bio-Bibliographicus, Notorum Hominum*, Osnabrück, 1973. 'Poland': pp. 1625 ff. .

0034   LORENTOWICZ, J., *La Pologne en France: Essai d'une bibliographie raisonnée*, Paris, 1935, vols. 1-3.

0035   MACIUSZKO, ZENY, *The Polish Short Story in English; A Guide and Critical Bibliography; with a foreword by W. J. Rose*, Detroit, Michigan, 1968.

0036   MADUROWICZ-URBAŃSKA, H., ed., *Bibliografia Historii Polski*, vol. 1, (Parts 1-2); vol. 2, (Parts 1-3); Warsaw, 1965-7.

0037   MANTEUFFEL, MARIAN, 'Les bibliothèques scientifiques en Pologne', *A.P.H.*, vol. 3, 1960, pp. 195-206.

0038   MEYER, KLAUS, *Bibliographie zur Osteuropäischen Geschichte*, Berlin, 1972, Pp. xlix + 649.

0039   *Monthly Catalogue of United States Government Publications. Decennial Cumulative Index*, 1951-60, 2 vols., Washington, 1968.

0040   SUPERINTENDENT OF DOCUMENTS, U.S. GOVERN-MENT (Washington, D.C.), *Monthly Catalogue of United States Government Publications*.

0041   MÜLLER, SEPP., *Schriftum über Galizien und sein Deutschtum*, Marburg, 1962.

0042 NERHOOD, H., *To Russia and Return: An Annotated Bibliography of Travellers' English Language Accounts of Russia, from the Ninth Century to the Present*, Columbus, Ohio, 1969.

0043 NOWAK, C.M. *Czechoslovak-Polish Relations, 1918-1939: A Selected and Annotated Bibliography*, Stanford, 1976, Pp. 220

0044 PELENSKY, E., *Ukraina: a Selected Bibliography of the Ukraine in Western European Languages*, Munich 1948, Pp. 111.

0045 PŁOSKI, S. *Bibliografia Historii Polski XIX wieku*, Wrocław, 1958-68, 2 vols..

0046 SENKOWSKA, M., 'Publications sur la période 1770-1830: Bibliographie polonaise', *A.H.R.F.*, vol. 36, 1964, pp. 391-9.

0047 SHAPIRO, D., *A Select Bibliography of Works in English on Russian History, 1801-1917*, Oxford, 1962, Pp. 106.

0048 SHUNAMI, SHLOMO, *Bibliography of Jewish Bibliographies*, Jerusalem, 1969, Pp. 998.

0049 SIEMEŃSKI, JOSEPH, *Guide des archives de la Pologne*, 1. *Archives de la Pologne ancienne: Archives d'Etat*, Warsaw, 1933, Pp. 120.

0050 SKWIROWSKA, STEFANIA, *Bibliographie des travaux des historiens polonais en langues étrangères parus dans les années 1945-68*, (Instytut Historii PAN), Wrocław-Warsaw, 1971, Pp. 91.

0051 STILLER, J., ed., *Schriftum über Polen, (ohne Posener Land), 1961-2 und nachträge*, J.G. Herder Institut, Marburg/Lahn, 1971 (previous 5 vols., 1943-60, RISTER, H. ed.).

0052 STURMINGER, WALTER, *Bibliographie und Ikonographie der Turkenbelagerungen Wiens 1529 und 1683*, [*Veröffentlichungen der Kommission für neuere Oesterreich*], XLI, Graz, 1955.

0053 SULKOWSKA, IRENA, 'Les Archives Centrales des Actes Anciens à Varsovie', *A.P.H.*, vol. 9, 1963, pp. 115-27.

0054 SYMONOLEWICZ, K., 'Studies in Nationality and Nationalism in Poland Between the Two Wars, 1918-1939: a Bibliographical Survey', *Bull. of the Polish Inst. of Arts and Sciences in America*, 1943, pp. 3-73.

0055 SZPORLUK, R., *List of Materials for the Study of the History of Poland: with a note of holdings in the libraries of Stanford University*, Stanford, 1962, Pp. 32.

0056 TABORSKI, B., *Polish Plays in English Translation: a Bibliography*, New York, Polish Institute of Arts and Sciences in America, 1968, Pp. 79.

0057 U.S.A.: LIBRARY OF CONGRESS, -(Slavic division.)*Newspapers of East Central and South Eastern Europe in the Library of Congress*, Washington, 1965, Pp. 204.

0058   VIGOR, P.H., ed., *Books on Communism and the Communist Countries*, London, 1971, Pp. 444.

0059   WEPSIEC, J., *Polish Serial Publications 1953-1962: an Annotated Bibliography*, Chicago, 1964, Pp. 506.

0060   WINTER, N.O., *The New Poland, Books for Libraries*, London, 1972.

0061   WYNAR, L., *Encylopedic Directory of Ethnic Newspapers and Periodicals in the United States*, Littleton, Colorado, 1972.

0062   ZABIELSKA, J., *Bibliography of Books in Polish or Relating to Poland, Published outside Poland, since 1 September 1939*, vols. 1,2,3, etc., Polish Library, London, 1966.

SEE ALSO:

TAMBORRA, (**0125**); WEDKIEWICZ, (**0127**); SCHMELZ,, (**1069**); YARMOLINSKY, (**1217**); AUFRICHT, (**1658**); BIRKOS, (**1660**); *Polish Research Guide*, (**1687**); LEMANSKI, (**1722**); MASON, (**1797**).

B. HANDBOOKS AND REFERENCE WORKS

The historical atlas (**0063**) is an excellent production, and like Tatomir (**0074**), a tabular chronology, Batowski (**0064**), a guide to place names, and Ihnatowicz (**0067**), an extremely useful collection of reference information, can be used by readers with a minimal knowledge of Polish.

The Concise Statistical Yearbook (**0065**) is the successor to 15 previous volumes dating back to 1957-8, and to the pre-war series, 1930-41.

Markert (**0068**) is a sound source of encyclopaedic information since 1918. Schöpflin (**0071**) contains more general, introductory essays, as does Keefe (**1711**).

Baedeker (**0077-9**) are first-rate period pieces. Nagel (**0082**) is marred by misprints; Uszyńska (**0084**) is a massive descriptive record, whilst the *Travel Guide* (**0083**) is detailed and accurate.*Radio Free Europe Research* (Appendix I) presents information based on current Polish sources.

1) GENERAL

0063   *Atlas Historyczny Polski*, ed., CZAPLIŃSKI, W. LADOGÓRSKI, T., (2nd edition), Wrocław, 1970, pp. 54 maps + 54 (text).

0064   BATOWSKI, HENRYK, Słownik Nazw Miejscowych Europy *Środkoweji Wschodniej, xix i xx wieku*, (A Dictionary of the Place Names of Central and Eastern Europe), Warsaw 1954, Pp. 86.

0065   *Concise Statistical Yearbook of the Polish People's Republic*, Central Statistical Office, Warsaw, vols. 1-15, 1959-73. (successor to *The Concise Statistical Yearbook of Poland*, vols. 1-9, Warsaw, 1930-38; vol. 10, 1939-41, Glasgow, 1941, Pp. 160).

0066   *Encyclopédie polonaise*, Lausanne-Paris, (Comité des publications encyclopédiques sur la Pologne à Fribourg en Suisse), 1919-20, vols. 1-3.

0067   IHNATOWICZ, IRENA, *Vademecum do Badan nad Historia*, *xix i xx wieku*, 2 vols., Warsaw, 1967.

0068   MARKERT, W., ed. *Osteuropa - Handbuch: Polen*, Köln-Graz, 1959, Pp. 829.

0069   POLONSKY, ANTONY., 'Libraries and Archives - Poland', *History*, vol. 56 (3), 1971, pp. 408-10.

0070   RETINGER, J.H., *All About Poland: Facts, Figures, Documents*, London 1940, (Revised 1941), Pp. 292.

0071   SCHÖPFLIN, G., ed., *The Soviet Union and Eastern Europe - Handbook*, London, 1970, Pp. 614.

0072 STEBELSKI, A., *Les Archives de la République Populaire de la Pologne*, Warsaw, 1965.

0073 STRAKHOVSKI, L.I., ed., *Handbook of Slavic Studies*, Cambridge, Mass., 1949, Pp. 753.

0074 TATOMIR, A., ed. *Tysiąc Lat Dziejów Polski (A Thousand Years of Polish History)*, Warsaw, 1961, Pp. 428.

0075 WOJCICKA, J., *Polish Abbreviations, a Selective List*, (2nd edition), Library of Congress, Washington, 1957, Pp. 164.

0076 WÜNDERLICH, E., ed., *Handbuch von Polen*, Leipzig, 1917, Pp. 463.

SEE ALSO;

MELLOR, **(0396)**; *Encyclopedia Judaica* (**1063**); *Peace Handbooks*, (**1631-45**); **KEEFE**, (**1711**); **KOSIŃSKI**, (**1715**); **LEWANSKI**, (**1722**); **WASSERMAN**, (**1766**).

2) GUIDE BOOKS

0077 BAEDEKER, KARL, *Russia, with Teheran, Port Arthur and Peking*, Leipzig, 1914. (Sections 1 and 2, General Government of Warsaw, and Western Russia), pp. 1-84. Reprinted, Newton Abbot, 1971.

0078 BAEDEKER, KARL, *Northern Germany*, (10th Edition), London-Leipzig, 1890.

0079 BAEDEKER, KARL, *Austria-Hungary*, (10th Edition), London-Leipzig, 1905.

0080 LORENTZ, S., *Guide to Museums and Collections in Poland*, Warsaw, 1974, Pp. 361.

0081 *Murray's Hand-book for Northern Europe: Finland and Russia*, London, 1849, Pp. 292.

0082 *Poland* (Nagel's Travel Guides), Geneva, 1964, Pp. 383.

0083 *Poland - A Travel Guide*, (Sport i Turystyka), Warsaw, 1970, Pp. 418.

0084 USZYŃSKA, Z., ed., *Guide to Poland*, Warsaw, 1960, 7 vols..

SEE ALSO:

LOZIŃSKI, (**1019**); KUBIYOVITCH, (**1158**); JEŻEWSKI, (**1181**).

C. HISTORIOGRAPHY

The most convenient introduction is Rose (**0102**). Halecki (**0093**) and Rose (**0103**) debate the main themes running through Polish Historiography. Grabski (**0091**) and Serejski (**0107**) present the two classic schools. Feldman (**0090**) and Handelsman (**0094**) outline pre-war writing. Valkenier (**0109**) (**0110**) treats post-war developments rather unsympathetically. Drzewieniecki (**0088**) and Wereszycki (**0112**) illustrate the problems which occupy historians in Poland at present.

Section 2, 'Foreign Historiography' shows how Polish history has been used by non-Polish historians for purposes of their own. In this field Serejski (**1383**) is an outstanding work.

Items from the collections of Polish contributions to the International Congresses of Historical Sciences at Oslo (1928), Rome (1955), Stockholm (1960), Vienna (1965) and Moscow (1970), are listed separately in the relevant subject sections.

1) POLISH HISTORIOGRAPHY

0085 BACKVIS, C., 'Polish Tradition and the Concept of History', *P.R.* vol. 6, 1961, pp. 125-58.

0086 BISKUP, MARIAN, 'Polish Research Work on the History of the Teutonic Order State Organisation in Prussia', 1945-59, *A.P.H.*, vol. 3, 1960 pp. 89-113; vol. 9, 1964, 59-76.

0087 CIENCIALA, ANNA, 'Marxism and History: Recent Polish and Soviet Interpretations of Polish Foreign Policy in the Era of Appeasement: an Evaluation', *E.E.Q.*, vol. 6, 1972, pp. 92-117.

0088 DRZEWIENIECKI, WALTER, 'The New "HISTORIA POLSKI" of the Polish Academy of Science', in *Studies in Polish Civilisation*, Wandycz, D., ed., New York, 1966, pp. 176-96.

0089 'Etat de Recherches', in, *La Pologne au XII Congrès International des Sciences Historiques à Vienne, Warsaw, 1965*, Section II, pp. 163-399.

0090 FELDMAN, J., 'Historical Studies in Poland', *S.E.E.R.*, vol. 2, 1923-4, pp. 660-66.

0091 GRABSKI, A.F., 'The Warsaw School of History', *A.P.H.*, vol. 26, 1972, pp. 153-70.

0092 HALECKI, O., 'The Moral Laws of History', *Catholic History Review*, vol. 42, 1956-7, pp. 409-40.

✓ 0093 HALECKI, OSCAR, 'Problems of Polish Historiography',

S.E.E.R., vol. 21, 1943, pp. 223-39.

0094 HANDELSMAN, MARCELI; DEMBINSKI, S.; HALECKI, O., *L'historiographie polonaise du XIX et XX siècles*, Warsaw, 1933, Pp. 37.

0095 HERBST, S., 'L'historiographie militaire polonaise,' *Revue Int. d'Histoire Militaire*, 1969, no. 2, pp. 397-402.

0096 KRÓL, MARCIN, 'Szymon Askenazy', *Polish Perspectives*, vol. 17, no. 7/8, 1974, pp. 36-41.

0097 KRUPNYTSKY, B., 'A Critique from the Ukrainian Point of View of the Traditional Division into Periods of Russian History', *Ukrainian Review*, vol. 1, 1954, pp. 5-12.

0098 MĄCZAK, ANTONI, 'The Style and Method of History', *Polish Perspectives*, vol. 16, no. 7/8, 1973, pp. 12-17.

0099 MADUROWICZ-URBANSKA, H., 'Revue des périodiques historiques polonaises', *A.P.H.*, vol. 4, 1961, pp. 195-225.

0100 MANTEUFFEL, T., 'Le rôle de l'Institut d'Histoire de l'Académie Polonaise des Sciences', *A.P.H.*, vol. 1, 1958, pp. 182-5.

0101 POLONSKY, A., 'The History of Inter-war Poland Today', *Survey*, no. 74-75, 1970, pp. 143-59.

0102 ROSE, W.J., 'Polish Historical Writing', *J.M.H.*, vol. 2, 1930, pp. 569-85.

0103 ROSE, W.J., 'Realism in Polish History', *J.C.E.A*, vol. 2, 1942-3, pp. 235-49; continued by HALECKI, OSCAR, 'What is Realism in Polish History?', *J.C.E.A.*, vol. 3, 1943-4, pp. 322-8.

0104 ROSE, W.J., 'Lelewel as Historian', *S.E.E.R.*, vol. 15, 1936-7, pp. 649-62.

0105 ROSE, W.J., *Warsaw Positivism*, London, 1942, Pp. 4.

0106 RUTKOWSKA, N., *Bishop A. Naruszewicz and his 'History of the Polish Nation': A Critical Study*, Washington, D.C, 1941.

0107 SEREJSKI, M.H., 'L'école historique de Cracovie et l'historiographie européenne', *A.P.H.*, vol. 26, 1972, pp. 127-52.

0108 SEREJSKI, M.H., 'Joachim Lelewel (1786-1861)', *A.P.H.*, vol 6, 1962-3, pp. 35-54.

0109 VALKENIER, E., 'The Soviet Impact on Polish Post-War Historiography', *J.C.E.A.*, vol. 11, 1950-52, pp. 372-96.

0110 VALKENIER, E., 'Sovietisation and Liberalism in Polish Post-War Historiography', *J.C.E.A.*, vol. 19, 1959-60, pp. 149-73.

0111 WEINTRAUB, W., 'Aleksander Brückner, 1856-1938', *S.E.E.R.*, vol. 25, 1945-7, pp. 122-33.

0112 WERESZYCKI, H., 'Polish Insurrections as a Controversial

Problem for Polish Historiography', *C.S.P.*, vol. 9, 1967, pp. 107-21.

0113 ZAHORSKI, A., 'L'historiographie militaire polonaise au cours des années 1944-60', *A.P.H.*, vol. 6, 1962, pp. 89-117.

0114 ZIFFER, B., *Poland - History and Historians*, New York, 1952, Pp. 107.

SEE ALSO:

POLONSKY, (**0069**); STEBELSKI, (**0072**); *Historia Polski*, (**0186**); FRUMKIN, (**0256**); GIEYSZTOR, (**0257**); GIETSZTOR, (**0286**); SIMONS, (**0290**); GIEYSZTOR, (**0323**); KURBIS, (**0487**); NIEDERHAUSER, (**0584**); KIENIEWICZ, (**0618**); ROSTWOROWSKI, (**0621**); HANDELSMAN, (**0637**); TAZBIR, (**0846**); MATCZAK, (**0867**); JASIENICA, (**0929**); ŚWIEŻAWSKI, (**0933**); FRIEDMAN, (**1087**); DUNDULIS, (**1121**); BISKUP, (**1128**); LABUDA, (**1254**); SEREJSKI, (**1383**); RYSZKA, (**1560**), SYMPOSIUM, (**1695**).

2) **FOREIGN HISTORIOGRAPHY OF POLAND**

0115 DOROSHENKO, D., 'A Survey of Ukrainian Historiography', *A.U.A.A.S.*, vols. 5-6, 1957.

0116 HRUSHEVSKY, M., 'The Traditional Scheme of "Russian" History and the Problem of a Rational Organisation of the History of the Eastern Slavs', *A.U.A.A.S.*, vol. 2, 1952, pp. 355-64.

0117 JASNOWSKI, J., 'Poland's Past in English Historiography', *P.R.*, vol. 3, 1958-9, pp. 21-35.

0118 JOLL, JAMES, 'Treitschke and the Prussian Legend,' *H.T.*, vol 2, 1952, pp. 186-90.

0119 KRUPNYTSKY, B., 'Bohdan Khmelnytsky and Soviet Historiography', *Ukrainian Review*, vol. 1, 1955, pp.

0120 MANNING, C.A., *A History of Slavic Studies in the United States*, Milwaukee, 1957, Pp. 117.

0121 MOCHA, F., 'The Karamzin-Lelewel Controversy', *S.R.*, vol. 31, 1972, pp. 592-611.

0122 POLOŃSKA-VASYLENKO, NATALYA DMITROVNA, *Two Conceptions of the History of Ukraine and Russia*, London, 1968, Pp. 79.

0123 RHODE, GOTTHOLD, 'The Institute for East European History', *Central Europe Journal*, vol. 22, 1974, pp. 122-5.

0124 RYSZKA, F., 'Poland - Some Recent Revaluations, *J. Cont. H.*, vol. 2, 1967, pp. 107-23.

0125 TAMBORRA, ANGELO, Gli studi di storia dell'Europa Orientale in Italia nell'ultimo ventennio, in *La Storiografia Italiana negli ultimi vent'anni*, Milan, 1969, pp. 991-1043.

0126 WANDYCZ, P., 'The Treatment of East Central Europe in History Textbooks', *S.R.*, vol. 16, 1957, pp. 515-23.

0127 WEDKIEWICZ, STANISLAS, *La Suède et la Pologne: Essai d'une bibliographie des publications Suèdoises concernant la Pologne*, Stockholm, 1918, pp. iii + 112.

0128 WINKLER, H.R., 'Sir Lewis Namier', *J.M.H.*, vol. 35, 1963, pp. 1-19.

SEE ALSO:

HALECKI, (**0226**); NAMIER, (**0157**); KURBIS, (**0487**);, NIEDERHAUSER, (**0584**); GÓRSKI, (**1132**); SEREJSKI, (**1383**); CARLYLE, (**1386**).

D. BIOGRAPHY AND MEMOIRS

This section includes biography, autobiography, memoirs, travel, obituaries, and several accounts of individuals' political activities which could not be conveniently fitted into other sections.

Of the old travellers, Coxe (**0140**) and Johnston (**0148**) are the most informative. Benyowski (**0134**) is highly exaggerated.

Of the literary biographies, a number, especially Gardner (**0143**) are markedly hagiographic. The best are Lednicki on Krasiński (**0152**) and Welsh on Mickiewicz and Krasicki, (**0181**), (**0182**).

For insights into everyday life, Pasek (**0160**) for the seventeenth century, and Slomka (**0173**) for the nineteenth, are unique.

From the mass of modern memoirs, Lednicki (**0153**) is outstanding.

Lady Namier's biography of her husband (**0157**) is of great interest to the historical profession, but contains relatively little about Poland.

0129 ADAMS, DOROTHY, *We Stood Alone*, New York, 1944, Pp. 284.

0130 ANDERSON, H. FOSTER, *What I Saw in Poland - 1946*, Slough, 1946, Pp. 194.

0131 (ANON.) *Jan - Portrait of a Polish Airman by his English Wife*, London, 1944, Pp. 256.

0132 (ANON.), *My Name is Million - (1939)*, London, 1944, Pp. 284.

0133 BARANSKI, JAN, *Mon pays perdu*, (1939-51), Paris, 1956, Pp. 188.

0134 BENYOWSKI, MAURITIUS AUGUSTUS, *Memoirs and Travels* (1746-86), London, 1904, Pp. 636.

0135 BETHELL, N., *Gomułka, His Poland and his Communism*, London, 1969, Pp. 296.

0136 BLIT, LUCJAN, *The Eastern Pretender, Bolesław Piasecki: his Life and Times*, London, 1965, Pp. 223.

0137 BULLOCK, W.H., *Polish Experiences, 1863-4*, London, 1864, Pp. 350.

0138 CAZELET, MAJOR V.H., *With Sikorski to Russia*, London, 1944, Pp. 55.

0139 CAZIN, PAUL., *Le Prince-Évêque de Varmie, Ignace Krasicki, 1735-1801*, Paris, 1940, Pp. 317.

0140 COXE, WILLIAM, *Travels in Poland and Russia*, London, 1802.

0141 CURIE, EVE., *Madame Curie: the Biography by her Daughter*, Translated by V. Sheean, London, 1938, (republished London, 1962, Pp. 411.).

0142 DYBOSKI, R., 'Count Leon Piniński', *S.E.E.R.*, vol. 17 (49), 1938, pp. 212-15.

0143 GARDNER, MONICA, *A. Mickiewicz - the National Poet of Poland*, London, 1911, Pp. 317.

0144 GIELGUD, ADAM, ed., *Memoirs of Prince Adam Czartoryski and his Correspondence with Alexander I*, London, 1888, Pp. 732, (Republished, 1965).

0145 HOTCHKISS, CHRISTINE, *Home to Poland*, London-New York, 1958, Pp. 247.

0146 JACHIMECKI, Z., 'Karol Szymanowski, 1883-1937', *S.E.E.R.*, vol. 17 (49), 1938, pp. 174-85.

0147 JOHNS, J.P., *Kościuszko - a Biographical Study with a Historical Background of the Times*, Detroit, 1965, Pp. 99.

0148 JOHNSTON, ROBERT, *Travels Through Part of the Russian Empire and the Country of Poland, along the Southern Shores of the Baltic*, London, 1816, (Reprinted, 1970).

0149 KELLOG, G., *Jadwiga - Poland's Great Queen*, New York, 1931, Pp. 304.

0150 KOROSTOWETZ, W.K., *The Rebirth of Poland, (1919-28)*, London, 1928, Pp. 317.

0151 LANDAU, R., *Piłsudski, Hero of Poland*, translated by Geoffrey Dunlop, London, 1930, Pp. 286.

0152 LEDNICKI, WACŁAW., *Zygmunt Krasiński, Romantic*

Universalist, New York, 1964, Pp. 228.

0153 LEDNICKI, WACŁAW, *Reminiscences: the Adventures of a Modern Gil Blas during the last War*, The Hague, 1971, Pp. 278.

0154 MALECKA, KATIE, *Saved from Siberia - the True Story of my Treatment at the Hands of the Russian Police*, London, 1913, Pp. 168.

0155 MARSHALL, JOSEPH, *Travels through Germany, Russia and Poland, in the Years 1769 and 1770*, London, 1772, Pp. 254, (Reprinted, London).

0156 MILYUKOV, P., 'Alexander Lednicki', *S.E.E.R.*, vol. 13 (39), 1935, pp. 677-80.

0157 NAMIER, LADY JULIA, *Lewis Namier - a Biography*, Oxford, 1971, Pp. xvii + 347.

0158 d'ORNANO, COUNT, *Life and Loves of Marie Walewska*, London, 1934, Pp. 287.

0159 PADEREWSKI, I.; LAWTON, MARY, *The Paderewski Memoirs*, London, 1939, Pp. 395.

0160 PASEK, JAN CHRYZOSTOM, *Les mémoirs de Jean-Chrysostome Pasek, gentilhomme polonais, 1656-88*, (trans. P. Cazin), Paris, 1929, Pp. 350. (to be published in English translation by Catherine P. Leach, University of California Press, Berkeley).

0161 PILSUDSKA, ALEXANDRA, *Memoirs of Madame Piłsudski*, London, 1940, Pp. 354. (Republished as *Piłsudski*, by Alexandra Piłsudska, New York, 1970.).

0162 PIŁSUDSKI, J., *Memoirs of a Polish Revolutionary and Soldier*, (trans. D.R. Gillie), London, 1931, Pp. 378. (Republished, New York, 1971, Pp. x + 377.)

0163 PIOTRKOWSKI, RUFIN., *My Escape from Siberia*, London, 1863, Pp. 386.

0164 POMIAN, J., ed., *Joseph Retinger: Memoirs of an Eminence Grise*, London, 1972, Pp. 265.

0165 RAWICZ, SLAVOMIR, *The Long Walk*, London, 1956, Pp. 241. [1939-42: apocryphal description of escape from Soviet internment.].

0166 RADZIWIŁŁ, M., *One of the Radziwiłłs*, London, 1971, Pp. 221.

0167 RAINA, PETER, *Gomułka - eine politische Biographie*, Köln, 1970, Pp. 194.

0168 REDDAWAY, W.F., *Marshal Piłsudski*, London, 1939, Pp. xiv + 334.

0169 ROSE, W.J., 'Paderewski, 1860-1941', *S.E.E.R.*, vol. 24 (63), 1946, pp. 66-80.

0170 ROSE, W.J., 'W. Sikorski', *S.E.E.R.*, vol. 23 (62), 1945, pp. 69-79.

0171 ROSE, W.J., 'W. Korfanty, 1867-1939', *S.E.E.R.*, vol. 19, pp. 316-18.

0172 SAPIEHA, VIRGILIA, *Polish Profile (1929-39)*, London, 1940, Pp. 289.

0173 SLOMKA, JAN, *From Serfdom to Self-Government: Memoirs of a Polish Village Mayor, 1842-1927*, (Translated by W. J. Rose), London, 1941, Pp. 275.

0174 STRYIENSKI, CASIMIR, ed., *Memoirs of Countess Potocka (1794-1818)*, London, 1900, Pp. 253.

0175 STYPUŁKOWSKI, Z., *Invitation to Moscow (1939-45)*, (preface by H. Trevor-Roper), London, 1951, Pp. 360.

0176 SZWEJKOWSKI, Z., 'Alexander Świętochowski, 1848-1938', *S.E.E.R.*, vol 19, 1940, pp. 228-36.

0177 VLACH, R., *Mickiewicz - l'exile et le poète*, New York, 1959, Pp. 138.

0178 WASILEWSKA, EUGENIA, *The Silver Madonna (1939-45)*, London, 1970, Pp. 216.

0179 WALISZEWSKI, K., *Marysieńka - Queen of Poland*, (Translated by Mary Lloyd), London, 1898, Pp. 297.

0180 WEIT, ERWIN, *Ostblock Intern - 13 Jahre Dolmetscher für die polnische Partei- und Staatsfuhrung*, Hamburg, 1970, Pp. 274.

0181 WELSH, DAVID, *Adam Mickiewicz*, New York, 1966, Pp. 168.

0182 WELSH, DAVID, *Ignacy Krasicki*, New York, 1969, Pp. 150.

0183 WIERZYNSKI, K., *The Life and Death of Chopin*, New York, 1949, Pp. xvi + 444. (Foreword by Artur Rubinstein).

0184 ZAGÓRSKI, WACLAW, *Seventy Days - (1944)*, London, 1957, Pp. 267.

SEE ALSO:

LELEWEL, (0104), (0108); NAMIER, (0128); WITOS, (0514); LIMANOWSKI, (0516); LIEBERMAN, (0524); DASZYŃSKI,, (0525); RADEK, (0532); LUXEMBURG, (0534); DMOWSKI, (0546); GRABSKI, (0547);HENRY VALOIS, (0580); BATORY, (0583); SOBIESKI, (0599), (0600), (0602), (0603); STANISLAS AUGUSTAS, (0614), (0616), (0620), (0623), (0978); PONIATOWSKI, (0624); KOCHANOWSKI, (0945); COPERNICUS, (0957); BRUCKNER, (0970); KOTTĄTAJ,, (0988); KONARSKI, (0990); STASZIC, (0991); KOŚCIUSZKO, (1193); PULAWSKI, (1196), (1199); PIŁSUDSKI, (1680); MIZWA, (1733); ROSE, (1804); LASSOTA, (1821).

E. GENERAL WORKS

An up-to-date and objective synthesis of Polish history is much needed. Both Gieysztor (**0185**) and Reddaway (**0188**), although containing many excellent contributions, are unwieldy and uneven. The former is marred by poor English, the latter by incomplete editing.

The Polish *Historia Polski* (**0186**) is still unfinished. Unlike the text, its maps, tables and bibliographies do not demand a knowledge of Polish. Despite obvious shortcomings, it compares very favourably with the Soviet '*Istoriya Pol'shi*' (**0187**).

The handiest factual summaries, Jobert (**0206**) and Portal (**0211**), are in French. Halecki (**0204**) is sound, but uninspiring for readers who do not appreciate the nationalist tradition. Roos (**0212**) is reliable, but scanty on earlier periods for which Bain (**0484**) is still valuable. *Encyclopaedia Britannica* (**0198**) is useful but out-of-date. Brandes (**0192**) and Lauen (**0207**) explore psychological factors convincingly. Sharpe (**0216**) is a brilliant personal essay. Syrop (**0217**) has written a popular, assertive volume. Wandycz (**0218**), the senior scholar in the field at present, has confined his recent survey to the nineteenth century.

Most of the other titles can best be described by the place and date of publication. Morfill (**0208**) made the first modern attempt to explain Polish History in England. Dyboski (**0195**) (**0197**) was trying to present the background of a newly independent state. Górka (**0203**), Newman (**0209**), Rose (**0213**), (**0214**) and Schmitt (**0215**) were trying to see beyond wartime catastrophes. Gołzawski (**0202**) is an émigré storybook for children.

Items in **SECTION 3** treat Poland in the context of East Central Europe as a whole. Halecki's two titles here (**0225**), (**0226**) are amongst his best work. Kolarz (**0229**) makes interesting reading. The most recent overall summary is by Palmer (**0230**).

1) MAJOR COMPOSITE WORKS

0185 GIEYSZTOR, A., et al., ed., *History of Poland*, Warsaw, 1968, Pp. 783.

0186 *Historia Polski*, Polish Academy of Sciences, Warsaw, 1957 -, vol. 1 to 1764 (in 3 parts), vol. 2 to 1864 (in 4 parts), vol. 3 to 1918 (in 2 parts), vol. 4 1918-39 (in 2 parts). (in Polish).

0187 '*Istoriya Pol'shi*', USSR Academy of Sciences, Moscow, 1954-65; vol 1 to 1848, vol. 2 1848-1917, vol. 3 1917-1944, vol. 4 1944-1964. (in Russian).

0188 REDDAWAY, W., ed., *The Cambridge History of Poland*, Cambridge, 1941-1950, vol. 1 to 1696, vol. 2 1696-1935.

SEE ALSO: DRZEWIENIECKI, (0088)

2) SHORTER SURVEYS

0189 ARNOLD, S.; ZYCHOWSKI, M., *Outline History of Poland*, Warsaw, 1962, Pp. 245.

0190 BENES, V.; POUNDS, N., *Poland*, London, 1970, Pp. 416.

0191 BRUCE BOSWELL, A., *Poland and the Poles*, London, 1919, Pp. 313.

0192 BRANDES, GEORGE, *Poland - a Study of the Land, People and Literature*, London, 1903, Pp. 310.

0193 BUELL, R.L., *Poland - Key to Europe*, London, 1939, Pp. 358.

0194 DROGOSŁAW, (Pseudonym), *Poland and the Polish Nation*, (Preface by P. Alden, M.P.), London 1917.

0195 DYBOSKI, R., *Poland in World Civilisation*, New York, 1950, Pp. 285.

0196 DYBOSKI, R., *Outlines of Polish History - a Course of Lectures*, London, 1925, Pp. 282.

0197 DYBOSKI, R., *Poland*, London, 1933, Pp. 430.

0198 *Encyclopaedia Britannica*, Chicago, 1967, vol. 18, 'Poland: III History', pp. 115-42.

0199 FOURNIER, EVA, *Poland*, (Vista Books), London, 1964, Pp. 191.

0200 GIEYSZTOR, A., *et al.*, *A Thousand Years of Polish History*, Warsaw, 1959, Pp. 103.

0201 GIEYSZTOR, A., et al., *Millenium*, Warsaw, 1961, Pp. 208.

0202 GOŁAWSKI, M., *Poland through the Ages: an Outline of Polish History for Young Readers*, London, 1971, Pp. 190.

0203 GÓRKA, OLGIERD, *Outline of Polish History*, London, 1942, Pp. 111.

0204 HALECKI, O., *History of Poland*, Chicago, 1966, Pp. 371.

0205 JELENSKI, K.A., 'White Eagle, Today and Yesterday', *Survey*, no. 35 (1961), pp. 12-25.

∨ 0206 JOBERT, A., *Histoire de la Pologne*, Paris, 1965, Pp. 127, (Que Sais-Je? no. 591).

0207 LAÜEN, HAROLD, *Polnische Tragödie*, Stuttgart, 1958 (Third Edition), Pp. 375.

0208 MORFILL, W.R., *Poland*, London, 1893, Pp. 389. (Reprinted, 1972)

GENERAL WORKS ON HISTORY

0209 NEWMAN, B., *The Story of Poland*, London, 1945, Pp. 206.

0210 PHILLIPS, W. ALISON, *Poland*, London, 1915, Pp. 256.

✓ 0211 PORTAL, R., et al., *La Pologne des origines à nos jours*, Paris, 1965.

0212 ROOS, H., *A History of Modern Poland*, (translated from the German by J. R. Foster), London, 1966, Pp. 303.

0213 ROSE,, W.J., *The Rise of Polish Democracy*, London, 1944, Pp. 253.

0214 ROSE, W.J., *Poland, Old and New*, London, 1948, Pp. 354.

0215 SCHMITT, BERNADOTTE, ed., *Poland*, Berkeley, 1945, Pp. 500.

0216 SHARPE, SAMUEL, *White Eagle on a Red Field*, Harvard, 1953.

0217 SYROP, KONRAD, *Poland between the Hammer and the Anvil*, London, 1968, Pp. 208.

0218 WANDYCZ, PIOTR, *The Lands of Partitioned Poland, 1795 - 1918*, Seattle, 1975 (History of East Central Europe Series, vol. 7. Pp. 450.

SEE ALSO:

SECTION Q (1); WAGNER,(0427);BAIN, (0484); IWANICKA, (0911); KNOX, (0913); KOT, (0915);KRIDL, (0917);LEDNICKI, (0918);SUPER, (0924); ŻÓŁTOWSKI, (1238).

3) EAST-CENTRAL EUROPE AS A WHOLE

0219 BROWN, J.F., *The New Eastern Europe: The Krushchev Era and After*, London, 1966, Pp. 306.

0220 BURKS, R.V., *The dynamics of Communism in Eastern Europe*, Princeton, 1961, Pp. xii + 243.

0221 EPSTEIN, F. T., ed., *Germany and the East; Selected Essays*, Bloomington, 1973.

0222 FARRELL, R.B., ed., *Political Leadership in Eastern Europe and the Soviet Union*, London, 1970, Pp. 359.

0223 FEJTO, FRANÇOIS, *A History of the People's Democracies: Eastern Europe since Stalin*, (translated from the French by D. Weissbort), London, 1974, Pp. 565.

0224 FISCHER-GALAȚI, STEPHEN, ed., *Man, State and Society in Eastern Europe*, New York - London, 1970, Pp. 343.

0225 HALECKI, OSCAR, *Borderlands of Western Civilisation - a History of East Central Europe*, New York, 1952, Pp. 503.

0226 HALECKI, OSCAR, *The Limits and Divisions of European History*, London, 1950, Pp. 242.

0227   IONESCU, GHITA, *The Break Up of the Soviet Empire in Eastern Europe*, London, 1965, Pp. 168.

0228   IONESCU, GHITA, *The Politics of the European Communist States*, London, 1967, Pp. 304.

✓ 0229   KOLARZ, W., *Myths and Realities in Eastern Europe*, London, 1946, Pp. 273.   *Um   940 k 83*

0230   PALMER, ALAN, *The Lands Between - A History of East Central Europe Since the Congress of Vienna*, London, 1970, Pp. 405.

0231   ROTHSCHILD, JOSEPH, *Communist Eastern Europe*, New York, 1964, Pp. 168.

0232   SCHAEFER, HENRY, *COMECON and the Politics of Integration*, New York, London, 1972, Pp. 200.

0233   SCHWARTZ, HENRY, *Eastern Europe in the Soviet Shadow*, New York, 1973, Pp. 117.

0234   SINGLETON, F.B., *Background to Eastern Europe*, Oxford, 1965, Pp. 226.

0235   SUGAR, P.F.; LEDERER, I.J., ed., *Nationalism in Eastern Europe*, Seattle, 1969, Pp. 465.

SEE ALSO:

OSBORNE, (**0321**); BRACKMANN, (**0485**); STAAR, (**0772**); SETON-WATSON, (**0790**); ZINNER, (**0809**); DVORNÍK, (**1230**); BRZEZINSKI, (**1604**); BYRNES, (**1605**); GRIFFITH, (**1608**); KERTESZ, (**1611**); KOLARZ, (**1613**); LEMBERG, (**1615**); REMINGTON, (**1621**); ROBERTS, (**1622**); WANDYCZ (**1624**); ROTHSCHILD, (**1748**).

F. ARCHAEOLOGY AND PREHISTORY

Despite appearances, this subject is often highly political, giving occasion for modern scores to be settled by recourse to ancient events.

Jazdżewski (**0247**) and Kastrzewski (**0248**) provide a wealth of material from which to proceed further.

0236   ANTONIEWICZ, J., 'Tribal Territories of the Baltic Peoples', *Acta Baltico-Slavica*, vol. 4, 1966, Pp. 7-27.'

0237   ANTONIEWICZ, WŁODZIMIERZ, *Sur l'atlas archéologique du monde et de la Pologne.*, (Ossolineum), Wrocław, 1966, Pp. 41.

0238   BIBBY, G. *The Testimony of the Spade*, (Fontana Library), London, 1957, (Chapter 26 - 'Biskupin', pp. 428-39).

0239   BUTZER, K.W., 'Physical Conditions in Eastern Europe, Western Asia and Egypt Before the Period of Agricultural and Urban Settlement', *Cambridge Ancient History*, (3rd Edition) vol. 1, part 1, Cambridge, 1970. (Chapter 2), pp. 35-69.

0240   CZECHANOWSKI, J., 'The Ancient Home of the Slavs', *S.E.E.R.*, vol. 25, 1945-7, pp. 356-72.

0241   DVORNÍK, F., *The Slavs - Their Early History and Civilisation*, Boston, 1956, Pp. 394.

0242   GĄSIOROWSKI, Z.J., 'The "Conquest" Theory of the Genesis of the Polish State, *Speculum*, vol. 30, 1955, pp. 550-60.

0243   GORDON CHILDE, V., 'The Origin of Neolithic Culture in Northern Europe', *Antiquity*, vol 23, 1949-50, pp. 129-35.

0244   GOUDY, A.P., 'Racial Origins', *C.H.P.*, vol. 1, Ch. 1, pp. 1-15.

0245   HENSEL,   WITOLD;   GIEYSZTOR,   ALEKSANDER, *Archaeological Research in Poland*, Warsaw, 1958, pp. 74.

0246   JAZDŻEWSKI, K., *Atlas to the Prehistory of the Slavs*, Łódź, 1948-9, 2 vols.

0247   JAZDŻEWSKI, K., *Ancient Peoples and Places - Poland*, London, 1965, Pp. 240.

0248   KASTRZEWSKI, J., *Les origines de la civilisation polonaise: préhistoire, protohistoire*, Paris, 1949, Pp. 671.

0249   PASZKIEWICZ, H., 'Are the Russians Slavs?', *Antemurale*, vol. 14, 1970, pp. 59-84.

0250   PEISKER, J., 'The Expansion of the Slavs', *C.Med.H.*, vol 2, Ch. 14, pp. 418-57.

0251   SULIMIRSKI, TED, 'The Problem of the Origin of the Slavs', *Journal of the Royal Anthrop. Inst. of G.B.*, vol 75, 1945, pp. 51-58.

0252   WIDAJEWICZ, J., *The Western Slavs on the Baltic*, Toruń, 1936, Pp. 49.

0253   WIŚLAŃSKI, T., *The Neolithic in Poland*, Wrocław, 1970, Pp. 520

SEE ALSO: SECTION J (3); LOWMIAŃSKI, (1134); CZARNECKI, (1676).

G. SOCIETY

This section is largely confined to settlement, population and class structure. It should be explored in conjunction with **Sections H** 'Economy' and **N**, 'Nationalities and Minorities'.

Two outstanding Polish works should be noted, Kieniewicz (**0288**) and Szczepański (**0317**). Zweig (**0300**) provides the most convenient guide to inter-war conditions. Lane, Kolankiewicz (**0309**) is a collection of studies applying the sociological method to post-war Poland. Zajączkowski (**0259**) has attempted a stimulating reappraisal of the Polish nobility.

1) GENERAL

0255   BARANOWSKI, B., et al., *Histoire de l'économie rurale en Pologne jusqu'à 1864*, Wrocław, 1966, Pp. 201.

0256   FRUMKIN, G., 'Pologne: dix années d'histoire démographique', *Population*, vol 4, 1949, pp. 695-712.

0257   GIEYSZTOR, IRENA, 'Research into Demographic History of Poland: a Provisional Summing-up', *A.P.H.*, vol 18, 1968, pp. 5-17.

0258   KOSSMANN, E.C., 'Zur Geschichte der polnischen Bauern und ihrer Freiheit', *Hist. Z.*, vol. 205, 1967, pp. 15-45.

0259   ZAJĄCZKOWSKI, ANDRZEJ, *Hauptelemente der Adelskultur in Polen*, Marburg/Lahn, 1967, Pp. 233.

SEE ALSO:

BARYCZ, (**0907**); LESTCHINSKY, (**1065**); JANOWSKA, (**1180**); ZUBRZYCKI, (**1183**).

2) MEDIAEVAL

0260   AUBIN, H.; RUTKOWSKI, J., 'The Lands East of the Elbe and German Colonisation Eastwards'; 'Poland, Lithuania, Hungary' in 'Mediaeval Agrarian Society in its Prime', *Cambridge Econ. Hist. of Europe*, vol. 1, 1966, ch. 7, pp. 449-506.

0261   BACKUS, O., 'The Problem of Feudalism in Lithuania, 1506-48', *S.R.*, vol. 21, 1962, pp. 639-59.

0262   BRUCE BOSWELL, A., 'Cultural and Social Conditions in the Middle Ages', *C.H.P.*, vol. 1, ch. 8, pp. 148-66.

0263   DVORNÍK, F., 'The First Wave of the *Drang nach Osten*', *C.H.J.*, vol. 7, 1943, pp. 129-45.

0264   GÓRSKI, KAROL, 'Les structures sociales de la noblesse polonaise au Moyen-Age,' *Le Moyen-Âge*, vol. 73, 1967, pp. 73-85.

0265   JEDLICKI, M.Z., 'German Settlement in Poland and the Rise of the Teutonic Order', *C.H.P.*, vol. 1, ch. 7, pp. 125-47.

0266   MANTEUFFEL, TADEUSZ, 'On Polish Feudalism', *Mediaevalia et Humanistica*, 1964, fasc. 16, pp. 94-104.

0267   RUTKOWSKI, J., 'La genèse du régime de la corvée dans l'Europe centrale depuis la fin du Moyen Age' in *La Pologne au VIème Congrès International des Sciences Historiques à Oslo (1928)*, Warsaw, 1930, pp. 211-17.

0268   RUTKOWSKI, J., 'Social and Economic Structure in the Fifteenth and Sixteenth Centuries', *C.H.P.*, vol. 1, ch. 20 (B), pp. 441-50.

0269   SKWARCZYŃSKI, P., 'The Problem of Feudalism in Poland up to the Beginning of the Sixteenth Century', *S.E.E.R.*, vol. 34, 1956, pp. 292-310.

0270   WOJCIECHOWSKI, Z., 'Les conditions des nobles et le problème de la féodalité en Pologne au moyen age', *Rev. Hist. Droit Fr. et Etr.*, vols. 25-26, 1936-7.

SEE ALSO:

GIEYSZTOR, (**0286**); WIŚNIOWSKI, (**0936**); BARTELS, (**1025**); BISKUP, (**1026**); KLIMAS, (**1124**); ZINS, (**1138**); GRABSKI, (**1294**); GRUDZIŃSKI, (**1698**).

3) 1569 - 1795

0271   BOBIŃSKA, C., 'Propriété foncière et luttes paysannes en Pologne méridionale au XVIIIème siécle', *A.H.R.F.*, vol. 36, 1964, pp. 279-93.

0272   DWORACZEK, W., 'La perméabilité des barrières sociales dans la Pologne du XVIeme siècle' *A.P.H.*, vol. 24, 1972, pp. 22-50.

0273   GIEYSZTOR, IRENA, 'Demographie historique polonaise du XVI à XVIII siècles: Sources, méthodes, résultats, et perspectives', *A.P.H.*, vol. 27, 1973, pp. 159-86.

0274   GOODWIN, A. ed., *The European Nobility in the Eighteenth Century*, (second edition), London, 1967.

0275   KOWECKI, J., 'Les transformations de la structure sociale en Pologne au XVIIIème siècle: la noblesse et la bourgeoisie', *A.P.H.*, vol. 26, 1972, pp. 5-30.

0276 LEŚNODORSKI, B., 'Le processus de l'abolition du régime féodal dans les territoires polonais aux XVIII et XIX siècles', *A.H.R.F.*, vol. 41, 1969, pp. 296-310.

0277 PTAŚNIK, J., *Gli Italiani a Cracovia del XVI et SVIII siecoli*, Rome, 1909, Pp. vii + 109.

0278 ROHMER, R., 'Une famille limousine en Pologne, 1645-1718', *R.H.D.*, vol. 49, 1935, pp. 339-61, and pp. 529-51; vol. 50, 1936, pp. 90-110.

0279 ROSE, W.J., 'Social Life before the Partitions', *C.H.P.*, vol. 2, ch. 4, pp. 72-87.

0280 VAUTRIN, H., *La Pologne au XVIIIème siècle vue par un précepteur franç*ais, Paris, 1966, Pp. 295.

0281 WOŁOWSKI, A., *La vie quotidienne en Pologne au XVIIème siè*cle, Paris, 1971, Pp. 342.

0282 WYCZAŃSKI, ANDRZEJ, 'En Pologne: l'économie du domaine nobiliaire moyen, 1500-1800', *Annales*, vol. 18, 1963, pp. 81-7.

0283 ZAJĄCZKOWSKI, ANDRZEJ, 'En Pologne: cadres structurales de la noblesse, 1500-1800', *Annales*, vol. 18, 1963, pp. 88-102.

0284 ŻYTOWICZ, LEONID, 'An Investigation into Agricultural Production in Masovia in the First Half of the Seventeenth Century,' *A.P.H.*, vol. 17, 1968.

SEE ALSO:

GIEYSZTOR, (**0257**); RUTKOWSKI, (**0267**); SKWARCZYŃSKI, (**0269**); LIPINSKI, (**0501**); FOX, (**0833**);KOT, (**0839**) (**0853**) (**0975**); SCHRAMM, (**0845**); LITAK, (**0976**); JOBERT, (**0982**), (**0983**); HERBST, (**1029**); LASKOWSKI, (**1035**); TOMKIEWICZ, (**1175**); KAMIŃSKI, (**1708**); STONE, (**1813**).

4) TOWNS

0285 FRANCASTEL, P., ed., *Les origines des villes polonaises*, Paris, 1960, Pp. 242.

0286 GIEYSZTOR, A., 'Les recherches sur l'histoire urbaine en Pologne', *A.P.H.*, vol. 8, 1963, pp. 79-90.

0287 GIEYSZTOR, A., 'From Forum to Civitas: Urban Changes in the Twelfth and Thirteenth Centuries', *La Pologne au XVII Congrès International des Sciences Historiques à Vienne, Warsaw, 1965*, pp. 7-30.

SOCIETY

SEE ALSO:

SECTIONS O; NOWAKOWSKI (0312); GIEYSZTOR, (0436) TOMKIEWICZ, (0950); COHEN, (1675); MICHALSKI, (1730); SZERMER, (1761); GUTKIND, (0312). DZIEWOŃSKI, (0302)

5) NINETEENTH CENTURY

0288   KIENIEWICZ, S., *The Emancipation of the Polish Peasantry*, Chicago, 1969, Pp. xix + 186.

0289   ROZDOLSKI, R., *Die grosse Steuer- und Agrarreform Josefs II: ein Kapitel zur österreichischen Wirtschaftsgeschichte*, Warsaw, 1961, Pp. 197.

0290   SIMONS, T.W., 'The Peasant Revolt of 1846 in Galicia: Recent Polish Historiography', *S.R.*, vol. 30, 1971, pp. 795-817.

0291   STANKIEWICZ,, ZBIGNIEW, 'Some Remarks on the Typology of Transition from Feudalism to Capitalism in Agriculture', *A.P.H.*, vol 28, 1973, pp. 169-89.

SEE ALSO:

SLOMKA, (0173); LÉSNODORSKI, (0276); KIENIEWICZ, (0650); JAKOBCZYK, (0671); ROSENTHAL, (0686); HANS, (0980); MENDELSOHN, (1081); THOMAS, ZNANIECKI, (1202); WYTRWAL, (1206); SLOMKA, (0173); BLEJWAS, (1661); BOREJSZA, (1664); BORKOWSKI, (1665); DASZYNSKA-GOLINSKA, (1677); HANDELSMAN, (1703); PIENKOS, (1741); SOBOCIŃSKI, (1755).

6) 1918-45

0292   BEREND, I.T., *Agriculture in Eastern Europe 1919-1939*, (Papers in East European Economics 35), Oxford, 1975, Pp. 84.

0293   GELLA, A., 'The Life and Death of the Old Polish Intelligentsia', *S.R.*, vol. 30, 1970, pp. 1-27.

0294   GROVE, W.R., *War's Aftermath*, New York, 1940, Pp. 223. [On U.S. Relief Work, 1918-21].

0295   HERTZ, A., 'The Social Background to Pre-war Polish Political Structure', *J.C.E.A.*, vol. 2, 1942, pp. 145-61.

0296   MALINOWSKI, W.R., 'The Pre-war Unionization of Polish Workers', *J.C.E.A.*, vol. 5, 1945, pp. 176-87.

0297   RADZIWILL, J., 'Poland since the Great War', *S.E.E.R.*, vol. 12, 1934, pp. 293-303.

0298   WYNOT, EDWARD, "The Society of Inter-War Warsaw: Profile of the Capital City in a Developing Nation, 1918-39', *E.E.Q.*, vol. 7, 1973, pp. 504-19.

0299   WYNOT, EDWARD, 'The Case of German Schools in Polish Upper Silesia, 1922-1939', *P.R.,* vol. 19, no. 2, 1974, pp. 47-69.

0300   ZWEIG, G., *Poland between Two Wars. A Critical Study of Social and Economic Changes*, London, 1944, Pp. 176.

SEE ALSO:

SYMONOLEWICZ, (**0054**); RADZIWILL, (**0166**); SAPIEHA, (**0172**); JASIENICA, (**0710**); JABŁOŃSKI, (**0711**); SZERUDA, (**0897**); HESSE, (**1057**); GLICKSMAN, (**1088**);

7) **POST-WAR SOCIETY**

0301   BANASIAK, S., 'Settlement of the Polish Western Territories, 1945-7', *P.W.A.*, vol 6, 1965, pp. 121-49.

0302   DZIEWOŃSKI, KAZIMIERZ, 'Urbanisation in Contemporary Poland', *Geografica Polonica*, 1964, no. 3, pp. 37-56.

0303   GRANT, NIGEL, *Society, Schools and Progress in Eastern Europe*, London, 1969, Pp. xxvi + 363.

0304   KALINKOWSKI, W., 'Poland' in *Urban Development in East-Central Europe,* GUTKIND, E.A. ed., London, 1972, Pp. xx + 475.

0305   KARSON, N., SZECHTER, S., *In the Name of Tomorrow: Life Underground in Poland*, New York, 1971, Pp. 285.

0306   KERSTEN, KRYSTYNA, 'The Transfer of German Population from Poland, 1945-7' *A.P.H.*, vol. 10, 1964, pp. 27-47.

0307   KING, E.J., ed., *Communist Education (Part II)*, London, 1963, Pp. 309.

0308   KOLAJA, J., *A Polish Factory: a Case Study of Worker Participation in Decision Making*, Kentucky, 1960, Pp. 157.

0309   LANE, D.; KOLANKIEWICZ, G., ed., *Social Groups in Polish Society*, London, 1973, Pp. 318.

0310   MATEJKO, ALEXANDER, 'Poland's New Social Structure', *East Europe*, vol. 22, 1973, no. 1, pp. 2-9.

0311   MATEJKO, ALEXANDER, 'The Industrial Workers', *C.S.P.*, vol. 15, 1973, pp. 90-100.

0312   NOWAKOWSKI, S., 'Town Dwellers versus Village Dwellers in Poland', *J. Cont. H.*, vol. 4, 1969, pp. 111-22.

0313   PIENKOS, 'The Polish Party Elite' *East Europe*, vol. 23, no. 27, 1974, pp. 19-24.

0314   PIRAGES, D.C., *Modernisation and Political-Tension Management: a Socialist Society in Perspective: a Case Study of Poland*, London - New York, 1972, Pp. xvi + 261.

0315   ROSSET, E., 'Demography of the New Poland', *A.P.H.*, vol. 16, 1967, pp. 109-38.

0316   SCHECHTMAN, J.B., 'The Polish-Soviet Exchange of Population', *J.C.E.A.*, vol. 9, 1949, pp. 289-314.

0317   SZCZEPAŃSKI, JAN, *Polish Society*, New York, 1970, Pp. 214.

0318   SZCZEPAŃSKI, JAN, 'Social Sciences and the Reform of the Education System' *C.S.P.*, vol. 15, 1973, pp. 134-43.

0319   ZAREMBA, A., 'Transformations in Contemporary Polish Society' *J.C.E.A.*, vol. 12, 1952.

SEE ALSO:

SECTIONS H (7c), K (12), L (8), N (4e); FABER, (1682); HARASYMIW, (1704); KOSINSKI, (1715); MATEJKO, (1727); MEYERS, (1735); PAULU, (1739); PIESOWICZ, (1742); TOPOLSKI, (1763).

H. ECONOMY

Apart from Rutkowski (**0322**), who stops at the Partitions, there is no adequate introduction to Polish economic history as a whole. But certain topics such as the Baltic Trade (**Section H (3)**) and the post-war economy (**Section H (7)**) have attracted considerable attention. For the earlier period the work of Małowist, (**0337**) and (**0356**) in particular, is essential. Zins (**0348**) concentrates on English commercial activities. Buist (**1668**) has unique information on Polish loans in the late 18th century. For the inter-war years, Modzilewski (**0376**) and Zweig (**0300**) present the basic information. The post-war economy is the subject of a continuing debate which can be followed in Alton (**0382**), Gambit (**0389**), *The Joint Committee Report*, a valuable set of essays (**0405**), Wilczyński (**0406**), Feiwel (**0412**) and Korboński (**0419**). **Section H 7d** concentrates on Polish foreign trade which is increasingly important to the economy. Kramer (**1716**) is a translation of the most important current Polish economic thought. Mieczkowski (**1732**) is a stimulating study. Wilczynski (**1768**) is unique for the importance of technology in Polish planning.

1) GENERAL

0320   BUJAK F., *Poland's Economic Development - a Short Sketch*, Warsaw, 1925, Pp. 67.

0321   OSBORNE, R.H., *East-Central Europe: a Geographical Introduction to Seven Socialist States*, London, 1967, Pp. 384. Chapter 8, 'Poland', pp. 227-82.

0322   RUTKOWSKI, JAN, *Histoire économique de la Pologne avant les Partages*, Paris, 1927, Pp. xii + 268.

SEE ALSO:

BARANOWSKI, (**0255**);   LIPIŃSKI, (**0501**);   POUNDS, (**1743**); WILCZYŃSKI, (**1768**).

2) MEDIAEVAL, TO 1569

0323   GIEYSZTOR, A., 'Villages désertes: Bilan de la récherche polonaise' in '*Villages Désertes et Histoire Economique, XI-XVII siècles*', Centre de Recherches Historiques de la VI section de L'Ecole Pratique des Hautes Études, Paris, 1965, pp. 607-12.

0324 ŁOWMIAŃSKI, H., 'Economic Problems of the Early Feudal Polish State', *A.P.H.*, vol. 3, 1960, pp. 7-32.

0325 MAŁOWIST, MARIAN, 'The Problem of Inequality of Economic Development in the later Middle Ages', *Ec.H.R.*, 2nd series, vol. 19, 1966, pp. 15-28.

0326 PANAITESCU, P.P., *La route commerciale de Pologne à la mer Noire au Moyen-Âge*, Bucarest, 1934, Pp. 24.

0327 POSTAN, M., 'The Trade of Mediaeval Europe: North', *Cambridge Econ. Hist. of Europe*, vol. 2, 1952, ch. 4, pp. 119-251.

SEE ALSO: MAŁOWIST, (**0356**); VON LOEWE, (**1127**); ATTMAN, (**1724**).

3) BALTIC TRADE

0328 BOGUCKA, M.,, 'Merchants' Profits in Gdansk Foreign Trade in the First Half of the XVII century', *A.P.H.*, vol. 23, 1971, pp. 73-90.

0329 BOGUCKA, M., 'Amsterdam and the Baltic in the First Half of the The Seventeenth Century', *Ec.HR.*, vol. 26, No. 3, 1973, pp. 433-47.

0330 CIEŚLAK, EDMUND, 'Bilan et structure du commerce de Gdansk dans la seconde moitié du XVIII siècle', *A.P.H.*, vol. 23, 1971, pp. 105-18.

0331 CIEŚLAK, EDMUND, 'Recherches polonaises sur l'histoire maritime du XVI au XVIII siècles', *A.P.H.*, vol. 23, 1971, pp. 162-77.

0332 HOSZOWSKI, S., 'The Polish Baltic Trade in the 15 - 18th Centuries' *Poland at the XI International Congress of Historical Sciences in Stockholm*, Warsaw, 1960, pp. 117-54.

0333 KLEYNTJENS, J., 'Les relations économiques des Pays-Bas avec la Pologne aux XIV et XV siècles', *Revue du Nord*, vol. 21, 1935, pp. 177-84.

0334 KOMASZYŃSKI, M., 'Les blés polonais sur les marchés de la France féodale', *Studia Hist. Oecon.*, vol. 3, 1968, pp. 63-91.

0335 KRANNHALS, D., *Danzig und der Weichselhandel im seine Blütezeit vom 16 zum 17 Jahrhundert*, Leipzig, 1942, Pp. xv + 143.

0336 MAŁOWIST, MARIAN, 'Poland, Russia and Western Trade in the Fifteenth and Sixteenth Centuries', *Past and Present*, no. 13, 1958, pp. 26-41; 'Rejoinder', *Past and Present*, no. 37, 1967, pp. 157-62.

0337 MAŁOWIST, MARIAN, 'The Economic and Social Development of the Baltic Countries from the Fifteenth to the Seventeenth Centuries', *Ec.H.R.*, 2nd series, vol. 12, 1959-60, pp. 177-89.

0338 MAŁOWIST, MARIAN, 'Le développement des rapports

économiques entre la Flandre, la Pologne et les pays limitrophes du XIII au XIV siècle', *Revue Belge de Philologie et d'Histoire*, vol. 10, 1931, pp. 1013-65.

0339   MAŁOWIST, MARIAN, 'Le commerce de la Baltique et le problème des luttes sociales en Pologne aux XV et XVI siècles', *La Pologne au X Congrès International des Sciences Historiques à Rome*, Warsaw, 1955, pp. 125-46.

0340   MAŁOWIST, MARIAN, 'A Certain Trade Technique in the Baltic Countries in the 16th - 17th centuries', *Poland at the XI International Congress of Historical Sciences in Stockholm*, Warsaw, 1960, pp. 103-16.

0341   MACZAK, ANTONI, 'The Sound Toll Accounts and the Balance of English Trade with the Baltic Zone, 1565-1646', *Stud. Hist. Oecon.*, vol. 3, 1968, pp. 93-113.

0342   MACZAK, ANTONI, 'The Balance of Polish Sea Trade with the West, 1565-1646', *Scand. Econ. Hist. Rev.*, vol. 18, 1970, pp. 107-25.

0343   MACZAK, ANTONI, 'La 'Eastland Company' anglaise et le commerce dans la Baltique dans la seconde moitié du XVIème siècle', *A.P.H.*, vol. 23, 1971, pp. 91-104.

0344   RATHS, R.W., *Der Weichselshandel in XVI Jahrhundert*, Marburg, 1927.

0345   RUSIŃSKI, W., 'The Role of Polish Territories in European Trade in the XVII and XVIII Centuries', *Studia Hist. Oecon.*, vol. 3, 1968, pp. 115-34.

0346   SZELAGOWSKI, A., GRAS, N.S.B. 'The Eastland Company in Prussia, 1579-1585', *T.R.H.S.*, 3rd series, vol. 6, 1912, pp. 163-84.

0347   WYCZAŃSKI, A., 'Tentative Estimate of Polish Rye Trade in the Sixteenth Century', *A.P.H.*, vol. 4, 1961, pp. 119-31.

0348   ZINS, H., *England and the Baltic in the Elizabethan Era*, Manchester, 1972, Pp. 347.

4) 1569-1795 (General)

0349   HOSZOWSKI, S., 'The Revolution of Prices in Poland in the 16th and 17th Centuries', *A.P.H.*, vol. 2, pp. 7-16.

0350   KULA, W., 'L'histoire économique de la Pologne du XVIIIème siècle', *A.P.H.*, vol. 4, 1961, pp. 113-46.

0351   KULA, W., 'Sur les transformations économiques de la Pologne au XVIIIème siècle', *A.H.R.R.*, vol. 36, 1964, pp. 261-77.

0352   LONNROTH, E., 'The Economic Policies of Governments - The Baltic States', *Cambridge Econ. Hist. of Europe*, vol. 3, 1963, ch. 6/iv, pp. 361-96.

0353 MAAS, WALTER, 'The 'Dutch' Villages in Poland', *Geography*, vol. 30, no. 174, 1951, pp. 263-8.

0354 MAŁOWIST, MARIAN, 'Evolution industrielle en Pologne du XIV au XVIII siècles', in *Studi in onore di Armando Sapori*, Milan, 1957, vol. 1, pp. 571-603.

0355 MAŁOWIST, MARIAN, 'Un essai d'histoire comparée: les mouvements d'expansion en Europe aux XV et XVI siècles', *Annales*, vol. 17, 62, pp. 923-29.

0356 MAŁOWIST, MARIAN, *Croissance et régression en Europe, XIV - XVII Siècles*, Ecole Pratique des Hautes-Etudes, VI section, (Cahiers des Annales 34), Paris, 1972, Pp. 223.

0357 TOPOLSKI, J., 'La régression économique en Pologne du XVIIème au XVIIIème siècle', *A.P.H.*, vol. 7, 1962, pp. 28-49.

0358 WYCZAŃSKI, A., 'La campagne polonaise dans le cadre des transformations du marché des XVI-XVIIème siècles', *Studia Hist. Oecon.*, vol. 2, 1967, pp. 57-81.

0359 ŻYTKOWICZ, LEONID, 'Grain Yields in Poland, Bohemia, Hungary and Slovakia in the XVI to XVIII Centuries', *A.P.H.*, vol. 24, 1972, pp. 51-73.

SEE ALSO:

ZYTOWICZ, (**0284**); RUTKOWSKI, (**0322**); LIPIŃSKI, (**0501**); BOGUCKA, (**1663**); BUIST, (**1668**).

5) NINETEENTH CENTURY

0360 BEREND, I.T., RANKE, G., *Economic Development in East-Central Europe in the 19th and 20th Centuries*, New York, 1974.

0361 BLUM, J., 'The Condition of the European Peasantry on the Eve of Emancipation' *Journal of Modern History*, vol. 46, 3, 1974, pp. 395-424.

0362 HEICKE, O., 'Polnische Forschung uber das Lodzer Industriegebeit - Literaturbericht', *Z. für Ost.,,* vol. 15, 1966, pp. 511-5.

0363 JEDLICKI, J., 'Industrial State Economy in the Kingdom of Poland in the Nineteenth Century', *A.P.H.*, vol. 2, 1959, pp. 155-66.

0364 KULA, W., *Les débuts du capitalisme en Pologne dans la perspective de l'histoire comparée*, Rome, 1960, Pp. 24.

0365 KURNATOVSKI, GEORGES, 'Les origines du capitalisme en Pologne', *Rev. d'Hist. Mod.*, vol. 8, 1933, pp. 236-67.

0366 LESKIEWICZ, J., 'Les débuts du capitalisme dans l'agriculture du Royaume de Pologne', *A.P.H.*, vol. 2, 1959, pp. 155-66.

SEE ALSO:

GROCHULSKA, **(0626)**; BUIST, **(1668)**; GASIOROWSKA, **(1690)**, **(1692)**; HANDELSMAN, **(1703)**.

6) 1918 - 1939

0367 DRABEK, Z., *Summary of Foreign Trade Matrices for East Europe 1920-1949* (Papers in East European Economics 28), Oxford, 1973, Pp. 42.

0368 DRABEK, Z., *Trade Performances of East European Countries, 1919-1939*, (Papers in East European Economics 37), Oxford, 1973, Pp. 89.

0369 'Economic Change in Eastern Europe from the First World War to the end of the Second World War: Conference Report', *Soviet Studies*, vol. 24, No. 3, 1973, pp. 468-79.

0370 EHRLICH, E., *Infrastructure and an International Comparison of Relationships with Indicators of Development in Eastern Europe 1920-50* (Papers in East European Economics 33-34), Oxford, 1973, Pp. 93.

0371 KAGAN, G., 'Agrarian Regime of Pre-war Poland', *J.C.E.A.*, vol. 3, 1943-4, pp. 241-269.

0372 KRUSZEWSKI, G., 'The German-Polish Tariff War (1925-1934) and its Aftermath', *J.C.E.A.*, vol. 3, 1943-4, pp. 294-315.

0373 LANDAU, Z., 'The Polish Economy of the Years 1918-1939 in Polish Postwar Publications', *A.P.H.*, vol. 5, 1962, pp. 141-63.

0374 LANDAU, Z., 'The Influence of Foreign Capital upon the Polish Economy, 1918-1939,' in *La Pologne au XII Congrès International des Sciences Historiques à* Vienne, Warsaw, 1965, pp. 113-45.

0374 LANDAU, Z., 'The Influence of Foreign Capital upon the Polish Economy, 1918-1939' in *La Pologne au XII Congrès International des Sciences Historiques à Vienne*, Warsaw, 1965, pp. 113-45.

0375 LANDAU, Z., TOMASZEWSKI, J., *The Main Social and Economic Problems of Poland Between the Wars*, (Papers in East European Economics 32), Oxford, 1973, Pp. 17.

0376 MODZILEWSKI, J., ed., *Pologne, 1919-39*, Neuchâtel, 1946-7, vols. 1-3.

0377 ORCZYK, J., 'The Main Features of the Agricultural Crisis in Poland, 1929-35', *Studia Hist. Oecon.*, vol. 3, 1968, pp. 221-41.

0378 PONIKOWSKI, W., LEŚNIEWSKI, V., 'Polish Agriculture' in *Agricultural Systems of Middle Europe*', ed., Morgan, J.S., New York, 1933.

0379 RADICE, E.A., *General Problems of the Area Between the Wars* (Papers in East European Economics 38), Oxford, 1973, Pp. 48.

0380 SOUTOU, GEORGE, 'La politique économique de la France en Pologne, 1920-4', *Rev. Hist.*, no. 509, 1974, pp. 85-116.

0381 STANIEWICZ, W., 'The Agrarian Problem in Poland between the wars', *S.E.E.R.*, vol. 43, 1964, pp. 23-33.

SEE ALSO: ZWEIG, (**0300**); BEREND, (**0292**), CARBONE, (**1779**).

7) SINCE 1945

a) GENERAL

0382 ALTON, A.P., *The Polish Post-War Economy*, Oxford-New York, 1955, Pp. 330.

0383 CHEŁSTOWSKI, STANISLAW, 'New Steps to Efficiency,' *Polish Perspectives*, vol. 16, No. 3, 1973, pp. 3-8.

0384 CHEŁSTOWSKI, STANISLAW, 'What's Good for the Economy', *Polish Perspectives*, vol. 17, No. 1, 1974, pp. 3-13.

0385 DOUGLAS, D.W., *Traditional Economic Systems: the Polish-Czech Example*, London, 1953, Pp. viii + 375.

0386 EHRLICH, S., ed., *Social and Political Transformations in Poland*, Warsaw, 1964, Pp. 329.

0387 FALLENBUCHL, Z.M., 'The Strategy and Development of Gierek's Economic Manoeuvre,' *C.S.P.*, vol. 15, 1973, pp. 52-70.

0388 FEIWEL, G.R., *Poland's Industrialisation Policy: a Current Analysis*, London, 1971, Pp. xxvi + 749.

0389 GAMBIT, J., 'The Polish Economy: Models and Muddles', *Survey*, vol. 17, 1971, pp. 74-89.

0390 GAMARNIKOW, M., 'Poland under Gierek: A New Economic Approach', *Problems of Communism*, Sept. - Oct., 1972, pp. 20-31.

0391 GLOD, STANLEY J., 'Poland's Role in East-West Trade', in *Studies in Polish Civilisation*, ed., Wandycz, D., New York, 1966, pp. 324-30.

0392 KUKLIŃSKI, A., 'Progress and Change in the Industrialisation of Poland', *Geografia Polonica*, vol. 3, 1964, pp. 57-70.

0393 LANDAU, ZBIGNIEW, 'Comparative Research on the Long-Range Economic Growth of Poland', *A.P.H.*, vol. 29, 1974, pp. 111-36.

0394   LESZCZYŃSKI, S., 'The Geographical Bases of Contemporary Poland', *J.C.E.A.*, vol. 7, 1948, pp. 357-73.

0395   MARER, PAUL, *Soviet and East European Foreign Trade 1946-69: A Statistical Compendium and Guide*, Bloomington, 1972, Pp. 408.

0396   MELLOR, ROY E.H., *Eastern Europe: A Geography of the Comecon Countries*, London, 1975, Pp. 384.

0397   MIECZKOWSKI, B., 'Estimates of Changes in Real Wages in Poland during the 1960s', *S.R.*, vol. 31, 1972, pp. 651-56.

0398   PRZYBYLA, J.S., 'Private Enterprise in Poland under Gomułka', *S.R.*, vol. 17, 1958, pp. 316-31.

0399   SHONFIELD, ANDREW, 'Hungary and Poland: the Politics of Economic Reform' *The World Today*, vol. 26, 1970, pp. 94-102.

0400   SKRZYPEK, STANISLAW, 'Soviet Aid to the East European Nations, 1955-62: an Evaluation', in *Studies in Polish Civilisation*, Wandycz, D. ed., New York, 1966.

0401   SMOGORZEWSKI, K.M., 'Polish Economy under Soviet Control', *S.E.E.R.*, vol. 32, 1954, pp. 385-405.

0402   SZWARC, KAROL, 'Streamlining the Economy,' *Polish Perspectives*, vol. 16, no. 7/8, 1973, pp. 24-30.

0403   SZWARC, KAROL, 'In Top Gear', *Polish Perspectives*, vol. 17, no. 2, 1974, pp. 3-8.

0404   TRZECIAKOWSKI, WITOLD, 'Foreign Trade: A Retrospective View', *C.S.P.*, vol. 15, 1973, pp. 71-89.

0405   U.S. CONGRESS: JOINT ECONOMIC COMMITTEE (93rd Congress), ed., *Reorientation and Commercial Relations of the Economies of Eastern Europe*, Washington, 1974, Pp. 771.

0406   WILCZYNSKI, J., *The Economics of Socialism*, London, 1970, Pp. 286.

0407   WILCZYNSKI, J., *Socialist Economic Development and Reforms*, London, 1972, Pp. 350.

0408   ZAUBERMAN, A., *Industrial Progress in Czechoslovakia, Poland and East Germany, 1937-62*, London, 1964, Pp. xiv + 338.

0409   ZIELINSKI, J.G., 'On the Effectiveness of the Polish Economic Reforms', *Soviet Studies*, vol. 22, 1971, pp. 406-32.

0410   ZIELINSKI, JANUSZ G., *Economic Reforms in Polish Industry*, (Economic Reforms in East European Industry), London, New York, Toronto, 1973, Pp. 333.

SEE ALSO:

Concise Statistical Yearbook, (**0065**); BIRKOS, (**1660**); FALLENBUCHL,

(1683); FLAKIERSKI, (1691); KRAMER, (1716); LAVIGNE, (1720); MIECZKOWSKI, (1732); RAJANA, (1744).

b) PLANNING

0411 FALLENBUCHL, Z.M., 'Comecon Integration', *Problems of Communism*, March-April, 1973, pp. 25-39.

0412 FEIWEL, G.R., *Problems in Polish Economic Planning: Continuity, Change and Prospects*, London, 1971, Pp. xviii + 471.

0413 FISHER, J.C., ed., *City and Regional Planning in Poland*, Ithaca, 1965, pp. 459.

0414 KASER, M., ZIELINSKI, J.G., *Planning in Eastern Europe*, London, 1970, Pp. 184.

0415 KASER, M., *COMECON - Integration Problems of the Planned Economies*, London, 1967, Pp. vi + 279.

0416 MIECZKOWSKI, B., 'Recent Discussions on Consumption Planning in Poland', *Soviet Studies*, vol. 22, 1971, pp. 609-22.

0417 MONTIAS, J., *Central Planning in Poland*, New Haven and London, 1962, Pp. xv + 410.

0418 MUTI, D.M., 'Discounting Methods in Polish Planning', *Soviet Studies*, vol. 23, 1971, pp. 309-17.

c) AGRICULTURE

0419 KORBOŃSKI, ANDRZEJ, *The Politics of Socialist Agriculture in Poland, 1945-60*, New York, 1965, Pp. xii + 330.

0420 KORBOŃSKI, ANDRZEJ, 'Peasant Agriculture in Socialist Poland since 1956: an Alternative to Collectivisation', in *Soviet and East European Agriculture*, ed., Karcz, J.F., Berkeley, 1967, pp. 411-35.

0421 LIPSKI, WITOLD, 'Changes in Agriculture', *C.S.P.*, vol. 15, 1973, pp. 101-7.

0422 SKRZYPEK, S., 'Agricultural Policies in Poland', *J.C.E.A.*, vol. 16, 1956, pp. 45-70.

d) FOREIGN TRADE : SPECIAL NOTE

Trade relations between Poland and the West are rapidly expanding. The following provide information on market potentials, commercial policies and business climate, trade statistics (often by firm), addresses of agencies, trade fair information, various reports and publications in all languages, and case studies in East-West Trade. The best are Wilczynski (0425) and Lauter (1719). Marer (1726) has a good bibliography. Essential reading for those doing business with Poland are *Eastwest Markets* and *Business International, Eastern Europe Report* (Periodicals)

0423 KASER, MICHAEL, 'East-West Trade: Comecon's Commerce,' *Problems of Communism*, July-August, 1973, pp. 1-16.

0424 LEWINS, L., *Trading in Poland*, Office of East-West Trade Development, Washington, 1973, Pp. 25.

0425 WILCZYNSKI, J., *The Economics and Politics of East-West Trade*, London, 1969.

SEE ALSO: (Periodicals): *East-West Commerce*; *East-West Trade Information*; *American Review of East-West Trade*; *Eastwest Markets*; MARER, **(0395)**, **(1726)**; U.S. Congress, **(0405)**; LAUTER, **(1719)**; STARR, **(1756)**; WILCZYNSKI, **(1768)**; ZWASS, **(1773)**; van BRABANT, **(1817)**.

I. CONSTITUTIONAL AND LEGAL HISTORY

This section should be explored in conjunction with Section J, 'Political History'. Owing to the Partitions, Polish Law and Constitution are rather fragmented subjects. Wagner (**0427**) is a recent survey and very useful. Considerable work has been done on the pre-Partition period, and in particular on the Constitution of 3 May 1791: see Kalinka (**0452**) and Klotz (**0453**). Konopczyński (**0454**) is a very erudite study of the most famous feature of the old constitution.

1) GENERAL

0426   STAREWICZ, A., HRYNIEWIECKI, J., ed., *The Polish Diet*, Warsaw, 1959, Pp. 124.

0427   WAGNER, W.J., *Polish Law throughout the Ages*, Stanford, 1970, Pp. 476.

SEE ALSO:

BARDACH (**0003**); KOSSMANN, (**0258**); MURZYNOWSKI, (**1734**)

2) MEDIAEVAL

0428   BARDACH, JULIUSZ, 'L'état polonais du haut moyen-âge,' *A.P.H.*, vol. 5, 1962-3, pp. 7-47.

0429   BARDACH, JULIUSZ, 'Le pouvoir monarchique en Pologne au moyen-âge', *Recueils de la Société Jean Bodin*, vol. 21, 1969, pp. 563-612.

0430   BARDACH, JULIUSZ, 'Gouvernants et gouvernés en Pologne au moyen-âge et aux temps modernes', *Standen en Landen*, vol. 36, 1965, pp. 255-85.

0431   BEŁCH, STANISŁAW, *Paulus Vladimiri, and his Doctrine Concerning International Law and Politics*, The Hague, 1965, 2 vols.

0432   DĄBROWSKI, JAN, 'Corona Regni Poloniae qu XIV siècle', *Bulletin International de L'Académie Polonaise des Sciences et des Lettres, Supplément M. 7*, Cracow, 1953, pp. 41-64.

0433   DĄBROWSKI, JAN, 'Die Krone des Polnischen Königtums im 14 Jahrhundert in *Corona Regni: Studien über die Krone als Symbol des Staates im späteren Mittelalter*, ed., Hellmann, M.; Darmstadt, 1961, pp. 399-548.

0434 DEVEIKE, J., 'The Legal Aspect of the last Religious Conversion in Europe', *S.E.E.R.*, vol. 32, 1954-4, pp. 117-31.

0435 EHRLICH, L., 'Polish Fifteenth-Century Doctrine of International Law', *Polish Perspectives*, vol. 7, no. 4, 1964, pp. 19-28.

0436 GIEYSZTOR, A., 'Les chartes de franchises urbaines et rurales en Pologne au XIII siècle,' in *Les libertés urbaines et rurales en Pologne du XI au XIV siècle: Colloque international de Spa 1966*, Bruxelles, 1968, Pp. 350.

0437 GIEYSZTOR, A., 'En Pologne médiévale: problèmes du régime politique et de l'organisation administrative du X au XIV siècles', *Annali della Fondazione Italiana per la storia Amministrativa*, vol. 1, 1964, pp. 135-56.

0438 GÓRSKI, KAROL, 'The Origins of the Polish Sejm', *S.E.E.R.*, vol. 44, 1966, pp. 122-38.

0439 GÓRSKI, KAROL, 'Les débuts de la représentation de la Communitas Nobilium dans les assemblées d'états de l'Est Européen', *Standen en Landen*, vol. 47, pp. 37-57.

0440 GÓRSKI, KAROL, 'Die Anfänge des Ständewesens im Nord-und Ostmitteleuropa in Mittelalter', *Standen en Landen*, vol. 40, 1966, pp. 43-59.

0441 GÓRSKI, KAROL, 'The Royal Prussian Estates in the Second Half of the XV century, and Their Relation to the Crown of Poland', *A.P.H.*, vol. 10, 1964, pp. 49-64.

0442 KNOLL, P.W., *The Rise of the Polish Monarchy: Piast Poland in East Central Europe, 1320-70*, Chicago, 1972, Pp. 276.

0443 LABUDA, G., 'L'intégration et la désintegration dans l'histoire du premier état polonais du X au XIII siècle', in *Studi in onore di A. Fanfani*, Milan, 1962, vol. 1, pp. 451-69.

0444 OLES, M., *The Armenian Law in the Polish Kingdom, 1356-1519: a Juridical and Historical Study*, Rome, 1966, Pp. 125.

0445 WOJCIECHOWSKI, Z., *L'état polonais au Moyen Age. Histoire des Institutions*, Paris, 1949, Pp. 365.

SEE ALSO:

GÓRSKI, (**0496**); GÓRSKI, (**0497**); BALZER, (**0566**); LEWIN, (**1078**), (**1079**); *The Problem of Unity...*, (**1125**); GÓRSKI, (**1133**)

3)   1569 - 1795

0446   BACKUS„ O., 'The Problem of Unity in the Polish-Lithuanian State', S.R., vol 22, 1963, pp. 411-31.

0447   BARDACH, J., 'L'union de Lublin', A.P.H., vol. 21, 1970, pp. 69-92.

0448   CUTTOLI, B., La Pologne an XVIII siècle et le Droit international , Paris, 1912, Pp. 146.

0449   CZAPLIŃSKI, W., 'The Polish Sejm', A.P.H., vol. 22, 1970, pp. 180-92.

0450   GÓRSKI, KAROL, 'Un Libre sur la théorie de la Représentation en Pologne au XVI siècle', Standen en Landen, vol. 40, 1966, pp. 89-108.

0451   HANDELSMAN, M., La constitution polonaise du 3 mai 1791 et l'opinion française, Paris, 1910.

0452   KALINKA, W., Die vierjährige polnische Reichstag, 1788-91, Berlin, 1896-8, 2 vols. .

0453   KLOTZ, J., L'oeuvre législative de la Diète de Quatre Ans, Paris, 1913, Pp. 588.

0454   KONOPCZYŃSKI, W., Le Libérum Veto (Translated from Polish by A. Korwin-Piotrowska), Paris, 1930, Pp. 297.

0455   LEŚNODORSKI, B., Les institutions polonaises au Siècle des Lumières, Warsaw, 1962, Pp. 41.

0456   LEŚNODORSKI, B., 'Le nouvel etat polonais du XVIIIème siècle: Lumières et traditions', in Utopie et Traditions au XVIIIème siècle', Paris, 1963, Pp. 147-63.

0457   MESNARD, P., '"La République" de Modrzewski comme philosophie de l'histoire des institutions polonaises', Rev. Hist. Droit Fr. et Etr., vol. 44, 1966, pp. 584-608.

0458   MICHALSKI, J., 'Les diétines polonaises au XVIII siècle', A.P.H., vol. 12, 1964-5, pp. 87-107.

0459   OKIRSHEVICH, L., The Law of the Grand Duchy of Lithuania, New York, 1953, Pp. 53.

0460   ROOS, H., 'Ständewesen und parlamentarische Verfassung in Polen, 1505-1771', Veröffentlichungen des Max-Planck-Instituts für Geschichte, Göttingen, 1969, vol. 27.

0461   ROUSSEAU, JEAN-JACQUES, Considérations sur le gouvernement de la Pologne et sa réformation projetée, (Paris, 1792).

0462   SKWARCZYŃSKI, PAUL, 'The Constitution of Poland before the Partitions', C.H.P., vol. 2, ch. 3, pp. 49-71.

0463   SKWARCZYŃSKI, PAUL, 'The Origin of the Name Pacta

Conventa in 1573', *S.E.E.R.*, vol. 37, 1958-9, pp. 469-76.

0464 SKWARCZYŃSKI, P., 'Les tractations autour de l'élection d'Henri de Valois comme Roi de Pologne, 1573, *Rev. Int. d'Hist. Pol. et. Const.*, vol. 5, 1955, pp. 173-317.

0465 TRUMPA, VINCENT, 'The Disintegration of the Polish-Lithuanian Commonwealth: a Commentary,' *Lituanus*, vol. 10, no. 2, 1964, pp. 24-32.

0466 WOJCIECHOWSKI, Z., 'Les éléments médiévaux dans l'organisation de l'état polonais du XVI au XVIII siècles', *Czasopismo Prawno-Historyczne*, vol. 1, 1948, pp. 5-24.

0467 WYTRZENS, G., *Die goldene Freiheit der Polen - aus den Denkwürdigkeiten Sr. Wohlgeboren des Herrn. Jan Chryzostom Pasek*, Wien, 1967, Pp. 478.

SEE ALSO:

STANKIEWICZ, (**0505**); ULAM, (**0508**); SKWARCZYŃSKI, (**0582**); GIEROWSKI, (**0607**); SASS, (**0611**); ASKENAZY(**0613**); KAPLAN, (**0617**); ROSTWOROWSKI, (**0622**); SAWCZYŃSKI, (**1040**); LEPSZY, (**1343**).

4) NINETEENTH CENTURY

0468 WINIARSKI, B., *Les institutions en Pologne au XIXème siècle*, Paris, 1921, Pp. 271.

SEE ALSO:

RAIN, (**0634**); RUDZKA, (**0656**); EISENBACH, (**1074**); GRYNWASER, (**1699**).

5) 1918-1976

0469 GROTH, A.J., 'Proportional Representation in Pre-war Poland', *S.R.*,vol. 23, 1964, pp. 103-16.

0470 GROTH, A.J., 'Polish Elections, 1919-28', *S.R.*, vol. 24, 1965, pp. 653-65.

0471 HARLEY, J.H., 'The New Polish Constitution', *S.E.E.R.*, vol. 15, 1936-7, pp. 135-42.

0472 GSOVSKI, V. GRZYBOWSKI, K., ed., *Government, Law and Courts in the Soviet Union and Eastern Europe*, London, 1959, 2 vols.

0473 GWIDŹ, ANDRZEJ, *The State System of the Polish People's*

Republic, Warsaw, 1966, Pp. 80.

0474 JONES, R.A. 'Polish Local Government Reorganised on Soviet Model', *S.R.*, vol. 10, 1951, pp. 56-68.

0475 LASOK, D., ed., *Polish Civil Law*, Leiden, 1973, Pp. 270. (first of a three volume translation).

0476 LOTARSKI, SUSANNE S., 'Reform of Rural Administration', *C.S.P.*, vol. 15, 1973, pp. 108-21.

0477 MODELSKI, IZYDOR B., 'Seym Committees in the Polish Political System,' Ph.D. Dissertation, Wayne State University, Detroit, 1973.

0478 ROZMARYN, S., *La Pologne*, (Librairie généeral de droit et de jurisprudence), Paris, 1963, Pp. 524.

0479 RUDZINSKI, A.W., 'Sovietisation of Civil Law in Poland', *S.R.*, vol. 15, 1956, pp. 216-43.

0480 SEIDLER, G.L., 'Marxist Legal Thought in Poland', *S.R.*, vol. 26, 1967, pp. 382-94.

0481 STAWARSKI, A., 'Law and Law Courts in Poland, 1919-39', *S.E.E.R.*, vol. 19, 1939-41, pp. 188-202.

0482 SZIRMAI, Z., ed., *Law in Eastern Europe*, No. 6, Leyden, 1962, Pp. 168; and *Ibid*. No. 16, Leyden, 1968, Pp. 304.

0483 TRISKA, JAN, F., ed., *Consitutions of the Communist Party States*, Stanford, 1968, Pp. 541.

SEE ALSO:

STAREWICZ, (**0426**); SOKOLEWICZ, (**1809**); PACZKOWSKJ, (**1801**)

J. POLITICAL HISTORY

Section **E** should be consulted for general political narratives. Sub-section **J** (1) below has references to works treating major periods of political history; **J** (2) is concerned with political ideas, and with political movements. Sub-sections **J**(3) - **J** (27c) deal with each of the specific periods of Polish history from the origins to the present day.

For early history, the choice of material tends to be strictly limited, and self-explanatory.

The early modern period can also be conveniently approached in detail through biographies of varying merit, such as Champion on the Valois (**0580**), the collected studies on Batory (**0583**), Morton on Sobieski (**0603**), Bain on Stanislas-August (**0614**) or Askenazy on Poniatowski (**0624**).

In the nineteenth century, the absence of a Polish State makes political history an integral part of Foreign Affairs (see Section **Q** (9)). On the Risings, Edwards (**0648**) and Michelet (**0653**) were contemporary sensations; the studies of R.F. Leslie (**0639, 0652**) are more recent, based on better sources. Prussian Poland is vividly recalled by Rose (**0682**).

On inter-war Poland, Polonsky (**0718**) and Rothschild (**0721**) stand out from a mass of lesser comment.

On the German Occupation, Broszat (**0731**) analyses Nazi policy to Poland in particular; Lemkin (**0740**) puts it into the context of occupied Europe as a whole. Cyprian, Sawicki (**0732**) present a Polish viewpoint. The Polish Resistance can be approached through personal memoirs, notably Bór-Komorowski (**0730**), Karski (**0738**) and Korboński (**0739**).

On the Soviet Occupation, Anon. (**0745**) paints a vividly descriptive picture. On Katyn, Zawodny (**0751**) is the most scholarly and dispassionate.

On the Warsaw Rising, the Polish Ambassador to the U.S.A. during the war, Ciechanowski (**0753**) is outstanding, although he only deals with the outbreak.

General surveys of the People's Republic are numerous, but Bromke, (**0760**) Morrison, (**0770**) Staar, (**0772**) and Syrop (**0217**), deserve mention. Szyr, (**0776**) is an official publication. The establishment of communist power, (Section **27b**) can only be studied in hostile accounts. Events in the Gomułka era can best be approached through Syrop (**0805**) and Bethell (**0135**).

1) MAJOR PERIODS - GENERAL

ıυΛ̩ 947/B16

0484 BAIN, R.N., *Slavonic Europe; a Political History of Poland and Russia, 1447-1796*, Cambridge, 1908, Pp. viii + 452.

0485 BRACKMANN, A., *The Political Development of Eastern Europe from the Tenth to the Fifteenth Centuries*, Boston, 1956.

0486 JABLONOWSKI, H., 'Poland to the Death of Sobieski, 1648-96', *N.C.M.H.*, Vol. 5, ch. 24, pp. 559-70.

0487 KURBIS, B., 'L'historiographie mediévale en Pologne' *A.P.H.*, vol. 6, 1962-3, pp. 7-34.

0488 MALOWIST, M., 'Les problèmes de la Pologne avant et après les grandes découvertes', *C.R. Acad. Polonaise*, 1963, pp. 196-206.

0489 NARKIEWICZ, O., *The Green Flag: Polish Populist Politics, 1867 - 1970*, London, 1976, Pp. 314.

0490 SKWARCZYŃSKI, P., 'Poland and Lithuania, 1569-1610', *N.C.M.H.*, vol 3, ch. 12, pp. 377-403.

SEE ALSO:

PŁOSKI, (**0045**); SENKOWSKA, (**0046**); WANDYCZ, (**0218**); CHOWANIEC, (**1406**); FRANKEL, (**1408**); *Peace Handbook*, (**1637**).

2) POLITICAL MOVEMENTS AND IDEAS

Feldman (**0495**) is a major work, and the only available study of nineteenth century political ideas as a whole. Brock (**0492**) together with Handelsman (**0498**), Coleman (**0504**), Szacki (**0506**) and Tazbir (**0507**), provide an introduction to modern Nationalism. The thought of earlier periods is not easily assessible, but Backvis (**0490**), Stankiewicz (**0505**) and Ulam (**0508**) bring the highlights of the sixteenth century into view.

The political origins of the present régime can be traced in **J** (**2d**) and **J** (**2e**). The Polish Marxists, Kołakowski (**0530**) and Schaff (**0535**) describe interesting ideological positions, one after disillusionment, the other before. Dziewanowski (**0539**) is a critical, but rather exploratory Party History.

Other political movements, of little significance outside Poland, have not attracted foreign scholars.

a) POLITICAL IDEAS

0491 BACKVIS, C., 'Les thèmes majeurs de la pensée politique polonaise au XVI siècle', *Annuaire de l'Institut de Philologie et d'Histoire Orientales et Slaves*, vol. 14, 1954-57, pp. 309 ff.

0492 BROCK, PETER, *Polish Nationalism*, New York, 1968.

0493 BROCK, PETER, *Nationalism and Populism in Partitioned Poland*. (Selected Essays), London, 1973, Pp. 219.

0494 BUJARSKI, G.T., 'Polish Liberalism, 1815-23', *P.R.*, vol. 17, 1972, pp. 3-37.

0495 FELDMAN, W., *Geschichte der politischen Ideen in Polen seit dessen Teilungen, 1795-1914*, Munich, 1917, Pp. 448.

0496 GÓRSKI, KAROL, 'Un traité polonais de politique du XV siècle et l'influence de Buridan en Pologne', *Standen en Landen*, vol. 39, 1966, pp. 65-83.

0497 GÓRSKI, KAROL, 'Les idées politiques de Lucas Watzenrode, évêque de Warmie, 1447-1512', *Standen en Landen*, vol. 48, 1969, pp. 37-76.

0498 HANDELSMAN, M., *Les idées françaises et la mentalité politique en Pologne au XIX siècle*, Paris, 1927, Pp. 213.

0499 LEDNICKI, W. 'Poland and the Slavophil Idea', *S.E.E.R.*, vol. 7, 1928, pp. 128-40, 649-62.

0500 LEŚNODORSKJ, B., 'La pensée politique de Rousseau en Pologne', *A.H.R.F.*, 1962, pp. 497-514.

0501 LIPIŃSKI, EDOUARD, *De Copernic à Stanislas Leszczyński: la pensée économique et démographique en Pologne*, Paris, 1961, Pp. xxiii + 342.

0502 MALARCZYK, JAN, *La fortuna di Machiavelli in Polonia*, Wrocław, 1962. (2nd ed enlarged, 1969, Pp. 54).

0503 MOREAU-REIBEL, J., 'Un tournant de la pensée politique en Pologne, aux XV-XVI siècles', *Rev. Int. d'Hist. Pol. et Const.*, vol. 5, 1955, pp. 224-35.

0504 COLEMAN, A.P., 'Language as a factor in Polish nationalism', *S.E.E.R.*, vol. 13 (37), 1934, pp. 155-72.

0505 STANKIEWICZ, W.J., *"The Accomplished Senator" of Laurentius Goślicki*, St. Andrews, 1964, Pp. 40.

0506 SZACKI, J., 'L'évolution du concept de "nation" en Pologne à la fin du XVIII et au début du XIX siècles', *Cah. Hist. Mond.*, vol. 9, 1965, pp. 59-79.

0507 TAZBIR, J., 'Recherches sur la conscience nationale en Pologne au XVII et XVIII siècles', *A.P.H.*, vol. 14, 1966, pp. 5-22.

0508 ULAM, A.B., 'A.F. Modrevius, Polish Political Theorist of the Sixteenth Century, *American Political Science Review*, vol. 40, 1946, pp. 485-94.

0509 WEINTRAUB, WIKTOR, 'Mickiewicz and Bakunin', *S.E.E.R.*, 1949, vol. 29 (70), pp. 72-83.

SEE ALSO:

KOLARZ, (0229); SUGAR, LEDERER, (0235); GÓRSKI, (0450); MESNARD, (0457); BROCK, (0518); JOBERT, (0942); KORANYI, (0955); BOROWY, (0969); BRUCKNER, (0970); CYNARSKI, (0972); ULEWICZ, (0977); KIENIEWICZ, (1270); SYMMONS, (1493); BLEJWAS, (1661); HANDELSMAN, (1702); KIENIEWICZ, (1713); ŁEPKOWSKI, (1725).

b) PEASANT MOVEMENT

0510   BROCK, P., 'The Polish Movement to the People', *S.E.E.R.*, vol. 40 (94), 1961, pp. 99-122.

0511   BROCK, P., 'B. Wysłouch - Founder of the Polish Peasant Party', *S.E.E.R.*, vol. 30 (74), 1951, pp. 139-63.

0512   BROCK, P., 'The Early Years of the Polish Peasant Party, 1895-1907', *J.C.E.A.*, vol. 14, 1954, pp. 219-35.

0513   BROCK, P., 'Zenon Swiętosławski, a Polish Forerunner of the Narodniki', *S.R.*, vol. 13, 1954, pp. 566-87.

0514   ROSE, W.J., 'Wincenty Witos', *S.E.E.R.*, vol. 25, 1946, pp. 39-54.

SEE ALSO: BROCK, (0493).

c) SOCIALISM

0515   BLIT, L., *The Origins of Polish Socialism - the History and Ideas of the First Polish Socialist Party, 1878-86*, London, 1971, Pp. ix + 160.

0516   BOROWY, W., 'B. Limanowski,' *S.E.E.R.*, vol. 14 (41), 1936, pp. 429-30.

0517   BROCK, P., 'Polish Socialists in early Victorian England', *P.R.*, vol. 6, 1961, pp. 33-53.

0518   BROCK, P., 'Socialism and Nationalism in Poland, 1840-6',*C.S.P.*, vol. 4, 1959, pp. 121-46.

0519   COTTAM, K.J., 'Bolesław Limanowski: a Polish theoretician of Agrarian Socialism', *S.E.E.R.*, vol. 51 (1), 1973, pp. 58-75.

0520   DZIEWANOWSKI, M.K., 'The Beginnings of Socialism in Poland', *S.E.E.R.*, vol. 29 (73), 1951, pp. 510-31.

0521   DZIEWANOWSKI, M.K., 'Social Democrats and Social Patriots', *S.R.*, vol. 10, 1951, pp. 14-25.

0522   HAUSTEIN, ULRICH, *Sozialismus und nationale Frage in Polen, 1875-1900*, Köln, 1969, Pp. 304.

0523 HOLZER, JERZY, 'The attitude of the P.P.S. and P.P.S.D. to the Russian Revolutions of 1917', *A.P.H.*, vol. 16, 1967, pp. 76-90.

0524 ORDEGA, A., 'Herman Lieberman', *S.E.E.R.*, vol. 23, 1945, pp. 147-8.

0525 ROSE, W.J., 'Ignacy Daszyński, 1886-1936', *S.E.E.R.*, vol. 15, 1937, pp. 445-8.

SEE ALSO:

STROBEL, (0724); TOBIAS, (1082); BROCK, (1219-21); BOREJSZA, (1664); BROCK, (1667).

d) MARXISM AND MARXISM-LENINISM

0526 BOBIŃSKA, C., 'Les débuts de la Première Internationale: Les polonais et la question polonaise,' in *La Pologne au XII Congrès International des Sciences Historiques à Vienne*, Warsaw, 1965, pp. 85-100.

0527 CIOŁKOSZ, A., 'Marx and the Polish Insurrection of 1863', *P.R.*, vol. 10, 1965, pp. 8-51.

0528 HISCOCKS, R., 'Some Liberal Marxists and Left-wing Catholics in Contemporary Poland', *Canadian Journal of Econ. Pol. Science*, vol. 30, 1964, pp. 12-21.

0529 JORDAN, ZBIGNIEW, *A Philosophy and Ideology: the Development of Philosophy and Marxism-Leninism in Poland since the Second World War*, Dordrecht, 1973, Pp. 600.

0530 KOŁAKOWSKI, LESZEK, *Marxism and Beyond*, [translated by J.Z. Peel], London, 1968, Pp. 240.

0531 LANGE, OSKAR, *Political Economy: Volume 1, General Problems*, (Translated by A.H. Walker,) Oxford, 1963; Volume 2, Oxford, 1971.

0532 LERNER, W., *Karl Radek - the Last Internationalist*, Stanford, 1970, Pp. 240.

0533 MACDONALD, H.M., 'Marx, Engels and the Polish National Movement', *J.M.H.*, vol. 13, 1941, pp. 321-34.

0534 NETTL, J.P., *Rosa Luxemburg*, London, 1966, 2 vols. .

0535 SCHAFF, ADAM, *A Philosophy of Man*, London, 1963, Pp. 139.

0536 SCHNEIDERMAN, S.L., *Warsaw Heresy*, New York, 1959, Pp. 253.

0537 VARGLA, T., et al., 'Poland: Bastion of Socialism', *World Marxixt Review*, vol. 17, no. 10, pp. 16-18.

SEE ALSO:

KERNIG, **(0028)**; LACHS, **(0032)**; SEIDLER, **(0480)**; DZIEWANOWSKI, **(0658)**; **(0659)**; SABALIUNAS, **(1749)**; SOLCHANYK, **(1810)**.

e) COMMUNIST PARTIES

0538 DEUTSCHER, I., 'The Tragedy of Polish Communism between Two Wars', *Les Temps Modernes*, March 1958, also published in *Marxism in our Time*, London, 1972, Pp. 312.

0539 DZIEWANOWSKI, M.K., *The Communist Party of Poland: an Outline of History*, Harvard, 1959, Pp. xvi + 369.

0540 DIEWANOWSKI, M.K., 'The Foundation of the Communist Party of Poland', *S.R.*, vol. 11, 1952, pp. 106-22.

0541 KIENIEWICZ, S., *Histoire de "La Tribune des Peuples"*, Wrocław, 1963.

0542 KOCHEŃSKI, A., TYCH, F., 'Le Parti Communiste polonais, 1918-38', *A. Feltrinelli*, 1960, vol. 3, pp. 630-55.

0543 KORBOŃSKI,, A., 'The Polish Communist Party, 1938-42', *S.R.*, vol. 26, 1966, pp. 430-44.

0544 STAAR, RICHARD, R., 'Polish Communist Party, 1918-48', *P.R.*, vol. 1, 1956, pp. 41-59.

0545 STROBEL, GEORG, W., *Quellen zur Geschichte des Kommunismus in Polen, 1878-1918: Programme und Statuten*, Köln, 1968, Pp. 342.

SEE ALSO:

VIGOR, **(0058)**; BLIT, **(0136)**; RAINA, **(0167)**; VARGLA, **(0537)**; STROBEL, **(0724)**; **SECTION J (27)**; SOLCHANYK, **(1166)**; VOLGYES, **(1765)**; PIENKOS, **(1802)**; RYBICKI, **(1805)**.

f) NATIONAL DEMOCRACY

0546 KOZICKI, S., 'Roman Dmowski', *S.E.E.R.*, vol. 18, 1939, pp. 118-28.

0547 ROSE, W.J., 'S. Grabski, 1879-1949', *S.E.E.R.*, vol. 28, 1949, pp. 229-31.

SEE ALSO:

DMOWSKI, **(1454)**. **(1464)**; GASIOROWSKI, **(1457)**.

g) SANACJA

0548 BOROWY, W., 'B. Pieracki', *S.E.E.R.*, vol. 13 (38), 1935, pp. 433-34.

0549 KRAKOWSKI, E., 'La pensée créatrice d'un chef - J. Piłsudski', *R.H.D.*, vol. 49, 1935, pp. 494-513.

0550 ROSE, W.J., 'W. Sławek', *S.E.E.R.*, vol. 18, 1939, pp. 204-6.

SEE ALSO:

BLIT, **(0136)**; LANDAU, **(0151)**; PIŁSUDSKI, **(0162)**; REDDAWAY, **(0168)** KENNET, **(0712)**; ROTHSCHILD, **(0722)**; WOOLF, **(0725)**.

3) ORIGINS OF THE POLISH STATE, 966-1079

0551 ANDRUSIAK, M., 'Kings of Kiev and Galicia ...', *S.E.E.R.*, vol. 33, 1954-5, pp. 342-50.

0552 DZIĘCIOŁ, W., *The Origins of Poland*, London, 1967, Pp. 309.

0553 HENSEL, WITOLD, *La naissance de la Pologne*, Wrocław, 1966, Pp. 255.

0554 HENSEL, WITOLD, *The Beginnings of the Polish State*, Warsaw, 1960, Pp. 180.

0555 KĘTRZYŃSKI, S., 'The Introduction of Christianity and the Early Kings of Poland', *C.H.P.*, vol. 1, ch. 2, pp. 16-42.

0556 MANTEUFFEL, T., GIEYSZTOR, A., ed., 'L'Europe aux IX et X siècles: Aux origines des etats nationaux', *Actes du Colloque international sur les origines des états européens*, (PAN), Warsaw, 1968, Pp. 527.

0557 ODLOŽILÍK, OTAKAR, 'The Contest for East Central Europe in the Eleventh Century', *P.R.*, vol. 2, no. 1, 1957, pp. 3-17.

0558 SZCZEŚNIAK, BOLESLAW, 'The Imperial Coronation of Gniezno in A.D. 1000', in *Studies in Polish Civilisation*, ed., Wandycz, D., New York, 1966, pp. 23-37.

0559 WOJCIECHOWSKI, Z, *Mieszko I and the Rise of the Polish State*, Toruń, 1936, Pp. 234.

SEE ALSO:

SECTION F; SMAL-STOCKI, **(1258)**; LADNER, **(1297)**; MANTEUFFEL, **(1301)**; SZCZEŚNIAK, **(1760)**.

4) THE DUKEDOMS, 1079 - 1333

✓ 0560 BRUCE BOSWELL, A., 'Poland, 1050-1303', *C.Med.H.*,vol. 6, ch. 13 (b), pp. 447-63.

0561 BRUCE BOSWELL, A., 'The Twelfth Century: From Growth to Division, 1079-1202', *C.H.P.*, vol. 1, ch. 3, pp. 43-59.

0562 BRUCE BOSWELL, A., 'Territorial Division and the Mongol Invasions, 1202-1300', *C.H.P.*, vol. 1, ch. 5, pp. 85-107.

0563 BUCZEK, DANIEL, 'Archbishop Jakub Świnka', 1283-1314, in *Studies in Polish Civilisation*, ed., Wandycz, D., New York, 1966, pp. 54-65.

0564 HOLZMANN, R., 'Über den Polenfeldzug Friedrich Barbarossas von Jahr 1157 und die Begründung der Schlesischer Herzogtümer,' *Zeitschrift des Vereins für Geschichte Schlesiens*, Bd. 56, 1922.

0565 SOBIESKI, JAKUB, 'Jean de Pologne à Louvain, 1253', *Cahiers de l'Institut d'Etudes Polonaises en Belgique*, no. 8, Brussels, 1950, Pp. 68.

5) CASIMIR THE GREAT AND SUCCESSOR, 1333 - 1386

0566 BALZER, O., *Les statuts de Casimir le Grand*, Paris, 1948, Poznań, 1947, Pp. 527.

✓ 0567 HALECKI, O., 'Casimir the Great, 1333-70', *C.H.P.*, vol. 1, ch. 9, pp. 167-87.

0568 HALECKI, O., 'From the Union with Hungary to the Union with Lithuania; Jadwiga, 1374-99', *C.H.P.*, vol. 1, ch. 10, pp. 188-209.

SEE ALSO: KNOLL, (**0442**), (**0931**); HALECKI, (**1700**).

6) THE EARLY JAGIELLONS, 1386 - 1506

0569 BALZER, O., *The Anniversary of the Battle of Grunwald*, London, 1941, Pp. 11.

0570 BRUCE BOSWELL, A., 'Poland and Lithuania in XIV and XV centuries', *C. Med. H.*, vol. 8, ch. 18, pp. 556-86.

0571 BRUCE BOSWELL, A., 'Jagiełło's Successors: the Thirteen Years' War with the Knights, 1434-66', *C.H.P.*, vol. 1, ch. 12, pp. 232-49.

0572 DĄBROWSKI, J., 'L'année 1444', *Bulletin International de l'Académie Polonaise des Sciences et des Lettres*, Cracow, 1952, Supplément 6, Pp. 45.

0573 ESZLARY, C. d', 'Le mariage de Władisław II Jagiellon et d'Anne de Foix, 1502', *Monuments de la Société de l'Histoire et Archéologie de la Bretagne*, vol. 45, 1969, pp. 5-39.

0574   HALECKI, O., 'Problems of the New Monarchy: Jagiełło and Vitold, 1400-34', *C.H.P.*, vol. 1, ch. 11, pp. 210-31.

SEE ALSO:

KELLOG, **(0149)**; BARDACH, **(0428)**; BISKUP, **(1026)**; HALECKI, **(1295)**; LASKOWSKI, **(1298)**; LASOCKI, **(1299)**; BACHUS, **(1659)**.

7) LATER JAGIELLONS, 1506-1572

0575   LEWALSKI, K.F., 'Sigismund I of Poland; Renaissance King and Patron', *Studies in the Renaissance*, vol. 14, 1966-7, pp. 49-72.

0576   PAJEWSKI, J., 'Zygmunt August and the Union of Lublin, 1548-72', *C.H.P.*, vol. 1, ch. 17, pp. 348-68.

0577   WOJCIECHOWSKI, Z., 'Les débuts du programme de l'exécution des lois en Pologne au début du XVIème siècle', *Rev. Hist. de Droit Franc. et Etr.*, vol. 29, 1951, pp. 173-92.

SEE ALSO: BARDACH, **(0447)**; DOLESEL, **(1130)**; KIRCHNER, **(1296)**.

8) THE INTERREGNA, 1572 - 1576

0578   BAIN, R.N., 'The Polish Interregnum, 1575', *E.H.R.*, vol. 4, 1889, pp. 645-66.

0579   CENIVAL de, P., 'La politique du Saint-Siège et l'élection de Pologne, 1572-1573', *Mélanges d'archéologie et d'histoire publiées par l'Ecole francaise de Rome*, vol. 36, 1916-17, pp. 109-203.

0580   CHAMPION, P., *Henri III, roi de Pologne*, Paris, 1944, vol. 1.

0581   ROTH, C., 'Dr Solomon Aszkanazi and the Polish Election, 1574-5', *Oxford Slavonic Papers*, vol. 9, 1960, pp. 8-20.

0582   SKWARCZYŃSKI, P., 'The Decretum Electionis of Henry of Valois', *S.E.E.R.*, vol. 37, 1958-9, pp. 113-30.

SEE ALSO: SKWARCZYŃSKI, **(0463)**, **(0489)**; DE PERSAN, **(1313)**.

9) BATORY, 1576-1586

0583   DABROWSKI, J., ed., *Étienne Batory, roi de Pologne, Prince de Transylvanie*, Cracow, 1935, Pp. 591.

0584   NIEDERHAUSER, E., 'Bathori dans l'historiographie polonaise et hongroise', *Publicationes Institutionis Philologicae et Slavicae Universitatis Debreceniensis*, 1964, vol. 47.

0585   NOWAK, F., 'The Interregna and Stephen Batory, 1572-86', *C.H.P.* vol. 1, ch. 18, pp. 369-91.

0586   SCOTT, C., SKWARCZYŃSKI, P., 'A Sixteenth Century Spanish Diplomat's View of Poland', *S.E.E.R.*, vol. 40, 1961-2, pp. 497-517.

SEE ALSO: SKWARCZYŃSKI, (**0489**); KARTTUNEN, (**1340**).

10) SIGISMUND III (ZYGMUNT III), 1587-1632

0587   BIAUDET, HENRY, *Les origines de la candidature de Sigismund Vasa au trône de Pologne en 1587*, Helsinki, 1911, Pp. 82.

0588   BIAUDET, HENRY, *Sixte-Quinte et la candidature de Sigismond Vasa au trône de Pologne en 1587. D'après des documents inédits des Archives Secrètes du Saint-Siège*, Helsinki, 1910, Pp. 22.

0589   LANCKORONSKA, K., 'Un portrait de Sigismund III par Rubens', *Antemurale*, vol. 11, 1967, pp. 173-6.

0590   NOWAK, F., 'Sigismund III, 1587-1632', *C.H.P.*, vol. 1, ch. 21, pp. 451-74.

0591   PÄRNÄNEN, J.A., *Le premièr séjour de Sigismond Vasa en Suède, 1593-1594: D'après la correspondence diplomatique du nonce apostolique, Germanico Malaspina*, Helsinki, 1933, Pp. 198.

SEE ALSO:

SKWARCZYŃSKI, (**0489**); JABLONOWSKI, (**0593**); BERGA, (**0862**); TALBOT, (**1321**); BARBOUR, (**1323**); MACISZEWSKI, (**1328**); THOMPSON, (**1332**); ŻÓŁKIEWSKI, (**1333**); CZAPLIŃSKI, (**1339**); KUJAWSKI, (**1342**); LEPSZY, (**1343**); REDDAWAY, (**1344**); SCHÜTZ, (**1346**).

11) LADISLAUS IV (WŁADYSŁAW IV), 1632-1648

0592   CZAPLIŃSKI, W., 'The Reign of Władysław IV, 1632-48', *C.H.P.*, vol. 1, ch. 22 (B), pp. 488-501.

0593   JABLONOWSKI, H., 'Poland and Lithuania, 1609-48', *N.C.M.H.*, vol. 4, ch. 19, pp. 585-601.

SEE ALSO:

MYCIŃSKI, (**0868**); KLEYNTJENS, (**1314**); REDDAWAY, (**1344**); SCHÜTZ (**1346**); SZCZEŚNIAK, (**1347**); WOLIŃSKI, (**1348**).

12) JOHN CASIMIR (JAN KAZIMIERZ), 1648 - 1668

0594 DE WEERD, H.E., 'Report of the Netherlands Ambassador at the Polish Court on Bohdan Khmelnytsky, 1654', *Ukrainian Quarterly*, vol. 13, 1957, pp. 56-8.

0595 KANE, W.T., 'Poland's Jesuit King', *Thought*, [New York], vol. 18, no. 69, June 1943, pp. 257-76.

0596 KORDUBA, M., TOMKIEWICZ, W., 'The Reign of John Casimir, 1648-68', *C.H.P.*, vol. 1, ch. 23, pp. 502-31.

0597 MARCINKOWSKI, K., *The Crisis of the Polish-Swedish War, 1655-1660*, Wilberforce, Ohio, 1951, Pp. 98.

0598 STOYE, JOHN, *Europe Unfolding, 1648-88*, London, 1969, Pp. 416. (chapters 1-3).

SEE ALSO:

KRUPNYTSKY, (0119); JABLONOWSKI, (0486); VERNADSKY, (1053); KRUPNYTSKY, (1324); LEWITTER, (1325); O'BRIEN, (1329); OHLOBYN, (1330); REDDAWAY, (1344).

13) 1668-1696: JAN SOBIESKI

0599 FORST-BATTAGLIA, O., 'Jan Sobieski, 1647-96', *C.H.P.*, vol. 1, ch. 24, pp. 532-56.

0600 LASKOWSKI, O., *Sobieski, King of Poland*, (Translated by F.C. Anstruther), Glasgow, 1944, Pp. 237.

0601 LASKOWSKI, O., *La campagne de Vienne, 1683*, Warsaw, 1933.

0602 LEWITTER, L.R., 'John III, Sobieski, Saviour of Vienna, *H.T.*, vol. 12, 1962, pp. 168-76, 242-52.

0603 MORTON, J.B., *Sobieski, King of Poland*, London, 1932, Pp. 286.

SEE ALSO:

STURMINGER, (0052); WALISZEWSKI, (0179); JABLONOWSKI, (0486); SZCZEŚNIAK, (1306); STOYE, (1307); DE FOURBIN, (1312); RUBINSTEIN, (1315); LEWITTER, (1326).

14) SAXON PERIOD, 1696 - 1763

0604 DZIEWANOWSKI, M.K., 'King Stanisław Leszczyński - Some Remarks and Question Marks', *J.G.O.*, vol. 16, 1968, pp. 104-16.

0605 FRANKOWSKI, T., 'La dynastie de Saxe sur le trône de Pologne', *R.H.D.*, vol. 45, 1931, pp. 119-40.

0606 GIEROWSKI, J.; KAMINSKI, A., 'The Eclipse of Poland', *N.C.M.H.*, vol. 6, ch. 20 (2), pp. 681-715.

0607 GIEROWSKI, J., 'La France et les tendances absolutistes du roi de Pologne, Auguste II', *A.P.H.*, vol. 17, 1968-9, pp. 49-70.

0608 KONOPCZYNSKI, W., 'The Saxon Period, 1697-1763', *C.H.P.*, vol. 2, ch. 1-2, pp. 1-48.

0609 LANGROD-VAUGHAN, M., *Stanisław Leszczynski, philosophe politique, souverain nominal et administrateur bienfaisant en Lorraine, 1737-1766*, Nancy, 1962.

0610 LEWITTER, L.R., 'Poland under the Saxon Kings', *N.C.M.H.*, vol. 7, ch. 16, pp. 365-90.

0611 SASS, C., 'The Election Campaign in Poland, 1696-7', *J.C.E.A.*, vol. 12, 1952, pp. 111-27.

0612 SCHLIMGEN, E., 'Stanislaus Leszczynski, King of Poland, reformer in exile', *Bul. Pol. Inst.*, vol. 3, 1944-45, pp. 621-49.

SEE ALSO:

LIPIŃSKI, (**0362**); HENTSCHEL, (**0974**); LEWITTER, (**1334**); (**1336**); GIEROWSKI, (**1349**); (**1350**); HASSINGER, (**1352**); LEWITTER, (**1355-1356**); KALISCH, (**1357**); ZIEKURSCH, (**1358**).

15) STANISLAUS AUGUSTUS (STANISLAW AUGUST), 1763-1795

0613 ASKENAZY, S., *Die letzte polnische Königswahl*, Göttingen, 1894, Pp. 158.

0614 BAIN, R.N., *The Last King of Poland and his Contemporaries*, London, 1909, Pp. 196.

0615 DEMBINSKI, R., 'The Age of Stanislas Augustus and the National Revival', *C.H.P.*, vol. 2, ch. 6, pp. 112-36.

0616 FORST-BATTAGLIA, O., *Stanislaus August Poniatowski und der Ausgang des alten Polenstaates*, Berlin, 1927, Pp. 393.

0617 KAPLAN, H.H., 'The election of the last King of Poland: Stanisław August Poniatowski', *P.R.*, vol. 2, no. 1, 1957, pp. 27-49.

0618 KIENIEWICZ, S., 'Les récentes études sur la Pologne au temps des Partages', *A.P.H.*, vol. 1, 1958, pp. 59-73.

0619 KUKIEL, M., 'Kościuszko and the Third Partition', *C.H.P.*, vol. 2, ch. 8, pp. 154-76.

0620 PALEWSKI, J.P., *Stanislaus-Auguste Poniatowski, dernier roi de Pologne*, Paris, 1946, Pp. 197.

0621 ROSTWOROWSKI, E., 'La Pologne pendant la seconde moitié du XVIII siècle: Bilan de recherches, 1945-56,' *Annales*, vol. 13, 1958, pp. 123-35.

0622 ROSTWOROWSKI, E., 'La Grande Diète, 1788-92 - réformes et perspectives', *A.H.R.F.*, vol. 36, 1964, pp. 309-28.

0623 ZERNACK, K., 'Stanislaus August Poniatowski', *J.G.O.*, vol. 15, 1967, pp. 370-92.

SEE ALSO:

SECTIONS Q (7, 8); BENYOWSKI, (0134); JOHNS(0147); HANDELSMAN, (0451); KALINKA, (0452); KLOTZ, (0453); FABRE, (0978); SCOTT, (1750).

16) DUCHY OF WARSAW, 1807-1815

0624 ASKENAZY, S., *Prince Joseph Poniatowski*, London, 1916, Pp. 16.

0625 CHEŁMIŃSKI, J., *L'Armeé du Duché de Varsovie*, Paris, 1913, Pp. 314.

0626 GROCHULSKA, B., 'Sur la structure économique du Duché de Varsovie, 1807-13', *A.H.R.F.*, vol. 36, 1964, pp. 349-63.

0627 HANDELSMAN, M., 'The Duchy of Warsaw', *C.H.P.*, vol. 2, ch. 11, pp. 236-56.

0628 HANDELSMAN, M., ed., *Instrukcje i Depesze Rezydentów Francuskich w Warszawie, 1807-18*, (Instructions and Communiqués of the French Agents in Warsaw, 1807-18), (Text in French), Kraków, 1914, 2 vols. Pp. 900.

0629 SENKOWSKA, M., 'Les majorats français dans le Duché de Varsovie', *A.H.R.F.*, vol. 36, 1964, pp. 373-86.

SEE ALSO:

d'ORNANO, (0158); STRYIENSKI, (0174); LEŚNODORSKI, (1000); KUKIEL, (1032); CHELMINSKI, (1673); JEDLICKI, (1707).

17) CONGRESS KINGDOM, 1815 - 1831

0630 ASKENAZY, S., 'Poland and the Polish Revolution 1815-31', *C.M.H.*, vol. 10, ch. 14, pp. 445-74.

0631 HANDELSMAN, M., 'The Congress Kingdom', *C.H.P.*, vol. 2, ch. 13 (A), pp. 275-94.

0632 LESLIE, R.F., 'Politics and Economics in Congress Poland, 1815-65', *Past and Present*, no. 8, 1955, pp. 43-63.

0633 PINGAUD, L., 'L'Empéreur Alexandre I, roi de Pologne', *R.H.D.*, vol. 31-2, 1917-18, pp. 513-40.

0634 RAIN, P., 'Alexandre I et la Pologne. Un essai en gouvernement constitutionnel, 1815-25', *R.H.D.*, vol. 26, 1912, pp. 74-101.

SEE ALSO: BUJARSKI, (**0494**); EISENBACH, (**1074**).

18) THE NOVEMBER RISING, 1830 - 1831

0635 BROCK, P., 'A Pacifist in Wartime: Wojciech Jastrezębowski', in *Studies in Polish Civilisation*, ed., Wandycz, D., New York, 1966, pp. 82-91.

0636 DUKER, A., 'The Polish Insurrection's Missed Opportunity, 1830-1831', *J.S.S.*, vol. 28, 1966, pp. 212-32.

0637 HANDELSMAN, M., 'L'état actuel des études relatives à l'histoire de 1830-31 en Pologne', *Revue d'Hist. Mod.*, vol. 6, 1931, pp. 469-80.

0638 LESLIE, R.F., 'Polish Political Divisions and the Struggle for Power, November 1830', *S.E.E.R.*, vol. 31, 1952, pp. 113-32.

0639 LESLIE, R.F., *Polish Politics and the Revolution of November 1830*, London, 1956, Pp. xii + 307.

0640 LEWAK, A., 'The Polish Rising of 1830', *S.E.E.R.*, vol. 9, 1930, pp. 350-60.

0641 KUKIEL, M., 'Les origines de la stratégie et de la tactique des insurrections polonaises au XVIII et au XIX siècles', *Revue Int. d'Histoire Militaire*, no. 12, 1952, pp. 526-45.

0642 MORLEY, C., 'The European Significance of the November Uprising', *J.C.E.A.*, vol. 11, 1952, pp. 407-16.

0643 WIECZERAK, J.W., 'The Polish Insurrection of 1830-1 in the American Press', *P.R.*, vol. 6, 1961, pp. 53-72.

SEE ALSO: SECTION P (2); WERESZYCKI, (**0112**).

19) 1831 - 1863

0644 LESLIE, R.F., 'Left-wing Political Tactics in Poland, 1831-46', *S.E.E.R.*, vol. 33, 1954, pp. 120-39.

0645 ROSEVEARE, IRENE, A, 'From Reform to Rebellion: A. Wielopolski and the Polish Question, 1861-3', *C.S.S.*, vol. 3, 1969, pp. 163-85.

0646 ZYZNIEWSKI, S.J., 'The Futile Compromise Reconsidered: Wielopolski and Russian Policy, 1861-3', *Am. H.R.*, vol. 70, 1965 (2), pp. 395-412.

SEE ALSO: LESLIE, **(0652)**; FELDMAN, **(0667)**; ROSEVEARE, **(1747)**; **SECTIONS Q,** 9 f, g.

20) THE JANUARY RISING, 1863 - 1864

0647   DZIEWANOWSKI, M.K., 'Herzen, Bakunin and the Polish Insurrection of 1863', *J.C.E.A.*.

0648   EDWARDS, S., *The Polish Captivity - An Account of the Present Position of the Poles*, London, 1863.

0649   KIENIEWICZ, S., 'A propos du centenaire de l'insurrection de 1863-4', *A.P.H.*, vol. 8, 1963, pp. 31-53.

0650   KIENIEWICZ, S., 'Polish Society and the Insurrection of 1863', *Past and Present*, no. 37, 1967, pp. 130-48.

0651   KULCZYCKA-SALONI, J., 'L'insurrection de 1863 dans la littérature polonaise', *A.P.H.*, vol. 11, 1965, pp. 5-21.

0652   LESLIE, R.F., *Reform and Insurrection in Russian Poland, 1856-65*, London, 1963, Pp. ix + 272.

0653   MICHELET, J., *La Pologne Martyr: Russie-Danube*, Paris, 1863, Pp. 365.

0654   PASIEKA, K.S., 'British Press and the Polish Insurrection of 1863', *S.E.E.R.*, 1963, vol. 42, pp. 15-37.

0655   PETROVICH, M.B., 'Russian Pan-slavists and the Polish Insurrection', *H.S.S.*, vol. 1, 1953, pp. 219-47.

0656   RUDZKA, WALENTYNA, 'Studies on the Polish Insurrectionary Government in 1863-4', *Antemurale*, vol. 8, 1967, pp. 397-481.

SEE ALSO:

WERESZYCKI, **(0112)**; BULLOCK, **(0137)**; PIOTRKOWSKI, **(0163)**; CIOLKOSZ, **(0527)**; KUKIEL, **(0641)**, **(1033)**; LINCOLN, **(1723)**.

21) RUSSIAN POLAND, 1864 - 1917

0657   CHMIELEWSKI, EDWARD, 'The Separation of Chełm from Poland, 1905,' *P.R.*, vol. 15, 1970, pp. 65-86.

0658   DZIEWANOWSKI, M.K., 'The Revolution of 1904-5 and the Marxist Movement of Poland', *J.C.E.A.*, vol. 12, 1952, pp. 259-75.

0659   DZIEWANOWSKI, M.K., 'The Polish Revolutionary Movement and Russia, 1904-7', *H.S.A.*, vol. 4, 1957, pp. 375-95.

0660   KORMANOWA, Z., 'Quelques aspects de l'histoire du Royaume de Pologne pendant la seconde moitié du XIX siècle', *A.P.H.*, vol. 5, 1962, pp. 183-98.

0661 LEWIS, RICHARD D., 'Labor-Management Conflict in Russian Poland: The Lodz Lockout of 1906-1907', *E.E.Q.*, vol. 7, no. 4, 1974, pp. 413-34.

0662 ROSE, W.J., 'Russian Poland in the later Nineteenth Century', *C.H.P.*, vol. 2, ch. 17, pp. 387-408.

0663 ROTH, P., *Die politische Entwicklung in Kongresspolen während der deutschen Okkupation*, Berlin, 1919.

SEE ALSO:

BAEDEKER, (**0077**); MALECKA, (**0154**); MILYUKOV, (**0156**); PIŁSUDSKA, (**0161**); PIŁSUDSKI, (**0162**); REDDAWAY, (**0168**); OLSZAMOWSKA, (**0894**); TOBIAS, (**1082**); STANDING, (**1476**); WHEELER-BENNETT, (**1478**); *Peace Handbooks*, (**1635-1636**).

22) PRUSSIAN POLAND, 1815 - 1918

0664 BLACK, C.E., 'Poznań and Europe in 1848', *J.C.E.A.*, vol. 8, 1948, pp. 191-206.

0665 BLANKE, RICHARD, 'The Development of Loyalism in Prussian Poland, 1886-1890, *S.E.E.R.*, vol. 52, 1974, pp. 548-65.

0666 DUFOURMANTELLE, M., *La politique de germanisation en Pologne prussienne: ses méthodes, ses résultats, ses effets*, Bruxelles, 1922

0667 FELDMAN, J., 'The Polish Provinces of Prussia and Austria after 1815: the "Springtime of Nations" ', *C.H.P.*, vol. 2, ch. 15, pp. 336-64.

0668 GENTZEN, F.H., *Grosspolen in Januaraufstand: Das Grossherzogtum Posen, 1854-64*, Berlin, 1958, Pp. 358.

0669 GROSSMANN, K., 'A Chapter in Polish-German Understanding - the German League for Human Rights', *P.R.*, vol. 15, no. 3, 1970, pp. 32-47.

0670 HAGEN, W., 'National Solidarity and Organic Work in Prussian Poland, 1815-1914', *J.M.H.*, vol. 44, 1972, pp. 38-64.

0671 JAKOBCZYK, W., 'The First Decade of the Prussian Settlement Commission's activities, 1886-97', *P.R.*, vol. 17, 1972, pp. 3-12.

0672 LAUBERT, M., *Die preussische Polenpolitik von 1772-1914*, Berlin, 1920, Pp. 204.

0673 LAUBERT, M., *Studien zur Geschichte der Provinz Posen in der ersten Hälfte des 19 Jahrhunderts*, Bd. 2, Posen, 1927, Pp. 190.

0674 MAI, JOACHIM, *Die preussisch-deutsche Polenpolitik, 1885-7: Eine Studie zur Herausbildung des Imperialismus in Deutschland*, Berlin, 1962, Pp. 231.

0675 MORROW, I.D., 'The Prussianisation of the Poles', *S.E.E.R.*, vol. 15, 1936, pp. 153-64.

0676 NEUBACH, HELMUT, *Die Ausweisungen von Polen und Juden aus Preussen, 1885-6. Ein Beitrag zu Bismarcks Polenpolitik, und zur Geschichte des deutsche-polnischen Verhaltnisses*, Wiesbaden, 1967, Pp. 293.

0677 ONSLOW, LORD, 'Polish Self-Help under Prussian Rule', *S.E.E.R.*, vol. 10, 1931, pp. 126-37.

0678 ORZECHOWSKI, MARIAN, 'Statistics and Language Maps as a Tool of Prussian Nationalish Policy', *P.W.A.*, vol. 6, 1965, pp. 197-217.

0679 POPIOŁEK, K., '1848 in Silesia: I - Prussian Silesia', *S.E.E.R.*, vol. 26, 1948, pp. 374-84.

0680 ROHL, J.C.G., 'A Document of 1892 concerning Prussia and Poland', *Hist.J.*, vol. 7, 1964, pp. 143-49.

0681 ROSE, W.J., 'Prussian Poland, 1850-1914', *C.H.P.*, vol. 2, ch. 18, pp. 409-31.

0682 ROSE, W.J., *The Drama of Upper Silesia - a Regional Study*, London, 1936, Pp. 349.

0683 ROSENTHAL, H.K., 'Nation or Class: The Bund der Landwirhte and the Poles', *Australian Journal of Politics and History*, vol. 19, 1973, pp. 200-4.

0684 ROSENTHAL, H.K., 'Poles, Prussians and Elementary Education in Nineteenth Century Posen,' *Canadian/American Slav. Studies*, VII, 1973, pp. 209-218.

0685 ROSENTHAL, H.K., 'The Election of Archbishop Stablewski', *S.R.*, vol. 28, 1969, pp. 265-75.

0686 ROSENTHAL, H.K., 'Rivalry between Notables and Townspeople in Prussian Poland: the First Round', *S.E.E.R.*, vol. 49, 1971, pp. 68-79.

0687 ROSENTHAL, H.K., 'The Problem of Caprivi's Polish Policy', *E.S.R.*, vol. 3, 1972, pp. 255-64.

0688 ROSENTHAL, H.K., 'Germans and Poles in 1890', *E.E.Q.*, vol. 5, 1971, pp. 302-12.

0689 ROSENTHAL, H.K., 'The Prussian View of the Pole - 1894', *P.R.*, vol. 17, no. 1, 1972, pp. 13-20.

0690 ROSENTHAL, H.K., 'Tactics and National Unity in Prussian Poland: The Necessary Disunities', *East Central Europe*, vol. I, 1974, pp. 65-70.

0691 SLAVENAS, JULIUS P., 'The Polish Parliamentarians in the North German Reichstag, 1867-1870', *P.R.*, vol. 19, 1974, pp. 71-76.

0692 TIMS, R., *Germanizing Prussian Poland. The H-K-T Society and the Struggle for the Eastern Marches in the German Empire, 1894-1919*, New York, 1941, Pp. 312.

0693 TOYNBEE, A.J., *The Destruction of Poland: a Study in German Efficiency*, London, 1916, Pp. 30.

0694 TRZECIAKOWSKI, LECH, 'The Prussian State and the Catholic Church in Prussian Poland, 1871-1914', *S.R.*, vol. 26, 1967, pp. 618-37.

0695 WEHLER, H-U., 'Die Polenpolitik im deutschen Kaiserreich, 1871-1918' in *Politische Ideologien und nationalstaatliche Ordnung*, Knixen, K.; Mommsen, W.J., ed., Munich, 1968.

SEE ALSO:

SECTION Q (3c); JOLL, **(0118)**; KNAPOWSKA, **(1440)**; GEISS, **(1468)**; *Peace Handbooks*, **(1633-1634)**, **(1640)**; JAKOBCZYK, **(1706)**; KORTH, **(1714)**; NEUBACH, **(1736)**.

23) AUSTRIAN POLAND, 1815 - 1918

0696 ANDRUSIAK, N., 'The Ukrainian Movement in Galicia', *S.E.E.R.*, vol. 14, 1935-6, pp. 163-75, 372-9.

0697 ESTREICHER, S., 'Galicia in the Period of Autonomy and Self-Government, 1848-1914', *C.H.P*, vol. 2, ch. 19, pp. 432-60.

0698 FELDMAN, J., 'The Polish Provinces of Prussia and Austria, 1815-48', *C.H.P.*, vol. 2, ch. 15, pp. 336-64.

0699 KANN, R.A., *The Multinational Empire - Nationalism and National Reform in the Habsburg Monarchy, 1848-1918*, New York, 1950, 2 vols.

0700 LINGELBACH, W.E., *Austria-Hungary*, London, 1906, (Republished London).

0701 KOENIG, S., 'Geographic and Ethnic Characteristics of Galicia', *J.C.E.A.*, vol. 1, 1941/2, pp. 55-65.

0702 POPIOŁEK, F., '1848 in Silesia: II The Duchy of Teschen', *S.E.E.R.*, vol. 26, 1948, pp. 384-89.

0703 RUDNICKI, J., *A Page of Polish History* (Translated by B.W. Massey), Lwów-London, 1944, Pp. 76.

0704 STEED, H.W., *The Habsburg Monarchy*, London, 1914, 2nd edition, Pp. xxxvi + 304.

0705 WANDYCZ, P., 'The Poles in the Austrian Empire', *A.H.Y.*, vol. 3, part 2, 1967, pp. 261-86.

0706 WENEDIKTER, RICHARD, 'Die Karpathenländer', in *Das*

Nationalitätenrecht des alten Oesterreichs, ed., Hugelman, K.G., Vienna, 1934.

0707   WERESZYCKI, H., 'The Poles as an Integrating and Disintegrating Factor', *A.H.Y.*, vol. 3, part 2, 1967, pp. 287-313.

SEE ALSO:

MULLER, (**0041**); SLOMKA, (**0173**); SIMONS, (**0290**); DOROSHENKO, (**0889**); MENDELSOHN, (**1081**); RUDNITSKY, (**1165**); *Peace Handbooks*, (**1632**), (**1641**); STILES, (**1757**).

24) THE FREE CITY OF CRACOW, 1815 - 1846

0708   KIENIEWICZ, S., 'The Free State of Cracow, 1815-46', *S.E.E.R.*, vol. 26, 1947, pp. 69-89.

25) SECOND REPUBLIC, 1918 - 1939

0709   DEVEREUX, ROY, *Poland Reborn*, London, 1922, Pp. 256.

0710   JASIENICA, PAWEL, 'The Polish Experience, (1918-19)', *J.Cont.H.*, 1968, vol. 3, (4), pp. 73-88.

0711   JABLONSKI, H., 'Les principaux groupes politiques de la société polonaise, 1918-19', *A.P.H.*, vol. 2, 1959, pp. 43-70; vol. 3, 1960, pp. 49-87.

0712   KENNET, LORD, 'Piłsudski', *C.H.P.*, vol. 2, ch. 25, pp. 589-615.

0713   MACARTNEY, C.A., PALMER, A.W., *Independent Eastern Europe - A History*, London, 1962, Pp. vii + 499.

0714   MACHRAY, R., *The Poland of Pilsudski*, London, 1936, Pp. 508.

0715   MURRAY, M., ed., *Poland's Progress, 1919-39*, London, 1944, Pp. xii + 152.

0716   OERTZEN, F.W. von, *So This is Poland*, London, 1932, Pp. 288.

0717   PENSON, J.H., 'The First Years of the Republic', *C.H.P.*, vol. 2, ch. 24, pp. 567-88.

0718   POLONSKY, A., *Politics in Independent Poland, 1921-39 - The Crisis of Constitutional Government*, London, 1971, Pp. 572.

0719   RAIN, P., 'La Pologne de 1919, était-elle valable?', *R.H.D.*, vol. 66, 1952, pp. 132-42.

0720   ROSE, W.J., *Poland's Political Parties, 1919-1939*, Surbiton, 1947, Pp. 28.

0721   ROTHSCHILD, JOSEPH, *Piłsudski's Coup d'Etat*, New York and London, 1966, Pp. xii + 435.

0722 ROTHSCHILD, JOSEPH, 'A Chapter in Polish Politics of the 1920's: (The BBWR)' in *Studies in Polish Civilisation*, ed., Wandycz, D., New York, 1966, pp. 99-116.

0723 SAROLEA, CHARLES, *Letters on Polish Affairs*, Edinburgh, 1922, Pp. 140.

0724 STROBEL, G.W., 'Arbeiterschaft und Linksparteien in Polen, 1928-38', *J.G.O.*, vol. 10, 1962, pp. 67-102.

0725 WOOLF, S.J., ed., *European Fascism*, London, 1968, Pp. 386 (chapter 8).

0726 WYNOT, EDWARD D., Jr., *Polish Politics in Transition: The Camp of National Unity and the Struggle for Power, 1935-39*, Athens (Georgia), 1974, Pp. 294.

0727 ZIELINSKI, HENRYK, 'Problèmes de la renaissance d'une Pologne indépendente, 1918-19', *Revue d'Histoire Moderne et Cont.*, vol. 16, 1969, pp. 105-13.

SEE ALSO:

POLONSKY, (**0101**); KOROSTOWETZ, (**0150**); LANDAU, (**0151**); PADEREWSKI, (**0159**); PIŁSUDSKA, (**0161**); PILSUDSKI, (**0162**); REDDAWAY, (**0168**); ROSE, (**0169**); ROSE, (**0170**); ROSE, (**0171**); HERTZ, (**0295**); MALINOWSKI, (**0296**); **SECTION I (5)**; DEUTSCHER, (**0538**); KOCHEŃSKI, (**0542**); STAAR, (**0544**); ROTHSCHILD, (**1038**); JOHNPOLL, (**1091**); **SECTION Q (11)**; REVIUK, (**1164**); BRATKOVSKI, (**1666**); GUNTHER, (**1701**); MENDELSOHN, (**1729**); ROTHSCHILD, (**1748**).

26) OCCUPATION AND RESISTANCE 1939 - 1945

a) GERMAN OCCUPATION

0728 ALDOR, F., ed., *Germany's Death Space: The Polish Tragedy*, London, (Undated) (1941?), Pp. 262.

0729 BARTOSZEWSKI, W., *Warsaw Death Ring, 1939-44*, Warsaw, 1968, Pp. 449.

0730 BÓR-KOMOROWSKI, TADEUSZ, *The Secret Army*, London, 1950, Pp. 407.

0731 BROSZAT, M., *Nationalsozialistische Polenpolitik, 1939-45*, Stuttgart, 1961, (revised ed., Frankfurt-Hamburg, 1965, Pp. 228).

0732 CYPRIAN, T.; SAWICKI, J., *Nazi Rule in Poland, 1939-45*, Warsaw, 1961, Pp. 261.

0733 DOBROSZYCKI, L., 'The Gestapo and the Polish Resistance Movement in the Radom Area', *A.P.H.*, vol. 4, 1961, pp. 85-118.

0734   *Documenta Occupationis Teutonicae*, Poznań, 1946-9, 4 vols.

0735   DURACZYŃSKI, EUGENIUSZ, 'Some Remarks on the Regional Characteristics of the Resistance Movement in Poland', *A.P.H.*, vol. 28, 1973, pp. 39-61.

0736   HOHENSTEIN, ALEXANDER (pseudonym), *Wartherländisches Tagebuch aus Jahren 1941-2*, Stuttgart, 1961, Pp. 319.

0737   HOESS, RUDOLF, *Commandant of Auschwitz*, London, 1959, Pp. 252.

0738   KARSKI, J., *Story of a Secret State* [on Polish resistance to the German occupation of Poland, 1939-44], London, 1945, Pp. 319.

0739   KORBOŃSKI, STEFAN, *Fighting Warsaw: the Story of the Polish Underground State 1939-45*, London, 1956, Pp. 495.

0740   LEMKIN, RAPHAEL, *Axis Rule in Occupied Europe*, Washington, 1944, Pp. 674.

0741   NUROWSKI, R., ed., *1939-1945 War Losses in Poland*, Warsaw, 1960, Pp. 135.

0742   *The Persecution of the Catholic Church in German Occupied Poland: Reports presented by Cardinal Hlond, Primate of Poland to Pope Pius XII ...*, London, 1941, Pp. 123.

0743   PIOTRKOWSKI, STANISLAW, ed., *Hans Frank's Diary*, Warsaw, 1961, Pp. 320.

0744   STEPNIOWSKI, T., 'La lutte armée de la résistance polonaise pendant les années de l'occupation hitlérienne', *Revue Int. d'Histoire Militaire*, no. 28, 1969, pp. 530-55.

SEE ALSO:

SECTION N (4d); ADAMS, **(0129)**; (ANON), **(0132)**; WASILEWSKA, **(0178)**; BARTOSZEWSKI, **(1006)**; AURICH, **(1056)**; POPIOŁEK, **(1151)**; *Poland*, **(1647-1651)**; AINSZTEIN, **(1657)**; GARLINSKI, **(1688, 1689)**; SERENY, **(1752)**.

b) SOVIET OCCUPATION, 1939 - 1941

0745   (ANON), *The Dark Side of the Moon*, (Preface by T.S. Eliot), London, 1946, Pp. 232.

0746   CZAPSKI, JOSEPH, *The Inhuman Land*, London, 1951, Pp. 301.

0747   FITZGIBBON, LOUIS, *Katyń - Crime Without Parallel*, London, 1971, Pp. 285.

0748   MACKIEWICZ, J., *The Katyń Wood Murders*, London, 1950, Pp. vi + 252.

0749 O'MALLEY, SIR OWEN, *Katyn: Dispatches of Sir Owen O'Malley to the British Government*, Chicago, 1973, Pp. 27.

0750 U.S.A. (82nd Congress), *Select Committee to Conduct an Investigation of ... The Katyn Forest Massacre: Hearings*, Washington, 1950.

0751 ZAWODNY, J.K., *Death in the Forest: The Story of the Katyń Forest Massacre*, London, 1971, Pp. xvii + 235.

SEE ALSO:

ZAGORSKI, **(0184)**; **SECTION Q (12)**; REDLICH, **(1745)**; KOMOROWSKJ, **(1790)**.

c) THE WARSAW RISING, 1944

0752 BRUCE, G., *The Warsaw Rising: 1 August to 2 October 1944*, London, 1972.

0753 CIECHANOWSKI, J., *The Warsaw Rising*, London/Cambridge, 1974, Pp. xi + 332.

0754 DESCHNER, G., *The Warsaw Rising* (Pan/Ballantine History of World War Two. Illustrated), London, 1972, Pp. 160.

0755 HOCHFELD, J., 'Social Aspects of the Warsaw Rising, 1944', *J.C.E.A.*, vol. 5, 1945, pp. 36-44.

0756 KRANNHALS, W. von, *Der Warschauer Aufstand*, Frankfurt, 1944, Pp. 445.

0757 ORLOWSKI, L., 'The Insurrection of Warsaw', *J.C.E.A.*, vol. 7, 1947, pp. 133-42.

SEE ALSO: KATZ, **(1710)**; LUKAS, **(1794)**.

27) POLISH PEOPLE'S REPUBLIC (P.R.L.)

a) GENERAL POLITICAL HISTORY

0758 BROMKE, ADAM, 'Nationalism and Communism in Poland', *Foreign Affairs*, vol. 40, 1960, pp. 635-643.

0759 BROMKE, ADAM, 'From "Falanga" to "Pax",' *Survey*, vol. 39, 1961, pp. 29-40.

0760 BROMKE, ADAM, *Poland's Politics: Idealism versus Realism*, Cambridge, Mass., 1967, Pp. 316.

0761 CIEPLAK, TADEUSZ N., 'Some Distinctive Characteristics of the

Communist System in the Polish People's Republic', *P.R.*, vol. 19, no. 1, 1974, pp. 41-66.

0762 GIBNEY, F., *The Frozen Revolution. Poland: a Study in Communist Decay*, New York, 1959, Pp. xiv + 269.

0763 GROTH, A.J., *People's Poland: Government and Politics*, Scranton (Pennsylvania), 1972.

0764 HALECKI, OSCAR, *Poland (East Central Europe under the Communists)*, New York, 1957, Pp. 601.

0765 HISCOCKS, R., *Poland - Bridge for the Abyss? An Interpretation of Developments in Post-war Poland*, London, 1963, Pp. vi + 359.

0766 IWANSKA, ALICJA, ed., *Contemporary Poland: Society, Politics, Economy*, Chicago, 1955, Pp. 578.

0767 JAROSZEWICZ, PIOTR, 'Thirty Years of People's Power', *World Marxist Review*, vol. 17, no. 7, 1974, pp. 1-4.

0768 KARSOV, N.; SZECHTER, S., *Monuments are not Loved*, London, 1970, Pp. 286.

0769 LEWIS, F., *The Polish Volcano - A Case Study of Hope*, London, 1959, Pp. xiv + 267. Also published as *A Case History of Hope: the Story of Poland's Peaceful Revolutions*, New York, 1958, Pp. 267.

0770 MORRISON, J.F., *The Polish People's Republic*, Baltimore, 1968, Pp. xi + 160.

0771 PIEKALKIEWICZ, J., 'Communist Administration in Poland within the Framework of Input-Output Analysis', *E.E.Q*, vol. 6, 1972, pp. 230-58.

0772 STAAR, RICHARD, F., *The Communist Regimes in Eastern Europe: an Introduction*, Stanford, 1967, Pp. xi + 387.

0773 STAAR, RICHARD F.,'Political Bureau of the Polish United Workers' Party', *S.R.*, vol. 15, pp. 206-15.

0774 STEHLE, H.J., *The Independent Satellite - Society and Politics in Poland since 1945*, London, 1965, Pp. 361.

0775 STRONG, ANNA, *I Saw the New Poland*, Boston, 1946.

0776 SZYR, EUGENIUSZ, *et al.* ed., *Twenty Years of the Polish People's Republic* (Illustrated), Warsaw, 1964, Pp. 313.

0777 WIATR, J.J., 'Political Parties, Interest, Representation and Economic Development in Poland', *American Political Science Review*, 1960, no. 64, pp. 1239-45.

0778 WOODS, WILLIAM, *Phoenix in the East*, Penguin Books, 1972, Pp. 202, (First published as *Eagle in the East*, London, 1968, Pp. 272.)

SEE ALSO:

WINTER, (0062); BETHELL, (0135); BLIT, (0136); RAINA, (0167); **SECTION K (10)**; BROWN, (0219); FISCHER-GALATI, (0224); IONESCU, (0227-0228); ROTHSCHILD, (0231); SINGLETON(0234); SUGAR, (0235); **SECTION I (6)**; EHRLICH, (0386); **SECTION K (10)**; HISCOCKS, (0528); CHECHINSKI, (1672); GOŁĘBIOWSKI, (1697); KERSTEN, (1712); PIEKALKIEWICZ, (1740).

b) ESTABLISHMENT OF THE P.R.L. 1944 - 1948

0779 CIECHANOWSKI, J., *Defeat in Victory*, London, 1948, Pp. 415.

0780 GROSS, F., 'The Fate of Poland', *J.C.E.A.*, vol. 8, 1948, pp. 242-55.

0781 HALPERN, ADA, *Liberation, Russian Style*, London, 1945, Pp. 598.

0782 JANCZEWSKI, G.H., 'The Origin of the Lublin Government,' *S.E.E.R.* vol. 50, 1972, pp. 410-33.

0783 JOHNSTON, R.R., *Poland 1945*, 1973.

0784 KORBOŃSKI, STEFAN, *Warsaw in Chains*, London, 1959, Pp. 319.

0785 KOWALSKI, J., 'Zur Entwicklung der Volksmacht in Polen in den Jahren 1944-6', *Jb. f.G. d.UdSSR.*, vol. 11, 1966 (3), pp. 3-28.

0786 LANE, A.B., *I Saw Freedom Betrayed*, London, 1949, Pp. 217.

0787 MALARA, JEAN, *La Pologne d'une occupation à l'autre, 1944-52*, Paris, 1952, Pp. 317.

0788 MIKOŁAJCZYK, S., *The Rape of Poland: - The Pattern of Soviet Domination*, New York, 1948, Pp. xiii + 309, also published as, *The Pattern of Soviet Domination*, London, 1948, Pp. xiv + 353.

0789 SCAEVOLA (pseudonym), *A Study in Forgery: the Lublin Committee and its Rule over Poland*, London, 1945, Pp. viii + 123.

0790 SETON-WATSON, H., *The East European Revolution*, London, 1956, (3rd edition), Pp. xix + 435.

0791 STAAR, RICHARD, F., *Poland 1944-62 - The Sovietisation of a Captive People*, New Orleans, 1962, Pp. 300.

0792 ZWERNIAK, S.M., *La justice soviétique*, Rome, 1945.

SEE ALSO:

ANDERSON, (0130); BARANSKI, (0133); STAAR, (0544); GOŁĘBIOWSKI, (1147); *U.S.A.*, (1654-1655); *U.S.S.R.*, (1656).

c) OCTOBER 1956 AND AFTER

0793 BIELECKI, F., *et al.*, *Pologne; Réalités et problèmes*, Warsaw, 1966, Pp. 440.

0794 BROMKE, ADAM, 'Poland under Gierek; A New Political Struggle', *Problems of Communism*, Sept/Oct, 1972, pp. 1-20.

0795 BROMKE, ADAM, STRONG, JOHN W., *Gierek's Poland*, New York, Washington, London, 1973, Pp. 219.

0796 CHRYPINSKI, VINCENT C., 'Political Change Under Gierek', *C.S.P.*, vol. 15, 1973, pp. 36-51.

0797 DEUTSCHER, ISAAC, *Russia in Transition and Other Essays*, New York, 1957, Pp. 245.

0798 FRELEK, RYSZARD, 'Into the Political Future', *Polish Perspectives*, vol. 17, no. 6, 1974, pp. 6-17.

0799 GRZYBOWSKI, K., 'Reform of Government in Poland,' *S.R.*, vol. 17, 1958, pp. 454-67.

0800 KAROL, K.S., *Visa to Poland*, London, 1959, Pp. 259.

0801 PEŁCZYNSKI, ZBIGNIEW A., 'The Downfall of Gomułka', *C.S.P.*, vol. 15, 1973, pp. 1-23.

0802 RAKOWSKI, MIECZYSLAW, F., 'December 1970: The Turning Point', *C.S.P.*, vol. 15, 1973, pp. 24-35.

0803 STAAR, RICHARD, F., 'Third Congress of the Polish Communist Party', *S.R.*, vol. 19, 1960, pp. 63-73.

0804 STAAR, RICHARD F., 'Poland: Old Wine in New Bottles', *Current History* (Philadelphia), vol. 64, 1973, pp. 197-201.

0805 SYROP, K., *Spring in October: The Polish Revolution of 1956*, London, 1957, Pp. xii + 267.

0806 WEYDENTHALL, JAN B. de., 'Academic Dissent as a Catalyst for Political Crisis in a Communist System', *P.R.*, vol. 19, no. 1, 1974, pp. 17-40.

0807 WHITE, PETER, T., 'Springtime of Hope in Poland', *National Geographic Magazine*, vol. 141, no. 4, 1972, pp. 467-501.

0808 WIATR, JERZY J., 'A Nation Reborn and Remodelled', *Polish Perspectives*, vol. 17, no. 6, 1974, pp. 66-75.

0809 ZINNER, P.E., ed., *National Communism and Popular Revolt in Eastern Europe. A Selection of Documents on Events in Poland and Hungary, February - November 1956*, New York, 1956, Pp. xx + 563.

SEE ALSO:

BETHELL, (**0135**); RAINA, (**0167**); WEIT, (**0180**); SCHAEFER, (**0232**); LEWIS, (**0769**); WIATR, (**0777**); CHECINSKI, (**1671**); BROMKE, (**1778**); DEAN, (**1781**); WOJCIK, (**1820**).

K. RELIGIOUS HISTORY

The historiography of religion in Poland is considerable for the early modern period, but deficient elsewhere. Manthey, (**0811**) is the only recent church history.

The work of Stanisław Kot dominates modern writing on the Reformation. Krasinski's classic study has been recently reprinted (**0842**). Halecki (**0890**) covers Catholic-Orthodox relations between the Conciliar Movement and the formation of the Uniate Church.

1) GENERAL

0810 HELM-PIRGO, MARIAN, *Virgin Mary, Queen of Poland: a Historical Essay*, New York, 1957, Pp. 32.

0811 MANTHEY, F., *Polnische Kirchengeschichte*, Hildesheim, 1965, Pp. 335.

0812 MEYSZTOWICZ, WALERIAN, *La Pologne dans la chrétienté: un coup d'oeil sur mille ans d'histoire, 966-1966*, Paris, 1966, Pp. 189.

0813 RĘCZLERSKI, W., *The Protestant Churches in Poland*, London, 1944.

0814 *Poland's Millenium of Catholicism*, (Scientific Society of the Catholic University of Lublin), Lublin, 1969, Pp. 627. (also published as *Le Millénaire du Catholicisme en Pologne*.)

0815 WAJSBLUM, M., 'The Quakers in Poland, 1661-1919', *P.R.*, vol. 11 (2), 1966, pp. 11-22.

SEE ALSO: BOHDANOWICZ, (**1044**).

2) THE ESTABLISHMENT OF CHRISTIANITY

0816 DAVID, P., *La Pologne et l'evangélisation de la Poméranie aux XI et XII siècles*, Paris, 1928, Pp. 66.

0817 DVORNIK, F., 'The Role of Bohemia and St. Adalbert in the Spread of Christianity in Poland', *P.R.*, vol. 5, no. 4, 1960, pp. 15-28.

0818 GIEYSZTOR, A., 'Les paliers de la pénétration du christianisme en Pologne aux X et XI siècles', in *Studi in onore di Amintore Fanfani*, Milan, 1962, vol. 1, pp. 327-67.

0819 ŁOWMIANSKI, H., 'The Slavic Rite in Poland and St. Adalbert', *A.P.H.*, vol. 24, 1972, pp. 5-21.

0820   VLASTO, A.P., *The Entry of the Slavs into Christendom*, Cambridge, 1970. (Chapter 3, 'The Western Slavs', pp. 86-154.)

SEE ALSO:

DEVEIKE, (0434); KĘTRZYŃSKI, (0555); BORWICZ, (1060); *Encyclopaedia Judaica*, (1063).

3) THE MEDIAEVAL CHURCH

0821   BUCZEK, D.S., 'Church, State and Holy See in Mediaeval Poland', *P.R.*, vol. 2, no. 3, 1966, pp. 62-6.

0822   DAVID, P., *Les Bénédictins et l'Ordre de Cluny dans la Pologne médiévale*, Paris, 1939, Pp. xxv + 113.

0823   DAVID, P., 'The Church in Poland, to 1250', *C.H.P.*, vol. 1, ch. 4, pp. 60-84.

0824   FABRE, P., 'La Pologne et le Saint Siège du X au XIII siècles,' in *Études d'histoire du moyen-âge dediées à Gabriel Monod*, Paris, 1896, pp. 163-76.

0825   GÓRSKI, KAROL, 'Le problème des influences liégeoises sur le Chapitre de Warmie aux XV et XVI siècles', *Standen en Landen*, vol. 32, 1964, pp. 15-26.

0826   HEIN, L., 'Der Sandomirer Knosens von 1570', *Kyrios*, N.F. vol. 3, 1963, pp. 65-77.

0827   KLOCZOWSKI, J., 'Les ordres mendiants et Pologne à la fin du moyen-âge', *A.P.H.*, vol. 15, 1969, pp. 5-38.

0828   MATCZAK, SEBASTIAN, 'An Archepiscopal Election in the Middle Ages: Jacob II of Gniezno', *P.R.*, vol. 8, no. 1, 1963, pp. 21-55.

0829   SCHLAUCH, M., 'A Polish Vernacular Eulogy of Wycliff', *Journal of Ecclesiastical History*, vol. 8, 1957, pp. 53-73.

0830   ŚWIDERSKA, H.M., 'A Polish Follower of Wycliffe', *University of Birmingham Historical Journal*, vol. 6, 1957, pp. 88-92.

SEE ALSO:

SECTION L (2); BEŁCH, (0431); GÓRSKI, (0497); BUCZEK, (0563); KAPELINSKI, (0879).

4) REFORMATION

0831   BETTS, R.R., 'Poland, Hungary and Bohemia: The Reformation in

Difficulties', *N.C.M.H.*, vol. 2, ch. 6, pp. 186-209.

0832   DAVID, P., *Le Protestantisme en Pologne jusqu'à 1570*, Montpellier, 1927.

0833   FOX, PAUL, 'The Reformation in Poland', *C.H.P.*, vol. 1, ch. 16, pp. 322-47.

0834   FOX, PAUL, *The Reformation in Poland: Some Social and Economic Aspects*, Baltimore, 1924, (Republished New York, 1971), Pp. viii + 153.

0835   HALL, B., *John à Lasko, 1499-1560: a Pole in Reformation England*, London, 1971, Pp. 31.

0836   HANS, N., 'Polish Protestants and their Connections in England, XVII-XVIII Centuries', *S.E.E.R.*, vol. 37, 1958, pp. 196-220.

0837   JOBERT, AMBROISE, *De Luther à Mohyla: La Pologne dans la crise de la chrétienté*, Paris, 1974, Pp. 484.

0838   JØRGENSEN, K.E.J., *Oekumenische Bestrebungen unter den polnischen Protestanten bis zum Jahre 1645*, Copenhagen, 1942, Pp. 410.

0839   KOT, STANISŁAW, *La Réforme dans la Grande Duché de Lithuanie: Facteur d'occidentalisation culturelle*, Brussels, 1953, Pp. 65.

0840   KOT, STANISŁAW, 'Opposition to the Pope by the Polish Bishops, 1557-60', *Oxford Slavonic Papers*, vol. 4, 1953, pp. 38-70.

0841   KOT, STANISŁAW, 'Polish Protestants and the Huguenots', *Proceedings of the Huguenot Society*, no. 17, 1945, pp. 303-10.

0842   KRASIŃSKI, WALERJAN, *Historical Sketch of the Rise, Progress and Decline of the Reformation in Poland*, London, 1838, 2 vols. .

0843   LEATHER, S., 'Notes on the Reformation in Poland', *C.M.H.*, vol. 2, ch. 17, pp. 634-8.

0844   PASCAL, G., *Jean de Lasco, baron de Pologne, evêque catholique, réformateur protestant*, Paris, 1894, Pp. 894.

0845   SCHRAMM, G., *Der Polnische Adel und die Reformation, 1548-1607*, Wiesbaden, 1965, Pp. 382.

0846   TAZBIR, J., 'Recherches sur l'histoire de la Réforme en Pologne', *A.P.H.*, vol. 2, 1960, pp. 133-53.

SEE ALSO: *Conférence Budapest*, **(0953)**; ŻANTUAN, **(1322)**.

5) THE SOCINIANS

0847   BENDER, D.H.S., 'The Anabaptists and Religious Liberty in the Sixteenth Century', *Archiv für Reformationsgeschichte*, vol. 44, 1953, pp. 32-57.

0848   CHMAJ, L., ed., *Studia nad Arianizmem*, (*Studies on Antitrinitarianism*), Warsaw, 1959, Pp. 563. (Summary in English).

0849   GÓRSKI, K., 'Some Aspects of the Polish Reformation in the XVI and XVII Centuries', *S.E.E.R.*, vol. 9, 1931, pp. 598-611.

0850   KOT, S., *Socinianism in Poland: The Social and Political Ideas of the Polish Antitrinitarians in The Sixteenth and Seventeenth Centuries*, Boston, 1957, Pp. xxvii + 229.

0851   KOT, S., 'Le mouvement antitrinitaire aux XVI et XVII siècles', *Humanisme et Renaissance*, vol. 4, 1937, pp. 16-58, 109-56.

0852   KOT, S., 'L'influence de Servet sur le mouvement antitrinitarien en Pologne et en Transylvanie' in *Autour de Michel Servet et de Sébastien Castellion*, Haarlem, 1953, pp. 72-115.

0853   KOT, S., 'Polish Brethren and the Problem of Communism in the Sixteenth Century', *Transactions of the Unitarian Historical Society*, vol. 11, no. 2, 1956, pp. 38-54.

0854   KOT, S., 'Szymon Budny, der grösste Häretiker lituanes im 16 Jahrhundert', Festschrift H.F. Schmidt, *Wiener Archiv*, vol. 2, 1956, pp. 63-118.

0855   KUPSCH, E., 'Der Polnische Unitarismus', *J.G.O.*, no. 5, 1957, pp. 401-40.

0856   LEVYTSKY, O., 'Socinianism in Poland and South-West Rus', *A.U.A.A.S.*, vol. 3, 1953, pp. 485-508.

0857   PIOLI, G., *Fausto Socino, Vita, opere, fortuna - Contributio alla storia del liberalismo religioso moderno*, Modena, 1952, Pp. 670.

0858   RUFFINI, F., 'Francesco Stancaro', *Ricerche Religiose*, vol. 8, 1932, pp. 395-408, 524-44; vol. 9, 1933, pp. 129-49, 237-56.

0859   RUFFINI, F., 'La Polonia del Cinquecento e le origini del Socinianismo', *La Cultura*, vol. 11, 1932, pp. 248-59.

0860   WILBUR, E.M., *A History of Unitarianism: Socinianism and its Antecedents*, Cambridge (Mass), 1946, Pp. xiii + 617.

0861   WILLIAMS, G.H., *The Radical Reformation*, London, 1962, Pp. xxxi + 924.

6) COUNTER-REFORMATION

0862   BERGA, A., *Un prédicateur de la Cour de la Pologne sous Sigismond III, Pierre Skarga: Etude sur la Pologne du XVI siècle et le Protestantisme polonais*, Paris, 1916, Pp. 376.

0863   BERNACKI, L., *La doctrine de l'Eglise chez le cardinal Hosius*, Paris, 1936, Pp. 290.

0864   GLEMMA, T., 'Le catholicisme en Pologne à l'époque d'Etienne Batory', in *Etienne Batory, roi de Pologne, prince de Transylvanie*,

Dąbrowski, J. ed., Cracow, 1935, pp. 335-74.

0865 HORAK, S.M., 'The Kiev Academy - a Bridge to Europe in the Seventeenth Century', *E.E.Q.*, vol. 2, 1968, pp. 117-37.

0866 KUNTZE, E., 'Les rapports de la Pologne avec le Saint-Siège à l'époque d'Etienne Bathory', in *Etienne Batory, roi de Pologne, prince de Transylvanie*, Dąbrowski, J., ed., Cracow, 1935, pp. 133-211.

0867 MATCZAK, SEBASTIAN, 'Stanislaus, Cardinal Hosius: Present State of Research', *P.R.*, vol. 6 (4), 1961, pp. 45-60.

0868 MYCIŃSKI, J., 'Quelques problèmes réligieux en Pologne sous le règne de Ladislas IV Vasa, 1632-42', *Revue du Nord*, vol. 49, 1967, pp. 409-19.

0869 OBERTYŃSKI, S., *Die florentiner Union der polnischen Armenier und ihr Bischofskatalog*, Rome, 1934, Pp. 68.

0870 PETROWICZ, G., *L'Unione degli Armeni di Polonia con la Santa Sede, 1626-86*, Rome, 1952, Pp. xiv + 334.

0871 PIERLING, P., *Le Saint-Siège, la Pologne et Moscou, 1582-1587*, Paris, 1885, Pp. 185.

0872 PIERLING, P., *Un Arbitrage Pontifical au XVI siècle entre la Pologne et la Russie, Mission diplomatique du P. Possevino 1581-1582*, Brussels, 1890, Pp. xxxvi + 274.

0873 PIERLING, P., *La Russie et le Saint-Siège - Études diplomatiques*, Paris, 1896-1912, 5 vols.

0874 POLLARD, A.F., *The Jesuits in Poland (The Lothian Essay)*, Oxford, 1892, Pp. viii + 98. (Republished New York, 1971.)

0875 ŚWIDERSKA, H., 'Stanisław Orzechowski, The Uneasy Years, 1550-59', *P.R.*, vol. 8, no. 3, 1963, pp. 3-45.

0876 UMIŃSKI, J., 'The Counter Reformation in Poland', *C.H.P.*, vol. 1, ch. 19, pp. 392-415.

SEE ALSO:

CÉNIVAL, (**0579**); BIAUDET, (**0587**), (**0588**); HALECKI, (**0890**); WYNAR, (**1055**); BIAUDET, (**1338**).

7) TOLERATION

0877 JOBERT, A., 'La tolérance religieuse en Pologne au XVI siècle, in *Studi in onore di Ettore lo Gatto e Giovanni Maver*, Florence, 1962, pp. 337-43.

0878 KAMEN, H., *The Rise of Toleration*, London, 1967, Pp. 256.

0879 KAPELINSKI, F., 'Paulus Vladimiri, 1369-1435, défenseur de la tolérance religieuse', *Rev. Int. d'Hist. pol. et const.*, vol. 5, 1955, pp. 201-14.

0880 KOT, STANISŁAW, *Georges Niemirycz et la lutte contre l'intolérance au XVII siècle*, The Hague, 1960, Pp. 78.

0881 LIBRACH, J., 'La paix religieuse en Pologne au temps de la Saint-Barthélemy', *Bull. de la Société de l'Histoire du Protestantisme*, vol. 14, 1968, pp. 507-20.

0882 TAZBIR, J., 'La tolérance religieuse en Pologne aux XVI et XVII siècles,' in *La Pologne au XII Congrès International des Sciences Historiques à Vienne*, Warsaw, 1965, pp. 31-48.

0883 WEINTRAUB, W., 'Tolerance and Intolerance in Old Poland', *C.S.P.*, vol. 13, 1971, pp. 21-43.

SEE ALSO: LEWIN, (**1078**).

8) ORTHODOX CHURCH

0884 AMMANN, A.M., *Abriss der Ostslavischen Kirchengeschichte*, Vienna, 1950, Pp. 748.

0885 GRAHAM, H.F., 'Peter Mogila, Metropolitan of Kiev', *Russian Review*, vol. 14, no. 4, 1955, pp. 345-56.

0886 JOBERT, A., 'L'Etat polonais, la liberté religieuse et l'Église orthodoxe au XVIIème siècle', *Rev. Int. d'Hist. pol. et const.*, vol. 5, 1955, pp. 236-43.

0887 MALVY, A.; VILLER, M., ed., *La confession orthodoxe de Pierre Moghila, métropolite de Kiev, 1633-46*, Rome, 1927, Pp. cxxxi + 223.

0888 POPPE, A., 'La tentative de réforme ecclésiastique en Russie au milieu du XIème siècle', *A.P.H.*, vol. 25, 1972, pp. 5-32.

SEE ALSO: WYNAR, (**1055**); LEWITTER, (**1336**).

9) THE UNIATE CHURCH

0889 DOROSHENKO, D., 'The Uniate Church in Galicia, 1914-17', *S.E.E.R.*, vol. 12, 1934, pp. 622-27.

0890 HALECKI, OSCAR, *From Florence to Brest, 1439-1596*, Rome, 1958, Pp. 444.

0891 LANCKORONSKA, K., 'Studies on the Roman-Slavonic Rite in Poland', *Orientalia Christiana Analecta*, Rome, 1961, Pp. viii + 196.

0892 PELESZ, J., *Geschichte der Union der ruthenischen Kirche mit Rom von den ältesten Zeiten bis auf die Gegenwart*, Würzburg-Wenna, 1878-81, 2 vols.

0893   VERNADSKY, G., *A History of Russia*, New Haven, 1959, vol. 4, Pp. xii + 348, (chapter 8).

10) MODERN RELIGIOUS HISTORY 1772 - 1918

0894   OLSZAMOWSKA, Z., 'Tentatives d'introduire la langue russe dans les églises latines de la Pologne orientale, 1865-1903', *Antemurale*, vol. 11, 1967, pp. 25-169.

0895   TAMBORRA, ANGELO, 'Catholicisme et le Monde Orthodoxe à l'époque de Pie IX', *Miscellanea Historiae Ecclesiasticae*, (Congrès de Moscou), no. 4, Louvain, 1972, pp. 179-93.

0896   ZATKO, J.J., 'The Organisation of the Catholic Church in Russia, 1772-84', *S.E.E.R.*, 1965, vol. 43, pp. 303-13.

SEE ALSO:

CAZIN, (**0139**); ROSENTHAL, (**0685**); TRZECIAKOWSKI, (**0694**); TAMBORRA, (**1477**); LESCOVER, (**1721**).

11) MODERN RELIGIOUS HISTORY 1918-1945

0897   SZERUDA, J., 'The Protestant Churches in Poland', *S.E.E.R.*, vol. 16, 1938, pp. 616-28.

12) MODERN RELIGIOUS HISTORY POST 1945

0898   BLIT, L., 'The Insoluble Problem, Church and State in Poland', *Religion in Communist Lands*, vol. 1, no. 3, 1973, pp. 8-11.

0899   DEMBINSKI, LUDWIK, 'Catholics and Politics in Poland', *C.S.P.*, vol. 15, 1973, pp. 176-83.

0900   DOLAN, F., 'Post-war Poland and the Church', *S.R.*, vol. 14, 1955, pp. 84-92.

0901   GSOVSKI, V., *Church and State behind the Iron Curtain*, New York, 1955, Pp. xxxi + 311.

0902   JORDAN, ALEXANDER T., ed., *A Strong Man Armed - Cardinal Wyszyński*, London, 1966, Pp. xiii + 187.

0903   MOSZYŃSKI, EDMUND, 'The Church on the Western Territories', *Polish Perspectives*, vol. 16, vol. 3, 1973, pp. 19-22.

0904   *The Roman Catholic Church in People's Poland*, (Central Priests' Committee of ZBOWiD), Warsaw, 1953, Pp. 129.

0905   STARON, STANISLAW, 'The State and the Church', *C.S.P.*, vol. 15, 1973, pp. 158-75.

0906   TUROWICZ, JERZY, 'Changing Catholicism in Poland', *C.S.P.*, vol. 15, 1973, pp. 151-71.

SEE ALSO: BROMKE, (1777)

L. CULTURAL AND INTELLECTUAL HISTORY

In this field, selection has of necessity been very arbitrary, especially on subjects such as Polish literature or fine arts which clearly require entire bibliographies to themselves.

Miłosz (**0921**) provides a comprehensive guide to literature, and Kot (**0915**) a learned essay on Polish learning.

In the mediaeval period, attention has been concentrated on the universities, in the Renaissance on contacts with Italy.

On the Enlightenment, the leading studies are by Jobert (**0982**) (**0983**) and Rose (**0990**).

The nineteenth century is dominated by literary giants, whose products are far too vast to be surveyed here. Senn (**1751**) describes inter-war Poland through the eyes of a famous Russian emigré-bibliophile.

Section (8), **SINCE 1945**, is mainly confined to intellectual revolt, and should be explored in conjunction with **Sections J 2 (d,e)**.

1) GENERAL

0907　BARYCZ, H., *The Development of University Education in Poland*, Warsaw, 1957, Pp. 59.

0908　BILIŃSKI, BRONISŁAW, *Tradizioni italiane all'Università Jagellonica di Cracovia*, Ossolineum, Wrocław, 1967, Pp. 124.

0909　BUCZEK, K., *The History of Polish Cartography*, Wrocław, 1966, Pp. 136 + 60 maps.

0910　GÖMÖRI, G., 'Polish Literature', in *World Literature since 1945: Critical Surveys of the Contemporary Literatures of Europe and the Americas*, Ivask, I., Wilpert, G., ed., New York, 1973, Pp. 503-24.

0911　IWANICKA, HALINA, *A Thousand Years of Poland's Heritage*, Chicago, 1966, Pp. 88.

0912　JEDLICKI, JERZY, 'Native Culture and Western Civilization', *A.P.H.*, vol. 28, 1973, pp. 63-85.

0913　KNOX, BRIAN, *The Architecture of Poland*, London, 1971, Pp. 161 + 216 plates.

0914　KOLBUSZEWSKI, S., 'Influences of Czech Culture in Poland', *S.E.E.R.*, vol. 18 (52), 1939, pp. 155-69.

0915　KOT, S., *Five Centuries of Polish Learning*, Oxford, 1944, Pp. 48.

0916　KRIDL, MANFRED, *A Survey of Polish Literature and Culture*, (Translated by O. Sherer-Virski), The Hague, 1956, Pp. 513.

0917 KRIDL, M., *et.al.*, *For Your Freedom and Ours: Polish Progressive Spirit Throughout the Centuries*, New York, 1943, Pp. 359. Also published as *The Democratic Heritage of Poland: For Your Freedom and Ours - an Anthology*, London, 1944, Pp. 236.

0918 LEDNICKI, WACLAW, *Life and Culture of Poland as Reflected in Polish Literature*, New York, 1944, Pp. 328.

0919 LEWALD, H. ERNEST, ed., *The Cry of Home. Cultural Nationalism and the Modern Writer*, Knoxville, 1972, Pp. 400.

0920 LISSA, Z., ed., *The Book of the First International Musicological Congress Devoted to the Works of Frederick Chopin, 1960*, Warsaw, 1965, Pp. 755.

0921 MIŁOSZ, CIESLAW, *A History of Polish Literature*, London, 1969, Pp. xiii + 570.

0922 PETERKIEWICZ, JERZY, ed., *Five Centuries of Polish Poetry, 1450-1950: An Anthology with Introduction and Notes*, London, 1950, Pp. 144.

0923 STACHIEWICZ, WANDA, 'The Jagiellonian University: a Historical Sketch', *P.R.*, vol. 9, no. 2, 1964, pp. 89-112.

0924 SUPER, PAUL, *The Polish Tradition*, London, 1944, pp. 215.

0925 WIRTH, ANDRZEJ, ed., *Polnisches Theater*, Neuwied, 1967, 2 vols.

SEE ALSO:

SECTIONS J (2), Q (3); COLEMAN, (0012);KUKULSKI, (0030); TABORSKI, (0056); BRANDES, (0192); DYBOSKI, (0195); EISENSTEIN, (1062); ESTREICHER, (1170); WŁOSZCZEWSKI, (1204); KREJCI, (1244); KRZYWICKI-HERBURT, (1717); ZIOMEK, (1772); SOWJNSKJ, (1811).

2) MEDIAEVAL

0926 BIRKENMAJER, ALEXANDER, *Études d'histoire des sciences et de la philosophie du Moyen Age*, Ossolineum, Wrocław, 1970, Pp. 698.

0927 CZARTORYSKI, P., 'L'idée de l'université et de la science à l'université de Cracovie', *Mediaevalia Philosophica Polonorum*, no. 14, 1969.

0928 DAVID, P., 'Etudiants polonais dans les universités françaises du moyen-âge', *Petit Ouvrier de France et de Pologne*, no. 9-10, 1929.

0929 JASIENICA, PAWEŁ, 'Recherches recentes sur la culture médiaévale polonaise', *Cahiers Pologne-Allemagne*, no. 3 (14), 1962, pp. 8-22.

0930 KOCZY, LEON, *Documents sur les origines de l'université de Cracovie, Comité du Millénaire de la Pologne en Belgique*, Dundee, 1967, Pp. 87.

0931 KNOLL, P., 'Casimir the Great and the University of Cracow', *J.G.O.*, vol. 16, 1968, pp. 232-49.

0932 ODLOŽILÍK, OTAKAR, 'Prague and Cracow Scholars', *P.R.*, vol. 9 (2), 1964, pp. 19-29.

0933 ŚWIEŻAWSKI, STEFAN, 'Aperçu sur les recherches des médiévistes polonais dans le domaine de l'histoire de la philosophie', *Miscellanea Mediaevalia*, vol. 2, 1963, pp. 110-25.

0934 ŚWIEŻAWSKI, STEFAN, 'Pour mieux connaître l'ambiance philosophique en Pologne mediévale', *Zeszyty Naukowe Katolickiego Uniwersytetu Lubelskiego*, vol. 4, 1961, pp. 81-118.

0935 TOMIAK, JANUSZ, J., 'The University of Cracow in the Period of its Greatness 1364-1569', *P.R.*, vol. 16, 1971, no. 2, pp. 25-44; no. 3, pp. 87-94.

0936 WIŚNIOWSKI, EUGENIUSZ, 'The Parochial School System in Poland toward the end of the Middle Ages', *A.P.H.*, vol. 27, 1973, pp. 29-44.

SEE ALSO:

BOSWELL, (**0262**); GOETEL-KOPFF, (**1017**); GROSS, (**1018**); MIŁOBEDZKI, (**1020**); FRIEDBERG, (**1292**).

3) RENAISSANCE

a) GENERAL

0937 BARYCZ, HENRYK, 'Les premiers contacts de Jan Łasicki avec la culture occidentale', *A.P.H.*, vol. 27, 1973, pp. 5-28.

0938 BILIŃSKI, BRONISLAW, *Gallileo Gallilei e il mondo polacco*, Ossolineum, Wrocław, 1969, Pp. 133.

0939 BIRNBAUM, H., 'Some Aspects of the Slavonic Renaissance', *S.E.E.R.*, vol. 47 (108), 1969, pp. 37-56.

0940 BRODY, E.C., 'Spain and Poland in the Age of the Renaissance. A Comparative Study', *P.R.*, vol. 15, no. 1, 1970, pp. 86-105.

0941 HALECKI, O.; KOMORNICKI, W., 'The Renaissance in Poland', *C.H.P.*, vol. 1, ch. 14, pp. 273-99.

0942 JOBERT, A., 'L'université de Cracovie et les grands courants de pensée du XVI— siècle', *Revue d'Histoire Moderne et Cont.*, vol. 1, 1954, pp. 213-25.

0943 KOT, STANISŁAW, 'L'Humanisme et la Renaissance en Pologne', *Bibliothèque d'Humanisme et Renaissance*, vol. 14, 1952, pp. 348-73; vol. 15, 1953, pp. 233-38.

0944 KOT, STANISŁAW, 'Le rayonnement de Strasbourg en Pologne à l'époque de l'humanisme', *Revue des Études Slaves*, vol. 27, 1951, pp. 184-200.

0945 LANGLADE, JACQUES, *Jean Kochanowski: L'Homme, le penseur, le poète lyrique*, Paris, 1932, Pp. 415.

0946 LEPSZY, K., 'La Renaissance en Pologne et ses liaisons internationales, *Centre Scientifique*, Paris, 1960, Pp. 19.

0947 NUCCI, N., *Il primo Rinasciamento italiano a Cracovia*, Budapest, 1931.

0948 SOKOLYSZYN, A., 'Sweipolt Fiol: the first Slavic Printer of Cyrillic Characters', *S.R.*, vol. 18, 1959, pp. 88-94.

0949 SOLMI, A., 'Il Rinasciamento italiano e la Polonia', *Europa Orientale*, vol. 16, 1936, pp. 257-71.

0950 TOMKIEWICZ, W., 'Le mécénat artistique en Pologne à l'époque de la Renaissance', *A.P.H.*, vol. 16, 1967, pp. 91-106.

0951 WEINTRAUB, W., 'Kochanowski's Renaissance Manifesto', *S.E.E.R.*, vol. 30 (75), 1952, pp. 412-24.

0952 ZANTUAN, K., 'Erasmus and the Cracow Humanists', *P.R.*, vol. 10, no. 2, 1965, pp. 3-36.

0953 La Renaissance et la Réformation en Pologne et en Hongrie, 1450-1650, Conférence Budapest - Eger 1961, *Studia Historica Academiae Scientarium Hungaricae*, Budapest, 1963, vol. 53, Pp. 562.

0954 Les Problèmes du Gothique et de la Renaissance et l'art de L'Europe Centrale, Conférence Budapest, 1965, being *Acta Historiae Artium Academiae Scientarium Hungaricae*, vol. 13, 1967.

0955 *Italia, Venezia e Polonia tra Umanesimo e Rinascimento: Atti del Convegno 1965*, BRAHMER, M., ed., Wrocław, 1967, Pp. xii + 376. including: BARYCZ, H., 'Italofilia e Italofobia nella Polonia del Cinque - e del Seicento, pp. 142-58; KORANYI, K. 'La costituzione di Venezia nel pensiero politico della Polonia,' pp. 206-14; GARBACIK, J., 'Le relazioni turco-polacche tra XVI e XVII secolo alla luce dei rapporti e dei dispacci dei baili veneziani a Constantinopoli', pp. 215-32; BRAHMER, M., 'La fortuna di Dante in Polonia', pp. 366-76.

SEE ALSO:

BACKVIS, (0491); STANKIEWICZ, (0505); LEWALSKI, (0575); TAMBORRA, (1242); CINI, (1269).

b) COPERNICUS

0956 ARMITAGE, ANGUS, *The World of Copernicus*, East Ardsley, 1971, Pp. 165. (a republication of *Sun, Stand Thou Still: the Life and Work of Copernicus*, London, 1947, and New York, 1963.)

0957 BIETKOWSKI, H., ZONN, W., *The World of Copernicus*, Warsaw, 1973, Pp. 167. (Illustrated.)

0958 BOGUCKA, MARIA, *Nicholas Copernicus. The Country and Times* (Trans. by Leon Szwajcer), Wrocław, 1973, Pp. 199.

0959 COPERNICUS, NICOLAUS, *Complete Works*. (Polish Academy of Sciences), London, 1972.

0960 CZARTORYSKI, P., ed., *Colloquia Copernicana: Conferences du Symposium de L'UIHPS, Torun, 1973*, Torun, 1973, Pp. 130.

0961 EVANS, CHARLOTTE,B., HOWARD,V, 'Nicholas Copernicus: A Renaissance Man', *E.E.Q.*, vol. 7, no. 3, 1973, pp. 231-47.

0962 HOYLE, F., *Nicolaus Copernicus*, London, 1973, Pp. 84.

0963 KAULBACH, F., *et al.*, ed., *Nicolaus Copernicus zum 500. Geburtstag*, Cologne-Vienna, 1973, Pp. xv + 270.

0964 MAHONEY, MICHAEL S., 'The Sublimity of the Mundane: The Impact of Copernicanism on Scientific Thought in the Sixteenth and Seventeenth Centuries', *P.R.*, vol. 18, no. 3, 1973, pp. 4-18.

0965 MĘKARSKI, STEFAN, *Nicholas Copernicus (Mikołaj Kopernik) 1473-1543*, London, 1973, Pp. 63.

0966 ROSEN, E., Trans., 'Three Copernican Treatises: The Commentariolus of Copernicus, the Letter against Werner, the Narratio Prima of Rheticus', *Columbia Records of Civilisation*, no. 30, New York, 1939, pp. 211.

0967 RYBKA, EUGENIUSZ, *Four Hundred Years of the Copernican Heritage*. (Trans. by M. Abrahamowicz), Cracow, 1964, Pp. 234.

SEE ALSO: LIPIŃSKI, (**0501**).

4) 1550 - 1750

0968 BIAŁOSTOCKI, JAN, 'Mannerism and "Vernacular" in Polish Art', in *Walter Friedländer zum 90 Geburtstag*, KAUFFMANN, E., SAUERLÄNDER, W., ed., Berlin, 1965, pp. 47-57.

0969 BOROWY, M., TATARKIEWICZ, W., 'Polish Literature and Art in the Eighteenth Century', *C.H.P.*, vol. 2, ch. 9, pp. 177-207.

0970 BRUCKNER, A., TATARKIEWICZ, W., 'Polish Cultural Life in the Seventeenth Century', *C.H.P.*, vol. 1, ch. 25, pp. 557-78.

0971 CIECHANOWIECKI, A., *Michał Kazimierz Ogiński und sein Musenhof zu Słonim*, Cologne-Graz, 1961, Pp. 212.

0972 CYNARSKI, S., 'The Shape of Sarmatian Ideology in Poland', *A.P.H.*, vol. 19, 1968, pp. 5-17.

0973 HALECKI, OSCAR, 'The Universities of the Polish-Lithuanian Commonwealth from the XVI to the XVII Centuries', *P.R.*, vol. 5, no. 3, 1960, pp. 21-30.

0974 HENTSCHEL, WALTER, *Die sächsische Baukunst des 18. Jahrhunderts in Polen*, Berlin, 1967, 2 vols.

0975 KOT, STANISŁAW, 'Nationum Proprietates', *Oxford Slavonic Papers*, vol. 6, 1955, pp. 1-43.

0976 LITAK, STANISŁAW, 'The Parochial School Network in Poland prior to the Establishment of the Commission of National Education', *A.P.H.*, vol. 27, 1973, pp. 45-66.

0977 ULEWICZ, T., 'Il problema del sarmatismo nella cultura e letteratura polacca', *Ricerche Slavistiche*, vol. 18, 1960.

SEE ALSO:

PASEK, (0160), (0467); BACKVIS, (0490); LIPIŃSKI, (0501); HORAK, (0865); POLLARD, (0874); ŚWIDERSKA, (0875); MARTEL, (1160).

5) ENLIGHTENMENT

0978 FABRE, J.M., *Stanislaus-Auguste Poniatowski et l'Europe des lumières*, Paris, 1952, Pp. 746.

0979 FABRE, J.M., *J-J Rousseau et le destin polonais*, Paris, 1961.

0980 HANS, N., 'Polish Schools in Russia, 1772-1831', *S.E.E.R.*, vol. 38, 1959, pp. 394-414.

0981 HINZ, H., 'The Philosophy of the Polish Enlightenment and its Opponents', *S.R.*, vol. 30, 1971, pp. 340-49.

0982 JOBERT, A., *La Commission d'education nationale en Pologne, 1773-94*, Paris, 1941, Pp. 500.

0983 JOBERT, A., *Magnats polonais et physiocrats français, 1767-1774*, Paris, 1941, Pp. 92.

0984 KURDYBACHA, L., 'The Commission for National Education in Poland, 1773-1794', *H of Ed.*, vol. 2, no. 2, 1973, pp. 133-46.

0985 LEŚNODORSKI, BOGUSŁAW, 'Le siècle des lumières en Pologne', *A.P.H.*, vol. 4, 1961, pp. 147-74.

0986 LEŚNODORSKI, BOGUSŁAW, *Les Jacobins polonais*, Paris, 1965, Pp. 367.

CULTURAL AND INTELLECTUAL HISTORY

0987 RACKAUSKAS, J.A., 'The Educational Commission of Poland and Lithuania 1773-1794: 200th Anniversary of its Establishment', *Lituanus*, vol. 19, no. 4, 1973, pp. 63-70.

0988 ROSE, W.J., 'Hugo Kołłątaj, 1750-1812', *S.E.E.R.*, vol. 29 (72), 1950, pp. 49-65.

0989 ROSE, W.J., 'Stanislas Konarski', *S.E.E.R.*, vol. 4, 1925, pp. 23-41.

0990 ROSE, W.J., *Stanislas Konarski, Reformer of Education in Eighteenth Century Poland*, London, 1929, Pp. 288.

0991 ROSE, W.J., 'Stanislaw Staszic, 1755-1826', *S.E.E.R.*, vol. 23, 1955, pp. 289-303.

0992 ROSTWOROWSKI, EMANUEL, 'Voltaire et la Pologne', in *Studies on Voltaire and the Eighteenth Century*, vol. 62, Geneva, 1968, pp. 101-21.

0993 WELSH, D.J., 'At the Sign of the Poets - Gröll's Printing House in Warsaw', *S.E.E.R.*, vol. 41 (96), 1962, pp. 208-16.

0994 WOŁOSZYŃSKI, R., WOŁTANOWSKI, A., 'Recherches sur le Siècle des Lumières en Pologne', *A.P.H.*, vol. 21, 1970, pp. 141-75.

SEE ALSO:

LEŚNODORSKI, **(0455)**, **(0456)**; ROUSSEAU, **(0461)**; BUJARSKI, **(0494)**; DEMBINSKI, **(0615)**; LEŚNODORSKI, **(0500)**, LOJEK, **(1724)**; MATERNICKI, **(1728)**; MICHALSKI, **(1730)**; RACKAUSKAS, **(1803)**; STONE, **(1815)**.

6) NINETEENTH CENTURY

0995 KIMBALL, STANLEY BOCHHOLZ, 'Poles at the All-Slavic Congress, 1868', *P.R.*, vol. 4, 1959, pp. 91-107.

0996 GARDNER, MONICA, 'The Great Emigration and Polish Romanticism', *C.H.P.*, vol. 2, ch. 14 B, pp. 324-35.

0997 KEEFER, L., 'The Influence of Mickiewicz on the Ballades of Chopin', *S.R.*, vol. 5, 1946, pp. 38-50.

0998 LEDNICKI, WACŁAW, 'Pushkin, Tyutchev, Mickiewicz and the Decembrists: Legends and Facts', *S.E.E.R.*, vol. 29 (73), 1951, pp. 375-402.

0999 LEDNICKI, WACŁAW, *Henryk Sienkiewicz: A Retrospective Synthesis*, The Hague, 1960, Pp. 81.

1000 LEŚNODORSKI, B., 'Les problèmes de L'acculturation: L'exemple du Duché de Varsovie', in *La Pologne au XII Congrès International des Sciences Historiques à Vienne*, Warsaw, 1965, pp. 63-83.

1001 LEWALSKI, K.F., 'Mickiewicz's "Konrad Wallenrod" - the Conflict between Politics and Art', *S.R.*, vol. 19, 1960, pp. 423-41.

1002 *Mickiewicz, Adam (1798-1855), Hommage de L'UNESCO à l'occasion du centième anniversaire de sa mort*, Paris, 1955, Pp. 277.

1003 WAGNER, A.M., 'Undivine Comedy - Krasiński and German Expressionism', *S.R.*, vol. 18-19, 1947, pp. 95-109.

1004 WEINTRAUB, WIKTOR, 'Adam Mickiewicz: the Mystic Politician', *H.S.S.*, vol. 1, 1953, pp. 137-78.

1005 ZBIERAŃSKA, K., 'Dante in Poland, a Retrospect', *P.R.*, vol. 11 (3), 1966, pp. 56-61.

SEE ALSO:

GARDNER, (0143); LEDNICKI, (0152); SZWEJKOWSKI, (0176); VLACH, (0177); WELSH, (0181); WELSH, (0182); WIERZYŃSKI, (0183); BROCK, (0492); FELDMAN, (0495); LEDNICKI, (0499);WEINTRAUB, (0509); KULCZYCKA, (0651); BOROWY, (1007); ZYGULSKI, (1023); COLEMAN, (1184); LEDNICKI, (1186); WALICKI, (1188); WINDAKIEWICZ, (1189); BLEJWAS, (1661); PIENKOS, (1741).

7) 1918 - 1945

1006 BARTOSZEWSKI, WŁADYSŁAW, 'Les études universitaires clandestines en Pologne occupée, 1939-45', *Cahiers Pologne-Allemagne*, 1962, no. 3 (14), pp. 38-52.

1007 BOROWY, W., 'The Centenary of a Great Poem: Mickiewicz's "Pan Tadeusz" ', *S.E.E.R.*, vol. 13, 1935, pp. 399-412.

1008 BUYNO, I., 'The Polish Academy of Sciences, 1873-1948', *S.E.E.R.*, vol. 27 (69), 1949, pp. 571-4.

1009 JACHIMECKI, Z., 'Karol Szymanowski, 1883-1937', *S.E.E.R.*, vol. 17 (49), 1938, pp. 174-86.

1010 McCALL, S., ed., *Polish Logic, 1920-1939*, Oxford, 1967, Pp. 406.

SEE ALSO:

CURIE, (0141); JACHIMECKI, (0146); PADEREWSKI, (0159).

8) SINCE 1945

1011 DONELLY, DESMOND, *The March Wind*, London, 1959, Pp. 256.

1012 MOND, GEORGES H., 'The Role of the Intellectuals', *C.S.P.* vol. 15, 1973, pp. 122-33.

1013 MAYEWSKI, P., ed., *The Broken Mirror: a Collection of Writings from Contemporary Poland*, London, 1959, Pp. 209.

1014 MILOSZ, CZESLAW, *The Captive Mind*, (Translated by Zielonko, J.), London, 1953, Pp. 251.

1015 SPEAIGHT, RICHARD, *Cultural Interchange with East Europe*, Sussex, 1971, Pp. 106.

1016 STILLMAN, E., ed., *The Bitter Harvest: Intellectual Revolt Behind the Iron Curtain*, London, 1959, Pp. xxxiii + 313.

SEE ALSO:

HISCOCKS, (**0528**); JORDAN, (**0529**); SCHAFF, (**0535**); GÖMÖRI, (**0910**); TRZECIAK, (**1021**); HARASYMIW, (**1704**).

9) FINE ARTS

1017 GOETEL-KOPFF, MARIA, 'Polish Mediaeval Art in the National Museum in Cracow', *The Connoisseur*, vol. 182, 1973, pp. 35-44.

1018 GROSS, P.B., 'Mediaeval Church Architecture in Poland', *P.R.*, vol. 12, 1967, pp. 41-67.

1019 LOZIŃSKI, J.Z., MIŁOBĘDZKI, A., ed., *Guide to Architecture in Poland*, Warsaw, 1967, Pp. 286.

1020 MIŁOBEDZKI, A., 'L'influence de l'Europe centrale et de l'Italie sur l'architecture de la Pologne meridionale, 1430-1530', *Acta Historiae Artium Academiae Scientiarum Hungaricae*, vol. 13, 1967, pp. 69-80.

1021 TRZECIAK, PRZEMYSLAW, *Building and Architecture in Poland, 1945-1966*, Warsaw, 1968.

1022 ZACHWATOWICZ, JAN, *Polish Architecture up to the Mid Nineteenth Century*, Warsaw, 1956. (Photographs with introductory text.)

1023 ZYGULSKI, ZDZISLAW, 'Princess Isabel and the Czartoryski Museum', *The Connoisseur*, vol. 182, 1973, pp. 15-25.

1024 *Handbuch der Deutschen Kunstdenkmäler [DEHIO]*, GALL, ERNST, ed., : *Deutschordensland Preussen*, Munich-Berlin, 1952, Pp. 504.

SEE ALSO:

LORENTZ, (**0080**); KNOX, (**0913**); BOCHNAK, (**1662**); MICHAOWSKI, (**1731**).

M. MILITARY HISTORY

Very little has been written in English on this subject, which figures prominently in Polish historiography. The recent collection of '*Histoire Militaire*' (**1030**) concentrates very largely on the twentieth century. Two numbers of the *Revue Internationale d'Histoire Militaire*, no. 12, (1952) and no. 28, (1969), are specifically devoted to Polish problems. Herbst (**0095**) summarises recent work in Poland.

Bartels (**1025**) and Biskup (**1026**) both deal with mediaeval military matters, whilst further outlines of the subject can be gleaned for the XVI century from Laskowski (**1035**), for the XVII century from Sawczyński (**1040**), for the XVIII century from Herbst (**1029**) and for the XIX century from Kukiel (**1032**) (**1033**).

Sikorski (**1041**) advocates policies which were not adopted by the Polish Army in the interwar period.

1025   BARTELS, K., *Deutscher Krieger in polnischen Diensten*, Berlin, 1922, Pp. 110.

1026   BISKUP, M., 'La Guerre de Treize Ans entre la Pologne et l'Ordre des Chevaliers Teutoniques, 1454-66', *Revue Int. d'Histoire Militaire*, no. 28, 1969, pp. 417-33.

1027   CYNK, J.B., *Polish Aircraft, 1893-1939*, London, 1971, Pp. xxii + 760.

1028   CYNK, J.B., *History of the Polish Airforce, 1918-68*, London, 1972, Pp. 307.

1029   HERBST, S., 'L'armée polonaise et l'art militaire au XVIII siècle', *A.P.H.*, vol. 3, 1960, pp. 33-68.

1030   *Histoire Militaire de la Pologne - problèmes choisis*, (Editions MON.), Warsaw, 1970, Pp. 570.

1031   KLECZKOWSKI, STEFAN, *Poland's First 100,000*, (Introduction by H. Wickham Steed,) London, 1940, Pp. 96.

1032   KUKIEL, MARIAN, 'Polish Military Effort in the Napoleonic Wars', *C.H.P.*, vol. 2, ch. 10 (B), pp. 220-35.

1033   KUKIEL, MARIAN, 'Problèmes des guerres d'insurrection au XIX siècle', *Antemurale*, vol. 2, 1959, pp. 70-9.

1034   KUKIEL, MARIAN, 'Notes on Two Moscow Campaigns', *The Army Quarterly*, vol. 45, 1942-3, pp. 79-85.

1035   LASKOWSKI, O., 'L'art militaire polonais aux XVI et XVII siècles', *Revue Int. d'Histoire Militaire*, no. 12, 1952, pp. 462-93.

1036   NOWAK, T., 'Kazimierz Siemienowicz, artilleur polonais du XVII siècle et son oeuvre', *Revue Int. d'Histoire Militaire*, no. 28, 1969, pp. 447-57.

1037   PACHONSKI, J., 'Les formations militaires polonaises de 1794 à 1807: Organisation, effectifs, faits d'armes', *Revue Int. d'Histoire Militaire*, no. 28, 1969, pp. 468-81.

1038   ROTHSCHILD, JOSEPH, 'The Military Background of Piłsudski's Coup d'Etat', *S.R.* vol. 21, 1962, pp. 241-60.

1039   RZEPNIEWSKI, A., 'Participation des aviateurs polonais à la Bataille d'Angleterre', *Revue Int. d'Histoire Militaire*, no. 28, 1969, pp. 515-29.

1040   SAWCZYŃSKI, A., 'Les institutions militaires polonaises au XVII siècle', *Revue Int. d'Histoire Militaire*, no. 12, 1952, pp. 494-525.

1041   SIKORSKI, WLADYSLAW, *La guerre moderne - son caractère, ses problèmes*, Paris, 1935, Pp. xiii + 246.

1042   STAPOR, Z., 'Les formations regulières polonaises dans la Bataille de l'Allemagne, avril-mai, 1945', *Revue Int. d'Histoire Militaire*, no. 28, 1969, pp. 574-85.

1043   WIMMER, J., 'L'effort financier et militaire de la Pologne au XVII siècle', *Revue Int. d'Histoire Militaire*, no. 28, 1969, pp. 434-46.

SEE ALSO:

STURMINGER, (0052);   HERBST, (0095);ZAHORSKI, (0113); LASKOWSKI, (0601);   CHELMÍNSKI, (0625);KUKIEL, (0641); ZÓŁKIEWSKI, (1333);   KUJAWSKI, (1342);   SCHÜTZ, (1346); SZCZESNIAK, (1347);   WOLIŃSKI, (1348);   PRZYBYLSKI, (1505); D'ABERNON, (1511);   DAVIES, (1513);   KUKIEL, (1521);   PILSUDSKI, (1523);   SIKORSKI, (1524);   KENNEDY, (1573);   KUKIEL, (1575); NEUGEBAUER, (1578);   ZALUSKI, (1588);   REMINGTON, (1621); WIMMER, (1624);   CHELMINSKI, (1673);   EVANS, (1681).

N. NATIONALITIES AND MINORITIES

The historiography of Poland's national minorities is largely confined to the twentieth century, when rival nationalist movements came into conflict. Horak (**1049**) presents the most recent general survey.

Writing on the Cossacks tends to be partisan. Longworth (**1052**) is culled exclusively from Russian sources. Vernadsky (**1053**) (**1054**) provides the best though incomplete introduction.

German settlement was important in the Middle Ages, but conflict did not emerge until the inter-war period, (**Section N (3)**).

The history of the Jews in Poland is a vast subject, rarely treated impartially. Dubnov (**1061**) is a classic work, whilst the *Encyclopaedia Judaica* (**1063**) provides a mine of information. Rabinowicz (**1092**) summarises the inter-war period, and Aufricht (**1658**) gives useful references.

On the Holocaust, the available literature is much greater, and the feelings much more intense, than can be described here. Lichten (**1100**) picks his way carefully between the various maelstroms. Reitlinger (**1103**) analyses the Final Solution. Bartoszewski (**1095**) presents a mass of material to confute charges about Polish indifference. Czerniachów (**1097**), Stroop (**1105**) and Zylberberg (**1109**) reported the horrors of the Warsaw Ghetto.

The history of the Ukrainians in Poland is treated in **SECTION O (5)**, 'The Ukraine'.

1) GENERAL

1044   BOHDANOWICZ, L., 'The Muslims in Poland', *Journal of the Royal Asiatic Society*, 1942, pp. 163-80.

1045   COTTAM, K.J., 'Limanowski and the Nationality Problems of the Polish Eastern Borderlands', *P.R.*, vol. 16, 1972, pp. 38-55.

1046   GOODHART, ARTHUR, *Poland and the Minority Races*, London, 1920, Pp. 198.

1047   GROTH, A., 'Dmowski, Piłsudski and the Ethnic Conflicts in pre-1939 Poland', *C.S.S.*, vol. 3, 1969, pp. 69-91.

1048   GROTH, A., 'Parliament and Ethnic Issues in Pre-war Poland', *S.R.*, vol. 27, 1968, pp. 564-80.

1049   HORAK, S., *Poland and her National Minorities, 1919-39*, New York, 1961, Pp. 259.

1050   ZAVRIAN, H., 'The Polish Armenian Colony', *Armenian Review*, 1951, pp. 13-16.

SEE ALSO:

SYMONOLEWICZ, (**0054**); PTAŚNIK, (**0277**); OLES, (**0444**); ROSENTHAL, (**0689**); OBERTYŃSKI, (**0869**); PETROWICZ, (**0870**).

2) COSSACKS

1051   HAVELOCK, H., 'The Cossacks in the Early Seventeenth Century', *E.H.R.*, vol. 13, 1898, pp. 242-60.

1052   LONGWORTH, P., *The Cossacks*, London, 1969, Pp. 409.

1053   VERNADSKY, G., *Bohdan, Hetman of Ukraine*, New Haven, 1941, Pp. 150.

1054   VERNADSKY, G., 'The Decline of Lithuania and the Rise of the Ukrainian Cossacks, 1526-66', in *Russia at the Dawn of the Modern Age*, Yale, 1959, (Chapter 7), pp. 220-68.

1055   WYNAR, L., 'The Ukrainian Cossacks and the Vatican in 1594', *Ukrainian Quarterly*, vol. 21, 1965, pp. 64-78.

SEE ALSO: Section O (5); WYNAR, (**1821**).

3) GERMANS

1056   AURICH, PETER, *Der Deutsch-Polnische September 1939 - eine Volksgruppe zwischen den Fronten*, Munich, 1969, Pp. 147.

1057   HESSE, J.C., 'National Minorities in Europe. The Germans in Poland', *S.E.E.R.*, vol. 16, 1937, pp. 93-101.

1058   KAPS, JOHANNES, *Die Tragödie Schlesiens, 1945-6*, Munich, 1953, Pp. 552.

1059   von NORMANN, Käthe, *Tagenbuch aus Pommern, 1945-6*, Bonn, 1955, Pp. 127.

SEE ALSO:

AUBIN, (**0260**); DVORNIK, (**0263**); JEDLICKI, (**0265**); WYNOT, (**0299**); BANASIAK, (**0301**); ROSENTHAL, (**0688-0690**); DEHIO, (**1024**); **Sections O (3, 4);** BREYER, (**1543**); *Germany, F.O.*, (**1629**); *Poland*, (**1648**).

4) JEWS

a) GENERAL

1060   BORWICZ, MICHEL, *1000 Years of Jewish Life in Poland*, Paris, 1955, Pp. 440.

1061   DUBNOV, S.M., *History of the Jews in Russia and Poland from the Earliest Times until the Present Day*, Philadelphia, 1916-1920, 3 vols.

1062   EISENSTEIN, M., *Jewish Schools in Poland. Their Philosophy and Development*, New York, 1950, Pp. xii + 112.

1063   *Encyclopaedia Judaica*, Jerusalem, 1971, vol. 13; 'Poland', pp. 710-90.

1064   *Encyclopaedia of the Jewish Diaspora, Poland Series*, 5 vols, 1. *Warsaw*, 2. *Brest-Litovsk*, 3. *Tarnopol*, 4. *Lwów*, 5. *Lublin*, Jerusalem, 1953-7.

1065   LESTCHINSKY, JACOB,, 'Aspects of the Sociology of Polish Jewry', *J.S.S.*, vol. 28, 1966, pp. 195-211.

1066   LICHTEN, JOSEPH L., 'Polish Americans and American Jews: Some Issues which Unite and Divide, *P.R.*, vol. 18, no. 4, 1973, pp. 52-62.

1067   MICHKINSKY, MOSHE, ed., *Gal-ed* ... [On the History of the Jews in Poland], vol. 1, Tel-Aviv, 1973, Pp. xxiv + 348. (English Summary).

1068   SACHAR, H.M., *The Course of Modern Jewish History*, London, 1958, Pp. 617.

1069   SCHMELZ, O, ed., *Jewish Demography and Statistics: Bibliography for 1920-1960*, Jerusalem, 1961; 'Poland', pp. 101-22.

1070   SZAJKOWSKI, ZOSA, *Jews, Wars and Communism*, 2 vols, New York, 1972-74. Pp. 714, 398.

1071   WEINRYB, BERNARD, *The Jews of Poland*, Philadelphia, 1973, Pp. xvi, 424.

SEE ALSO: SHUNAMI, (**0048**).

b) PRE - 1918

1072   BERGER, SOLOMON, *The Jewish Commonwealth of Zborow*, New York, 1967, Pp. 154.

1073   DUKER, A.G., 'Polish Frankism's Duration: a Preliminary Investigation,' *J.S.S.*, vol. 25, 1963, Pp. 287-333.

1074   EISENBACH, A., 'Les droits civiques des Juifs dans le Royaume de Pologne, 1815-63', *Rev. Etudes Juives*, vol. 123, 1964, pp. 19-84.

1075 GOLDBERG, JACOB, 'Poles and Jews in the 17th and 18th Centuries. Rejection or Acceptance', *J.G.O.*, NF, XXII, 1974, pp. 248-283.

1076 HUNDERT, GERSHON, 'Recent Studies Relating to the History of the Jews in Poland from Earliest Times to the Partition Period', *P.R.*, vol. 18, no. 4, 1973, pp. 84-99.

1077 LERSKI, GEORGE J., 'Jewish-Polish Amity in Lincoln's America', *P.R.*, vol. 18, no. 4, 1973, pp. 34-51.

1078 LEWIN, ISAAC, 'The Protection of Jewish Religious Rights by Royal Edicts in Ancient Poland', *Bul. Pol. Inst.*, 1942-3, vol. 1, pp. 556-77.

1079 LEWIN, ISAAC, 'The Historical Background of the Statute of Kalisz, 1264', in *Studies in Polish Civilisation*, ed. Wandycz, D., New York, 1966, pp. 38-53.

1080 KREMER, M., 'Jewish Artisans and Guilds in Former Poland, 16th-18th Centuries', *VIVO* (Annual of Jewish Social Sciences), 1956-7, pp. 211-42.

1081 MENDELSOHN, E., 'From Assimilation to Zionism in Lvov', *S.E.E.R.*, vol. 49, 1971, pp. 521-34.

1082 TOBIAS, H.J., *The Jewish Bund in Russia from its Origins to 1905*, Stanford, 1972, Pp. xvii + 409.

1083 VETULANI, Adam, 'The Jews in Mediaeval Poland', *Jewish Journal of Sociology*, vol. 4, 1964, pp. 274-94.

SEE ALSO:

ROTH, (0581); DUKER, (0636); NEUBACH, (0676); BASKERVILLE, (1218); *Peace Handbook*, (1642).

c) 1918 - 1939

1084 BENDOW, JOSEF, *Der Lemberger Judenpogrom (November 1918 - Jänner 1919)*, Wien, 1919, Pp. 167.

1085 COHEN, I., 'My Mission to Poland, 1918-19', *J.S.S.*, vol. 13 (2), 1951, pp. 149-72.

1086 DAVIES, NORMAN, 'Great Britain and the Polish Jews, 1918-21', *J.Cont.H.*, vol. 8, no. 2, 1973, pp. 119-42.

1087 FRIEDMAN, PHILIP, 'Polish Jewish Historiography between the Two Wars, 1918-39', *J.S.S.*, vol. 11, 1949, pp. 373-408.

1088 GLICKSMAN, Wm. M., *In the Mirror of Literature: The Economic Life of the Jews in Poland as Reflected in Yiddish Literature, 1914-39*, New York, 1966, Pp. 254. *um* 301.83/649

1089 HELLER, C.S., 'Assimilation: a Deviant Pattern Among the Jews of Inter-war Poland', *Jewish J Soc*, vol. 15, no. 2, 1973, pp. 221-37.

1090 HUNCZAK, TARAS, 'A Reappraisal of Symon Petliura and Ukrainian-Jewish Relations, 1917-21', *J.S.S.*, vol. 31, 1969, pp. 163-213.

1091 JOHNPOLL, B.K., *The Politics of Futility: the General Jewish Workers Bund of Poland, 1917-43*, Cornell, 1967, Pp. xix + 298.

1092 RABINOWICZ, HARRY, M., *The Legacy of Polish Jewry. A History of Polish Jews in the Inter-war Years, 1919-39*, New York, 1965, Pp. 256.

1093 SEGAL, S., *The New Poland and the Jews*, London, 1938, pp. 223.

SEE ALSO:

SOHN, **(1179)**; COHEN, **(1675)**; FISHMAN, **(1685)**.

d) 1939 - 1945: THE HOLOCAUST

1094 APENSZLAK, JACOB, ed., *The Black Book of Polish Jewry: An Account of the Martyrdom of Polish Jewry under the Nazi Occupation*, New York, 1943, Pp. 343.

1095 BARTOSZEWSKI, W., LEWIN, Z., ed., *Righteous Among Nations: How Poles Helped the Jews, 1939-45*, London, 1972, Pp. lxxxvii + 834.

1096 BERNFES, ALEXANDER BEN, *"The Warsaw Ghetto No Longer Exists". In Their Own Words and Photographs the Full Story of the Nazi's Extermination of the Polish Jews*, London, 1973, Pp. 70.

1097 CZERNIACHÓW, ADAM, *Warsaw Ghetto Diary, 1939-42*, ed., N. Blumental.

1098 KRAKOWSKI, S., 'The Slaughter of Polish Jewry: a Polish "Reassessment" ', *Wiener Lib Bull.*, vol. 121, May 1973, pp. 392-401.

1099 KUPERSTEIN, ISAIAH, 'Rumors: A Socio-Historical Phenomenon in the Ghetto of Lodz', *P.R.*, vol. 18, 1973, pp. 63-83.

1100 LICHTEN, JOSEPH, L., 'Some Aspects of Polish-Jewish Relations during the Nazi Occupation', in *Studies in Polish Civilisation*, ed., Wandycz, D., New York, 1966, pp. 154-75.

1101 MEED, VLADKA, *On Both Sides of the Wall: Memoirs from the Warsaw Ghetto*, (Translation from Yiddish, second edition) Ghetto Fighter's House and Hakibbutz Hameuched Publishing House, 1973, Pp. 341.

1102 MIRSKY, M., SMOLAR, H., 'Commemoration of the Warsaw

Ghetto Uprising in Poland: Reminiscences', *Sov.Jew.Aff.*, vol. 3, no. 1, 1973, pp. 98-103.

1103   REITLINGER, G., *The Final Solution - an Attempt to Exterminate the Jews of Europe, 1939-45*, London, 1953, Pp. xii + 622.

1104   RINGELBLUM, EMMANUEL, *Polish-Jewish Relations during the Second World War*, Jerusalem, 1974, Pp. 330.

1105   STROOP, JURGEN, *The Report of Jurgen Stroop: concerning the Uprising in the Ghetto of Warsaw and the Liquidation of the Jewish Residential Area*, Warsaw, 1958, Pp. 124.

1106   TENENBAUM, JOSEPH, *Underground: the Story of a People*, New York, 1952, Pp. 532.

1107   TRUNK, ISIAH, *Judenrat: The Jewish Councils in Eastern Europe Under Nazi Occupation*, New York, 1972, Pp. xxxv + 664.

1108   TUSHNET, LEONARD, *To Die with Honour: The Uprising of the Jews in the Warsaw Ghetto*, New York, 1965, Pp. 128.

1109   ZYLBERBERG, MICHAEL, *A Warsaw Diary, 1939-45*, London, 1969, Pp. 220.

SEE ALSO: NUSSBAUM, (**1737**).

e) SINCE 1945

1110   AINSZTEIN, R., 'Anti-Semitism in Catholic Poland', *N Hum*, vol. 89, Dec. 1973, pp. 262-76.

1111   DOBROSZYCKI, L., 'Restoring Jewish Life in Post-War Poland', *Sov Jew Aff*, vol. 3, no. 2, 1973, pp. 58-72.

1112   FEJTO, F., *Les Juifs et l'antisémitisme dans les pays communistes, entre l'intègration et la sécession*, Paris, 1960, Pp. 273.

1113   KORZEC, P., 'The Steiger Affair', *Sov Jew Aff.*, vol. 3, no. 2, 1973, pp. 38-57.

1114   LENDEVAI, PAUL, *Anti-semitism in Eastern Europe*, London, 1972, Pp. vi + 393.

1115   NIEMIRA, P., 'The Situation of the Jews in Poland', *J.C.E.A.*, vol. 11, 1951, pp. 172-83.

1116   WALICHNOWSKI, TADEUSZ, *The Tel-Aviv - Bonn Axis and Poland*, Warsaw, 1968, Pp. 87.

1117   WEINRYB, BERNARD, 'Poland' and 'Polish Jewry' in *The Jews in the Soviet Satellites*, ed., Meyer, P. *et al.*, Syracuse, 1953, Pp. 637, (chapters 2 and 3, pp. 207-369).

SEE ALSO:

SECTIONS J (26); Q (12); CHECINSKI, (1670); (1672).

5) KASHUBS

1118 BROCK, PETER, 'Florjan Cenova and the Kashub Question',
E.E.Q., vol. 11, 1968, pp. 252-94.

1119 LORENTZ, F., *et al.,The Cassubian Civilisation*, London, 1935,
Pp. 407.

1120 MACDONALD, G., 'The Kashubs', *S.E.E.R.*, vol. 19, 1940, pp. 265-
76.

6) UKRAINIANS

SEE: SECTION O (5).

O. REGIONAL AND LOCAL HISTORY

Lithuanians, Prussians or Ukrainians may be surprised to find their countries categorised under Polish regional history. But the list below is only intended as the barest introduction to areas whose histories frequently overlapped with that of Poland. Local history is usually directed towards a local readership, and only occasional items can be found in English.

On Lithuania, Senn (**1126**), Jurgela (**1123**) and Gerutis (**1122**) present national viewpoints. On Prussia, there is the excellent work of Carsten (**1129**). On the Ukraine, Allen (**1154**) complements Hrushevsky (**1156**). On Cracow, Morawski (**1171**) is a classic account, and Adamczewski (**1169**) is a balanced, useful guide.

1) LITHUANIA

1121   DUNDULIS, B., 'A Historiographic Survey of Lithuanian-Polish Relations', *Lithuanian Quarterly*, Winter, 1971.

1122   GERUTIS, ALBERTAS, ed., *Lithuania - 700 Years*, New York, 1969, Pp. 458.

1123   JURGELA, C.R., *History of the Lithuanian Nation*, New York, 1948, Pp. 544.

1124   KLIMAS, P., *Ghillebert de Lannoy in Medieval Lithuania*, New York, 1945, Pp. 96.

1125   *(Symposium)*, 'The Problem of Unity in the Lithuanian State - a Discussion', *S.R.*, vol. 22, 1963, pp. 411-50.

1126   SENN, A.E., *The Emergence of Modern Lithuania*, Princeton, 1959, Pp. 272.

1127   VON LOEWE, K., 'Commerce and Agriculture in Lithuania, 1400-1600', *Ec.H.R.* 2nd Series, vol. 26, 1973, pp. 23-37.

SEE ALSO:

ANTONIEWICZ, (**0236**); BACKUS, (**0261**); DEVEIKE, (**0434**); BACKUS, (**0446**); BARDACH, (**0447**); OKIRSHEVICH, (**0459**); TRUMPA, (**0465**); BOSWELL, (**0570**); HALECKI, (**0574**); KOT, (**0839**); KOT, (**0854**); RACKAUSKAS, (**0987**); VERNADSKY, (**1054**); ZÓLTOWSKI, (**1238**); BOHDANOWICZ, (**1289**); RHODE, (**1303**); KRAKOWSKI, (**1418**); CONFLIT, (**1499**); SENN, (**1506**); BACHUS, (**1659**); COHEN, (**1675**); KAMINSKI, (**1708**); SABALIUNAS, (**1749**); STUKAS, (**1758**); RACKAUSKAS, (**1803**).

2) PRUSSIA

1128 BISKUP, MARIAN, 'The Role of the Order and the State of the Teutonic Knights in the History of Poland', *Pol. West Aff.*, 1966, no. 2, pp. 337-65.

1129 CARSTEN, F.L., *The Origins of Prussia*, Oxford, 1955, Pp. 309.

1130 DOLESEL, S., *Das preussisch-polnische Lehnverhältnis unter Herzog Albrecht von Preussen, 1525-68*, Cologne, 1967, Pp. 260.

1131 GÓRSKI, KAROL, 'The Teutonic Order in Prussia', *Mediaevalia et Humanistica*, 1966, vol. 17, pp. 20-37.

1132 GÓRSKI, KAROL, 'L'Ordre Teutonique: un nouveau point de vue', *Rev. Hist.*, vol. 230, 1963, pp. 285-94.

1133 GÓRSKI, KAROL, 'La ligue des états et les origines du régime représentatif en Prusse' in *Album Helen Maud Cam: Études presentées à la Commission Internationale pour l'Histoire des Assemblées des Etats'*, Paris-Louvain, 1960, vol. 1, pp. 173-86.

1134 ŁOWMIAŃSKI, HENRYK, *The Ancient Prussians*, Toruń, 1936, Pp. 109.

1135 TYMIENIECKI, K., *History of Polish Pomerania*, Poznań, 1929, Pp. 181.

1136 WOJCIECHOWSKI, Z., *The Territorial Development of Prussia in Relation to the Polish Homelands*, Toruń, 1936, Pp. 78.

1137 ZAJĄCZKOWSKI, S., *The Rise and Fall of the Teutonic Order in Prussia*, Toruń. 1935. Pp. 97.

1138 ZINS, H., 'Aspects of the Peasant Rising in East Prussia, 1525', *S.E.E.R.*, vol. 38, 1959, 178-87.

SEE ALSO:

SECTIONS J (22), Q (3c); GÓRSKI, (0441); DEHIO, (1024).

3) DANZIG

1139 ASKENAZY, S., *Danzig and Poland*, (Translated by W.J. Rose), London, 1921, Pp. 132.

1140 GIANNINI, A., *The Problem of Danzig*, Rome, 1933, Pp. 26.

1141 KEYSER, ERICH, 'Neue Forschungen zur Geschichte Danzig und Pommerellens bis zum 13 Jahrhundert', *A. für Ost.*, vol. 16, 1967, pp. 676-91.

1142 KIMMICH, C.M., *The Free City of Danzig and German Foreign Policy, 1919-34*, New Haven, 1968, Pp. 196.

1143 MAMEL, J.A., *Danzig and the Polish Problem*, New York, 1933.

1144 MASON, J.B., *The Danzig Dilemma*, Stanford, 1946, Pp. 377.

1145 WILDER, J.A., 'The Danzig Problem from Within', *S.E.E.R.*, vol. 15 (44), 1937, pp. 357-67.

SEE ALSO:

CIEŚLAK, (**1310**), (**1311**); PIWARSKI, (**1490**); DOPIERALA, (**1549**); SZERMER, (**1761**).

4) SILESIA

1146 DERLATKA, T., ed. *et al.*, *Western and Northern Poland*, (Zachodnia Agencja Prasowa), Poznań, 1962, Pp. 534.

1147 GOLĘBIOWSKI, J.W., 'L'attitude de la Pologne à l'égard de la population autochtone de la Silésie d'Opole, 1945-7', *A.P.H.*, vol. 13, 1966, pp. 41-64.

1148 HARRINGTON, JOSEPH F., Jr., 'Upper Silesia and the Paris Peace Conference', *P.R.*, vol. 19, no. 2, 1974, pp. 25-45.

1149 KAECKENBEECK, G.S.F.C., *The International Experiment of Upper Silesia*, New York, 1942, Pp. 867.

1150 MACHRAY, R., *The Problem of Upper Silesia*, London, 1945, Pp. 134.

1151 POPIOŁEK, KAZIMIERZ, *Silesia in German Eyes, 1939-45*, Katowice, 1964.

1152 ROSENTHAL, HARRY, K., 'National Self-Determination: The Example of Upper Silesia', *J.Cont.H.*, vol. 7, 1972, pp. 231-41.

1153 ZIELIŃSKI, HENRYK, 'The Social and Political Background to the Silesian Risings', *A.P.H.*, vol. 26, 1972, pp. 73-108.

SEE ALSO:

ROSE, (**0170**); WYNOT, (**0299**); POPIOŁEK, (**0679**), (**0702**); ROSE, (**0682**); KAPS, (**1058**); CAMPBELL, (**1497**); CECIL, (**1498**).

5) UKRAINE

1154 ALLEN, W.E.D., *The Ukraine - A History*, Cambridge, 1940, Pp. xvi + 404.

1155 CZUBATYJ, N., 'The Modern Ukrainian Nationalist Movement', *J.C.E.A.*, vol. 4, 1944, pp. 281-303.

1156 HRUSHEVSKY, M., *A History of the Ukraine*, (Translated from Ukrainian), New Haven, 1941, Pp. xix + 629.

1157　KUBIYOVITCH, V., KOSYK, W., *La Pologne et les regions occidentales de la Ukraine*, Paris, 1966, Pp. 40.

1158　KUBIYOVITCH, V., ed., *Ukraine: a Concise Encyclopaedia*, Toronto, 1967-71, 2 vols.

1159　MANNING, CLARENCE, *The Story of the Ukraine*, New York, 1947, Pp. 236.

1160　MARTEL, ANTOINE, *La langue polonaise dans les pays ruthènes, Ukraine et Russie Blanche, 1569-1667*, Lille, 1938, Pp. 318.

1161　McNEILL, W., *Europe's Steppe Frontier*, Chicago, 1964, Pp. 252.

1162　PIKHAINI, REG. S., 'Ukrainian - Polish Problem in the Dissolution of the Russian Empire 1914-17', *New Review of Books*, 1962, pp. 115-19.

1163　RESHETAR, J., *The Ukrainian Revolution 1917-20*, Princeton, 1952, Pp. xi + 363.

1164　REVIUK, E., *Polish Atrocities in the Ukraine*, New York, 1931.

1165　RUDNITSKY, I., 'Ukrainians in Galicia under Austrian Rule', *A.H.Y.*, vol. 3, 1967, pp. 394-429.

1166　SOLCHANYK, R., 'The Foundation of the Communist Movement in Eastern Galicia, 1919-21', *S.R.*, vol. 30, 1971, pp. 774-94.

1167　STACHIW, M., SZETENDERA, J., *Western Ukraine at the Turning Point of Europe's History, 1918-28*, Scranton, Pa., 1969, vol. 1, to May 1919, pp. 324.

1168　TYSZKIEWICZ, M., *Documents historiques sur l'Ukraine et ses relations avec la Pologne*, Lausanne, 1919, Pp. 72

SEE ALSO:

PELENCKY, (**0044**); KRUPNYTSKY, (**0097**); **SECTION N** (**2**); DOROSZENKO, (**0115**); HRUSHEVSKY, (0116); KRUPNYTSKY, (**0119**); POLONSKA-VASYLENKO,, (**0122**); ANDRUSIAK, (**0551**); DE WEERD, (**0594**); ANDRUSIAK, (**0696**); LEVYTSKY, (**0856**); HORAK, (**0865**); GRAHAM, (**0885**); POPPE, (**0888**); HUNCZAK, (**1090**); ZÓLLOWSKI, (**1238**); SKRZYPEK, (**1507**); DOROSHENKO,)**1679**); FEDYSHYN, (**1684**).

6) CRACOW

1169　ADAMCZEWSKI, JAN, *In Cracow*, Warsaw, 1973, Pp. 298.

1170　ESTREICHER, KAROL, 'Cracow - Centre of Polish Culture', *The Connoisseur*, vol. 182, 1973, pp. 25-35.

1171　MORAWSKI, C., *Histoire de l'université de Cracovie: Moyen Âge et Renaissance*, Paris-Kraków, 1900-05, 3 vols. Pp. 311, 297, 359.

1172 PEKALA, JERZY, 'Cracow in the Pages of History', *The Connoisseur*, vol. 182, 1973, pp. 1-2.

SEE ALSO:

SEREJSKI, (**0107**); PTAŚNIK, (**0277**); STACHIEWICZ, (**0923**); CZARTORYSKI, (**0927**); KOCZY, (**0930**); KNOLL, (**0931**); ODLOŽILÍK, (**0932**); TOMIAK, (**0935**); ZANTUAN, (**0952**); ZYGULSKI, (**1023**).

7) WARSAW

1173 BEAUVOIS, D., 'Varsovie, 1815-30', *Revue d'Histoire Moderne et Contemp.*, vol. 18, 1971, pp. 91-105.

1174 KOZLOWSKI, E., 'La défense de Varsovie en Septembre 1939', *Revue Int. d'Histoire Militaire*, no. 28, 1969, pp. 501-14.

1175 TOMKIEWICZ, W., 'Varsovie au XVII siècle', *A.P.H.*, vol. 15, 1967, pp. 39-64.

1176 WILLIAMSON, DAVID, 'The New Warsaw', *Geographical Magazine*, vol. 38 no. 8, 1965, pp. 596-607.

SEE ALSO:

GRABSKI, (**0091**); WYNOT, (**0298**); KORBONSKI, (**0739**), (**0784**), (**1223**).

8) MISCELLANEOUS

1177 BAILLY, ROSA, *A City Fights for Freedom - the rising of Lwów in 1918-19*, London, 1956, Pp. 396.

1178 HALECKI, O., 'The Place of Częstochowa in Poland's Millennium', *Catholic Historical Review*, vol. 52, 1967, pp. 494-508.

1179 SOHN, D., *Białystok*, New York, 1951, Pp. 386. (1200 Pictures with Yiddish and English text.)

SEE ALSO:

DAVID, (**0816**); *Encyclopaedia of the Diaspora*, (**1064**); BERGER, (**1072**); MENDELSOHN, (**1081**); BENDOW, (**1084**); ZÓLTOWSKI, (**1238**); SYMMONS(**1493**); *Peace Handbooks*, (**1636**); *Poland*, (**1652-1653**); COHEN, (**1675**); VAKAR, (**1764**).

P. EMIGRATION

The Polish émigré community is considerable, as is the growing literature about it. Zubrzycki (**1183**) supplies the statistics. **Section 2** deals with the political emigration of the nineteenth century. Wytrwal (**1205-1206**) and Howe (**1705**) provide the most recent surveys of the Poles in America. Thomas and Znaniecki (**1202**) constitutes an extraordinary scholarly achievement and has been partially reprinted, (N.Y., 1958). The local studies are of interest but indifferent quality. On the Poles in Great Britain, Patterson (**1224**) and Zubrzycki (**1226**) present reliable information.

The history of Polish Jewry in exile is a vast and separate subject of its own. Baskerville (**1218**) is a period piece, which needs to be supplemented by (**1063**), (**1066**) and (**1068**).

1) GENERAL

1180   JANOWSKA, HALINA, 'Research on Economic Emigration', *A.P.H.*, vol. 27, 1973, pp. 187-208.

1181   JEZEWSKI, B.O., *Poles Abroad: Yearbook and Directory*, London-New York, 1948 *et seq.* .

1182   ROSE, W.J., 'National Minorities in Europe. IV. The Poles in Germany', *S.E.E.R.*, vol. 15, 1936, pp. 165-76.

1183   ZUBRZYCKI, J., 'Emigration from Poland in the Nineteenth and Twentieth Centuries', *Population Studies*, vol. 6, 1953, pp. 248-72.

2) THE GREAT EMIGRATION

1184   COLEMAN, A.P., 'The Great Emigration', *C.H.P.*, vol. 2, ch. 14 (A), pp. 311-23.

1185   DZIEWANOWSKI, M.K., '1848 and the Hotel Lambert', *S.E.E.R.*, vol. 22. 26, 1948, pp. 361-74.

1186   LEDNICKI, W., 'Mickiewicz at the Collège de France', *S.E.E.R.*, vol. 20, 1941, pp. 149-73.

1187   SOKOLNICKI, M., *Les origines de l'émigration polonaise en France, 1831-2*, Paris, 1910, Pp. 239.

1188   WALICKI, A., 'The Paris Lectures of Mickiewicz and Russian Slavophilism', *S.E.E.R.*, vol. 46, 1968, pp. 155-75.

1189   WINDAKIEWICZ, S., 'The Anglomania of Mickiewicz', *S.E.E.R.*, vol. 8, 1929-30, pp. 131-9.

SEE ALSO:

GARDNER, (0996); BROCK, (1219-1221); GÖMÖRI, (1431); HANDELSMAN, (1432); SKWARCZYŃSKA, (1434); TESLAR, (1435).

3) THE POLES IN NORTH AMERICA: GENERAL

1190 FOX, P., *The Poles in America*, New York, 1922, Pp. xii + 143. (Republished 1970).

1191 LERSKI, JERZY, *A Polish Chapter in Jacksonian America: The United States and the Polish Exiles of 1831*, Wisconsin, 1958, Pp. xi + 242.

1192 HAIMAN, M., *Polish Past in America, 1608-1865*, Chicago, 1939, Pp. 178.

1193 HAIMAN, M., *Kościuszko in the American Revolution*, New York, 1943, Pp. 198.

1194 HAIMAN, M., *Poland and the American Revolutionary War*, Chicago, 1932, Pp. 308.

1195 HEYDENKORN, BENEDICT, ed., *Past and Present, Selected Topics on the Polish Group in Canada*, Toronto, 1974, Pp. 224.

1196 KONOPCZYŃSKI, W., *Casimir Puławski* (Translated by I. Makarewicz), Chicago, 1947, Pp. 62.

1197 KOS-RABCEWICZ-ZUBKOWSKI, L., *The Poles in Canada*, Montreal, 1968, Pp. xvi + 202.

1198 MAKOWSKI, W.B., *History and Integration of the Poles in Canada*, Niagara Falls, 1967, Pp. 274.

1199 MANNING, C.A., *Soldier of Liberty - Casimir Puławski*, New York, 1945, Pp. 304.

1200 FOX, PAUL, *The Poles in the Americas*, New York, 1972, 2 vols. .

1201 RENKIEWICZ, FRANK, ed., *The Poles in America 1608-1972. A Chronology and Fact Book*, New York, 1973, Pp. 128. (Ethnic Chronology Series, no. 9).

1202 THOMAS, WM. I, ZNANIECKI, FLORIAN, *The Polish Peasant in Europe and America: Monograph of an Immigrant Group*. vol. 1, *Primary Group Organisation*, Boston, 1918, P.p. 526; vol. 2, *Primary Group Organisation*, Boston, 1918, Pp. 589; vol. 3, *The Life Record of an Immigrant*, Boston, 1919, Pp. 418; vol. 4, *Disorganisation and Reorganisation in Poland*, Boston, 1920, Pp. 337; vol. 5, *Organisation and Disorganisation in America*, Boston, 1920, Pp. 345.

1203 WANKOWICZ, MELCHIOR, *Three Generations*, Toronto, 1973, Pp. 418.

1204   WŁOSZCZEWSKI, S., *A History of Polish American Culture*, Trenton, 1946, Pp. 151.

1205   WYTRWAL, J.A., *Poles in American History and Tradition*, Detroit, 1969, Pp. 485.

1206   WYTRWAL, J.A., *America's Polish Heritage. A Social History of the Poles in America*, Detroit, 1961, Pp. 350.

4) THE POLES IN NORTH AMERICA: LOCAL

1207   HAIMAN, M., *Polish Pioneers of Virginia and Kentucky*, Chicago, 1937, Pp. 84.

1208   HAIMAN, M., *Poles in New York in the Seventeenth and Eighteenth Centuries*, Chicago, 1938, Pp. 64.

1209   HAIMAN, M., *Polish Pioneers of California*, Chicago, 1940, Pp. 83.

1210   HAIMAN, M., *Poles in the Early History of Texas*, Chicago, 1936, Pp. 64.

1211   HAIMAN, M., *Polish Pioneers of Pennsylvania*, Chicago, 1941, Pp. 72.

1212   KOSBERG, MILTON L., *The Polish Colony of California, 1876-1914*, San Fransisco, 1972, Pp. 80.

1213   MOSTWIN, DANUTA, 'The Profile of a Transplanted Family', *P.R.*, vol. 19, no. 1, 1974, pp. 77-89.

1214   NAPOLSKA, MARY REMIGIA, *The Polish Immigrant in Detroit to 1914*, Chicago, 1946, Pp. 110.

1215   OBIDZINSKI, E., 'Polish Americans in Buffalo', *P.R.*, vol. 14 (1), 1969, pp. 28-39.

1216   PRZYGODA, J., *Texas Pioneers from Poland: a Study in the Ethnic History*, San Antonio-Los Angeles, 1971, Pp. xi + 171.

1217   YARMOLINSKY, A., *Early Polish Americana: A Bibliographical Study*, New York, 1937.

5) THE POLES IN GREAT BRITAIN. TO 1939

1218   BASKERVILLE, B., *The Polish Jew - His Social and Economic Value*, London, 1906, Pp. 336.

1219   BROCK, P., 'Joseph Cowen and the Polish Exiles', *S.E.E.R.*, vol. 32, 1953-4, pp. 52-69.

1220   BROCK, P., 'Polish Democrats and English Radicals, 1832-62: A Chapter in the History of Anglo-Polish Relations', *J.M.H.*, vol. 25, 1953, pp. 139-56.

1221   BROCK, P., 'The Polish Revolutionary Commune in London',

S.E.E.R., vol. 36, 1956, pp. 116-29.

1222 DAVIES, NORMAN, 'The Poles in Great Britain, 1914-19', *S.E.E.R.*, vol. 50, 1972, pp. 63-89.

1223 KORBOŃSKI, STEFAN, *Warsaw in Exile* (Translated by D.J. Welsh), London, 1966.

1224 PATTERSON, SHEILA, 'The Polish Exile Community in Britain', *P.R.*, vol. 6 (3), 1961, pp. 69-97.

1225 TANNAHILL, J.A., *European Volunteer Workers in Britain*, Manchester, 1958, Pp. x + 143.

1226 ZUBRZYCKI, J., *Polish Immigrants in Britain*, The Hague, 1956, Pp. 219.

SEE ALSO:

PIŁSUDSKA, (**0161**); POMIAN, (**0164**); RACZYŃSKI, (**015921**); RADZIWILL, (**0166**); OPPMAN, (**1800**).

Q. FOREIGN RELATIONS

Poland's foreign relations form a vast subject which cannot be satisfactorily encapsulated, although Ascherson (**1227**) for the recent period, and Halecki (**1230**) can be recommended. **Section 3** provides a country-by-country analysis, with German and Russian relations inevitably dominant. Broszat (**1246**) and Labuda (**1254**) present both sides of Polish-German relations, whilst Konovalov (**1277**) and Lednicki (**1279**) introduce Polish-Russian relations. German-Russian relations where Poland is centrally involved, are analysed by Lord (**1399**) (**1449**), Carr (**1482**) and Riekhoff (**1539**). Bottcher (**1264**) provides a good bibliography of current British writing on Poland and Europe in newspapers and journals; Spencer (**1370**) is relevant to British foreign policy and the Polish question in the 1760's.

On mediaeval affairs, Gieysztor (**1293**) is a slim survey, whilst Halecki (**1295**) provides a controversial study of a brilliant episode. Dvornik (**1290**) includes Polish affairs in the wider setting of Slavonic Europe.

There is little by way of a summary of the foreign policy of the old *Rzeczpospolita*, although certain aspects, such as French relations (**Q 3c, Fc**), and particular periods such as the Revolt of the Ukraine (**Q 5e**) or the reign of Sobieski (**J 13**), are well covered.

The eighteenth century Sections (**Q (6), (7), (8)**) should be followed in conjunction with the corresponding political sections (**J 14, 15**).

1) GENERAL

1227   ASCHERSON, NEAL, 'Poland's Place in Europe', *The World Today*, vol. 25, 1969, no. 12, pp. 520-9.

1228   BAGIŃSKI, H., *Poland and the Baltic, the Problems of Poland's Access to the Sea*, Edinburgh, 1942, Pp. xx + 211.

1229   GASZTOWTT, TADEUSZ, *La Pologne et L'Islam; Notes historiques*, Paris, 1907, Pp. 355.

1230   HALECKI, OSCAR, 'Poland's Place in Europe, 966-1966, in *Studies in Polish Civilisation* , ed., Wandycz, D., New York, 1966, pp. 15-22.

1231   KUCHARZEWSKI, J., *La Pologne et l'Europe*, Lausanne, 1920.

1232   LESLIE, R.F., *The Polish Question. Poland's Place in Modern History*, Historical Association Pamphlet, London, 1964, Pp. 39.

1233   LUKACS, J.A., 'Poland's Place in the European State System', *P.R.*, vol. 7, 1962, pp. 47-58.

1234   RETINGER, J.H., *Poland's Place in Europe*, London, 1947.

1235   ROSE, W.J., *Poland's Place in Europe. Three Lectures*, Edinburgh, 1946.

1236   WOOLSEY, L.H., 'The Polish Boundary Question - a Historical Summary', *American Journal of International Law*, vol. 38, 1944, pp. 441-8.

1237   ZÓŁTOWSKI, A., *Border of Europe: a Study of the Polish Eastern Provinces*, London, 1950, pp. xvi + 348.

1238   ZÓŁTOWSKI, A., *East and West in European History*, London, 1945, Pp. 47

2) DIPLOMACY

1239   PONINSKI, A., 'Les traditions de la diplomatie polonaise', *R.H.D.*, vol. 39, 1925, pp. 366-81.

1240   PRZEŹDZIECKI, R., *Diplomatie et protocole à la cour de Pologne*, Paris, 1934-37, vols. 1-2.

1241   *Receuil des actes diplomatiques, traités et documents concernants la Pologne*: vol. 1, ed., Lutostanski, K., *Les Partages de la Pologne*; vol. 2, ed., Filasiewicz, S., *La Question Polonaise pendant la Guerre Mondiale*, Warsaw, 1918-20.

1242   TAMBORRA, ANGELO, 'Cristoforo Warszewicki e la Diplomazia del Rinascimento in Polonia', in *Italia, Venezia e Polonia*, Brahmer, M., ed., Wrocław, 1967, pp. 159-205.

SEE ALSO:

PRZEŹDZIECKI, (1319); (1331); DZIEWANOWSKI, (1407).

3) GENERAL: BY COUNTRIES

a) POLAND - BELGIUM

SEE

KLEYNTJENS, (0333); SOBIESKI, (0565); GÓRSKI, (0825); BETLEY, (1428); PERELMAN, (1430).

b) POLAND - CZECHOSLOVAKIA

1243   HEYMAN, F.J., *Poland and Czechoslovakia*, Englewood Cliffs (New Jersey), 1966, Pp. viii + 181.

1244   KREJCI, K., 'Polish Influences on Czech Culture', *S.E.E.R.*, vol. 19, 1940, pp. 110-22.

1245   ROSE, W.J., 'Czechs and Poles as Neighbours', *J.C.E.A.*, vol. 2, 1941, pp. 153-71.

SEE ALSO:

NOWAK, (**0043**); ODLOŽILÍK, (**0557**); DVORNIK, (**0817**); ŁOWMIAŃSKI; (**0819**); VLASTO, (**0820**); KOLBUSZEWSKI, (**0914**); GĄSIOROWSKI, (**1457**); WISKEMANN, (**1496**); LAROCHE, (**1502**); TAPIÉ, (**1508**); WITT, (**1510**); GROMADA, (**1533**); GĄSIOROWSKI, (**1530**); CIENCIALA, (**1547**); GROMADA, (**1552**); TABORSKY, (**1582**); WANDYCZ, (**1586**).

c) POLAND - GERMANY

1246   BROSZAT, M., *200 Jahre deutsche Polenpolitik*, Munich, 1963, Pp. 269.

1247   CZAPLIŃSKIZ, W., WRZESIŃSKI, W., 'The Polish Western Frontier', *A.P.H.*, vol. 29, 1974, pp. 195-206.

1248   DRZEWIENIECKI, W.M., *The German-Polish Frontier*, Chicago, 1959, Pp. 166.

1249   FELDMAN, J., *Polish-German Antagonisms in History*, Toruń, 1935, Pp. 80.

1250   GAYRE, G.R., *Teuton and Slav on the Polish Frontier: a Diagnosis*, London, 1944, Pp. 76.

1251   GOETTINGEN RESEARCH COMMITTEE, *The German Eastern Territories beyond Oder and Neisse in the Light of the Polish Press*, Wurzburg, 1958, Pp. 112.

1252   KACZMARCZYK, Z., 'One Thousand Years of the History of the Polish Western Frontier', *A.P.H.*, , vol. 5, 1962, pp. 79-106.

1253   LABUDA, G., 'The Territorial, Ethnical and Demographic Aspects of Polish-German Relations in the Past', *P.W.A.*, vol. 3, 1962.

1254   LABUDA, G., 'A Historiographic Analysis of the German "Drang nach Osten" ', *P.W.A.*, vol. 5, 1964, pp. 221-65.

1255   LYSEK, PAWEL, *Poland's Western and Northern Territories - a Millenium of Struggle*, New York, 1973, Pp. 23.

1256   MARVEY, S.M., *A thousand years of German aggression*, London, 1943, Pp. 116.

1257   POLIAKOW, V. [AUGUR], *Eagles Black and White - the Fight for the Sea*, New York - London, 1929, Pp. 205.

1258   SMAL-STOCKI, R., *Slavs and Teutons - the oldest Germanic-*

Slavic Relations, Milwaukee, 1950, Pp. x + 108.

1259   'Germans and Poles, 1840-1940 - a Symposium', being *P.R.*, vol. 17, 1972, no. 1, pp. 86ff.

SEE ALSO:

SECTIONS J (22), (26a); **O** (3,4,5); **N** (3,4,5); **Q** (8); **Q** (12); STILLER, (0051); WUNDERLICH, (0076); JOLL, (0118); EPSTEIN, (0221); WYNOT, (0299); BANASIAK, (0301); SZCZEŚNIAK, (0558); BALZER, (0569); OERTZEN, (0716); KOT, (0944); CARSTEN, (1129); ROSE, (1182); FRIEDBERG, (1292); CZAPLIŃSKI, (1305); BASLER, (1460); BURKE, (1461); CONZE, (1462); GEISS, (1468); GROSFELD, (1469); WHEELER-BENNETT, (1478); CARR, (1482); CAMPBELL, (1497); WISKEMANN, (1496); CECIL, (1498); MORROW, (1503); GĄSIOROWSKI, (1531); RIEKHOFF, (1538-1539); BREYER, (1543); CIENCIALA, (1546); DALLIN, (1548); GĄSIOROWSKI, (1550-1551); JĘDRZEJEWICZ, (1554); BIERZANEK, (1601); BLUHM, (1602); GIERTYCH, (1607); JORDAN, (1610); KOKOT, (1614); WIEWIORA, (1626); ZDZIECHOWSKI, (1627); *Germany*, (1629); *Great Britain*, (1630); *Peace Handbooks*, (1633-1634), (1640); *Poland*, (1646-1651); CZARNECKI, (1676); EVANS, (1681); FEDYSHYN, (1684); GARLINSKI, (1688-9); JAKOBCZYK, (1706); KORTH, (1714).

d) POLAND - FRANCE

1260   GĄSIOROWSKI, W., ed., *La Pologne et la France à travers les siècles*, Paris-Lausanne, 1917.

1261   GRAPPIN, H., 'Normandie et Pologne', *Revue des Etudes Slaves*, vol. 15, 1935, pp. 224-8.

1262   KOROWIN, M.S., *Dix siècles de relations franco-polonaises*, Paris, 1945, Pp. 79.

1263   *Recueil des Instructions données aux Ambassadeurs et ministres de France depuis les traitées de Westphalie jusqu'à la Révolution française. Pologne ....*, Franges, L., ed., (1648-1729 and 1729-1794), Paris, 1888. 2 vols..

SEE ALSO:

SECTION Q (9b); LORENTOWICZ, (0034); ROHMER, (0278); VAUTRIN, (0280); SOUTOU, (0380); HANDELSMAN, (0451); ROUSSEAU, (0461); HANDELSMAN, (0498); ASKENAZY, (0624); HANDELSMAN, (0628); SENKOWSKA, (0629); DAVID, (0921); FABRE, (0979); KUKIEL, (1032); COLEMAN, (1184); DZIEWANOWSKI, (1185); LEDNICKI, (1186); SOKOLNICKI, (1187); WALICKI, (1188); BOYÉ, (1359); DÉFOURNEAUX, (1361); DESPREAUX, (1362); KONOPCZYNSKI, (1364); OLIVA, (1367);

GROSSBART, (1376); DOYON, (1397); BOBR-TYLINGO, (1444); BOREJSZA, (1452a); WANDYCZ, (1455), (1528), (1540); LAROCHE, (1537); CIENCIALA, (1545); JEDRZEJEWICZ, (1535); NOEL, (1558); SAKWA, (1561); *France*, (1628); BOREJSZA, (1776; CARLEY, (1780).

e) POLAND - GREAT BRITAIN

1264   BOTTCHER, W., *et al.*, ed., *Britische Europaideen, 1940-1970*, Dusseldorf, 1970-3, 2 vols.

1265   HALECKI, OSCAR, 'Anglo-Polish Relations in the Past', *S.E.E.R.*, vol. 12, 1934, pp. 659-69.

1266   STEUART, A. FRANCIS, ed., *Papers relating to the Scots in Poland, 1576-1793*, Edinburgh, 1915, Pp. xxxix + 362.

1267   TOMASZEWSKI, W., ed., *The University of Edinburgh and Poland: a Historical Review*, Edinburgh, 1968, Pp. ix + 95.

SEE ALSO:

SECTIONS P (5); Q (5); Q (12b); CROWTHER, (0001); HINDS, (0021); JASNOWSKI, (0117); WINKLER, (0128); NAMIER, (0156); PASIEKA, (0654); ŚWIDERSKA, (0830); HALL, (0835); HANS, (0836); PASCAL, (0844); RZEPNIEWSKI, (1039); COHEN, (1085); DAVIES, (1086); WINDAKIEWICZ, (1189); LODGE, (1366); REDDAWAY, (1369); ANDERSON, (1385); CARLYLE, (1386); HORN, (1387); KONOPCZYŃSKI, (1389); STRUVE, (1402); WEBSTER, (1425); BLOCH, (1429); TESLAR, (1435); WEBSTER, (1436); WEISSER, (1437); GLEASON, (1445); GRZEBIENIOWSKI, (1446-1447); HARLEY, (1448); MOSSE, (1450); WERESZYCKI, (1451); D'ABERNON, (1511); MACFARLANE, (1522); CIENCIALA, (1545); BETHELL, (1567); GARLINSKI, (1568); JEDRZEJEWICZ, (1571); ROZEK, (1580); VOIGT, (1584); ZALUSKI, (1588); UMIASTOWSKI, (1599); WHITE, (1767); OPPMAN, (1800); SCOTT, (1806).

f) POLAND - ITALY

1268   BRONARSKI, A., *L'Italie et la Pologne au cours des siècles*, Lausanne, 1945, Pp. 204.

1269   CINI, L., ed., *Venezia, e la Polonia nei secoli dal XVII al XIX. Atti del convegno, 1963*. (Civiltà Veneziana, Studii 19), Venice-Rome, 1965, Pp. xix + 431.

1270   KIENIEWICZ, S., *La Polonia e il Risorgimento italiano*, Rome, 1961, Pp. 35.

SEE ALSO:

TAMBORRA, (0125); PTAŚNIK, (0277); PIOLI, (0857); RUFFINI, (0858); BILIŃSKI, (0908); BILIŃSKI, (0938); NUCCI, (0947); SOLMI, (0949); *Italia, Venezia e Polonia* ..., (0955); KIENIEWICZ, (1409).

g) POLAND - PERSIA (IRAN)

1271 KOŚCIAŁKOWSKI, S., *L'Iran et la Pologne à travers les siècles,* Teheran, 1943, Pp. 58.

h) POLAND - RUMANIA

1272 JORGA, N., *Polonais et Roumains; Relations politiques, économiques et culturelles,* Bucarest, 1921, Pp. 95.

1273 ŁUKASIK, S., *Pologne et Roumanie - aux confins des deux peuples et des deux langues,* Paris, 1939, Pp. 442.

i) POLAND - RUSSIA AND USSR

1274 COATES, Z.K. and W.P., *Six Centuries of Russo-Polish Relations,* London, 1948, Pp. 235.

1275 HALECKI, OSCAR, 'Polish-Russian Relations, Past and Present', *Review of Politics,* vol. 5, 1943, pp. 332-8.

1276 HALECKI, OSCAR, 'Poland's Eastern Frontiers, 981-1939', *J.C.E.A.,* vol. 2, 1941, pp. 191-207.

1277 KONOVALOV, E., *Pologne et Russie,* Paris, 1946, Pp. 468.

1278 KRAKOWSKI, E., *Pologne et Russie,* Paris, 1946, Pp. 468.

1279 LEDNICKI, W., *Russia, Poland and the West, Essays in Literature and History,* New York, 1954, Pp. 419.

1280 WARTH, R.D., 'The Russian "Enigma": Some Recent Studies by Western Writers', *J.M.H.,* vol. 22, 1960, pp. 346-55.

1281 ZALESKI, Z-L., *Le dilemme russo-polonais - les deux conceptions de l'ordre et de la liberté,* Paris, 1920, Pp. 232.

SEE ALSO:

SECTIONS J (17), (18), (19), (20), (21), (26b); Q (5e,f), (6), (8), (9), (11c), (12c); CROWTHER, (0013); SHAPIRO, (0047); CIENCIALA, (0087); VALKENIER, (0109-0110); HRUSHEVSKY, (0116); KRUPNYTSKY, (0119); MOCHA, (0121); POLONSKA-VASYLENKO, (0122); CAZALET, (0138); KOROSTOWETZ, (0150); MILYUKOV, (0156); PIOTRKOWSKI, (0163); SCHAEFER, (0232); SCHECHTMAN, (0316);

BAIN, (0484); LEDNICKI, (0499); HOLZER, (0523); LERNER, (0532); NETTL, (0534); KORBOŃSKI, (0543); DZIEWANOWSKI, (0647); PETROVICH, (0655); ZWERNIAK, (0792); POPPE, (0888); LEDNICKI, (0998); WEINTRAUB, (1004); RESHETAR, (1163); BOHDANOWICZ, (1289); DVORNÍK, (1291); KIRCHNER, (1296); RHODE, (1303); CARR, (1405); ZYZNIEWSKI, (1412); MORLEY, (1420-1421); HANDELSMAN, (1432); CHMIELEWSKI, (1453); MICHAELS, (1455); DALLIN, (1463); DZIEWANOWSKI, (1466-1467); GRZYBOWSKI, (1471); WHEELER-BENNETT, (1478); CARR, (1482); ELCOCK, (1500); SKRZYPEK, (1507); JACKSON, (1534); KORBEL, (1536); BUDUROWYCZ, (1544); BRZEZINSKI, (1604); GRIFFITH, (1608); KOLARZ, (1613); LEMBERG, (1615); REMINGTON, (1621); WANDYCZ, (1624); *Poland*, (1646); *U.S.S.R.*, (1656); DAVIES, (1518); GĄSIOROWSKI, (1693); BARRAT, (1775); LUKAS, (1794).

j) POLAND - SPAIN

1282 BRODY, E.C., 'Poland in Calderon's "Life is a Dream" - Poetic Illustration or Reality?, *P.R.*, vol. 14, no. 2, 1969, pp. 21-62.

1283 MEYSZTOWICZ, V., ed., *Documenta Polonica ex Archivo Generali Hispaniae in Simancas*, Parts I-VII (1514-1791), Rome 1963-9, 7 vols. .

SEE ALSO: SCOTT, (0586); BRODY, (0940); ZIOMEK, (1772).

k) POLAND - SWITZERLAND

1284 GIEYSZTOR, A., *et al.* ed., *Echanges entre la Pologne et la Suisse du XIV au XIX Siècles*, Geneva, 1964, Pp. 237.

1285 HANDELSMAN, M., ed., *Pologne-Suisse: Recueil d'etudes historiques*, Warsaw-Lwów, 1938, Pp. 170.

1286 KOT, S., 'Basel und Polen, XV-XVII Jahrhundert', *Zeitschrift für Schweizerische Geschichte*, no. 30, 1950, pp. 71-91.

l) POLAND - U.S.A.

1287 KOVRIG, R., *The Myth of Liberation: East - Central Europe in U.S. Diplomacy and Politics since 1941*, Baltimore, Pp. xiii + 360.

SEE ALSO:

SECTION P (3, 4); MANNING, (0120); WANDYCZ, (0126); SHARPE, (0216); GROVE, (0294); LERSKI, (1077); LICHTEN, (1066); WIECZERAK, (0643); GERSON, (1458); MAMATEY, (1474); KUSIELEWICZ, (1479); FISHER, (1485); JANTA, (1489);

GASIOROWSKI, (1532); BYRNES, (1605); KERTESZ, (1611); *U.S.A.*, (1654-1655).

4) MEDIAEVAL, to 1569

1288 BABINGER, F., 'Von Amurath zu Amurath: Vor- und Nachspiel der Schlacht bei Varna (1444)', *Oriens*, vol. 3, 1950, pp. 229-65.

1289 BOHDANOWICZ, A., 'La Horde d'Or, la Pologne et la Lithuanie (1242-1430)', *Revue int. d'Hist. pol. et const.*, vol. 5, 1955, pp. 186-200.

1290 DVORNÍK, FRANTIŠEK, *The Slavs in European History and Civilisation*, New Jersey, 1962, Pp. xxxviii + 688.

1291 DVORNÍK, F., 'The Kievan State and its relations with Western Europe', *T.R.H.S.*, vol. 29, 1947, pp. 27-46.

1292 FRIEDBERG, M., 'Polish and German Culture (Native Elements and German Influences in the Structure and Civilisation of Medieval Poland)', *S.E.E.R.*, vol. 26, 1947, pp. 282-5.

1293 GIEYSZTOR, A., *La Pologne et l'Europe au Moyen Age*, Warsaw, 1962, Pp. 14, (also published by the Centre Scientifique, Paris, 1964, Pp. 44).

1294 GRABSKI, A.F., 'La Pologne et les polonais vus par les étrangers du X au XIII siècles', *A.P.H.*, vol. 12, 1965, pp. 22-43.

1295 HALECKI, OSCAR, *The Crusade of Varna: a Discussion of Controversial Problems*, New York, 1943, Pp. 96.

1296 KIRCHNER, W., 'The Russo-Livonian Crisis, 1555 - Extracts from Joachim Barwitz's Report of 19 Feb. 1555', *J.M.H.*, vol. 19, 1947, pp. 142-51.

1297 LADNER, GERHARD, 'The Holy Roman Empire of the Tenth Century and East Central Europe', *P.R.*, vol. 5, no. 4, 1960, pp. 3-14.

1298 LASKOWSKI, O., *The Battle of Grunwald and the German Drang nach Osten*, London, 1942, Pp. 22.

1299 LASOCKI, Z., *Un diplomate polonais, Nicholas Lasocki, au Congrès d'Arras en 1435*, Paris, 1928, Pp. 78.

1300 LEPSZY, K., 'La Pologne et la souveraineté sur la Baltique au milieu du XVI siècle', *Rev. Hist. Econ. Soc.*, vol. 40, 1962, pp. 32-47.

1301 MANTEUFFEL, T., 'L'état de Mesco I et les relations internationales au X siècle', *Rev. Hist.*, vol. 228, 1962, pp. 1-16.

1302 ODLOŽILÍK, OTAKAR, 'Bohemia and Poland in Medieval Plans of European Organisation', *Bul. Pol. Inst.*, vol. 1, 1942-3, pp. 432-9.

1303 RHODE, G., *Die Ostgrenze Polens. Politische Entwicklung, Kulturelle Bedeutung und geistige Auswirkung*. Bd. 1, *Im*

Mittelalter bis zum Jahre 1401, Cologne-Graz, 1955, Pp. 457.

1304   ZIENTARA, BENEDYKT, 'Foreigners in Poland in the 10th-15th Centuries: Their Role in the Opinion of Polish Medieval Community', *A.P.H.*, vol. 29, 1974, pp. 5-27.

SEE ALSO:

BEŁCH, (0431); MAŁOWIST, (0488); MANTEUFFEL, (0556); ODLOŽILÍK, (0557); BOSWELL, (0571); DĄBROWSKI, (0572); ESZLARY, (0573); BUCZEK, (0821); FABRE, (0824); GÓRSKI, (0825); KOT, (0840); BISKUP, (1026); KLIMAS, (1124); ZAJĄCZKOWSKI, (1137); SMAL-STOCKI, (1258); SZCZEŚNIAK, (1760).

5) FOREIGN RELATIONS OF THE *RZECZPOSPOLITA* 1569-1696

a) GENERAL

1305   CZAPLIŃSKI, W., 'Les territoires de l'ouest dans la politique de la Pologne, 1572-1764', *A.P.H.*, vol. 9, 1964, pp. 5-27.

1306   SZCZEŚNIAK, B., 'The Diplomatic Relations between John III Sobieski and the Emperor Hsi', *Journal of the American Oriental Society*, vol. 89, 1969, pp. 157-61.

SEE ALSO:

DE WEERD, (0594); KUNTZE, (0866); PIERLING, (0871), (0872).

b) POLAND - HOLY ROMAN EMPIRE

1307   STOYE, J., *The Siege of Vienna, 1683*, London, 1964, Pp. 349.

1308   LEITSCH, W., 'Moskau und die Politik des Kaiserhofes im XVII Jahrhundert', *Wiener Archiv*, vol. 4, 1960, *et seq.*.

1309   KOCZY, L., 'The Holy Roman Empire and Poland', *Antemurale*, 2, 1955, pp. 50-66.

c) POLAND - FRANCE

1310   CIESLAK, EDMUND, *Les rapports des residents français à Gdańsk au XVIII siècle*, Warsaw, 1965-9, 2 vols. .

1311   CIESLAK, EDMUND, *Residents Français à Gdańsk au XVIII siècle: leur rôle dans les relations franco-polonaises*, Warsaw, 1969, Pp. 20.

1312   DE FOURBIN, 'Toussaint de Forbin et l'élection de Jean Sobieski

(1674)', *R.H.D.*, vol. 23, 1909, pp. 497-517.

1313 DE PERSAN, MARQUIS, 'La mission diplomatique en Pologne de Jacques Faye d'Espeisses et Guy du Faur de Pibrac, 1574-4', *R.H.D.*, vol. 18, 1904, pp. 74-108, pp. 200-36.

1314 KLENTJENS, J., 'Une ambassade polonaise en 1633', *R.H.D.*, vol. 48, 1934, pp. 355-69.

1315 RUBINSTEIN, S., *Les Relations entre la France et la Pologne de 1680-3*, Paris, 1913, Pp. 164.

SEE ALSO:

CHAMPION, (**0580**); DZIEWANOWSKI, (**0604**); GIEROWSKI, (**0607**); LANGROD-VAUGHAN, (**0609**); SCHLIMGEN, (**0612**); KOT, (**0841**).

d) POLAND - GREAT BRITAIN

1316 *Elementa ad fontium editiones: Institutum Polonicum Historicum Romae*, ed., TALBOT, C.H., *Res Polonicae Elisabetha I Angliae Regnante, Conscriptea ex Archivis Publicis Londiniarum*, (1578-1608), Rome, 1961, Pp. xvi + 311; *Res Polonicae ex Archivo Musei Britannici*, Part I (1598), Rome, 1965, Pp. xvii + 175; Part II (1411-1616), Rome, 1967, Pp. vii + 311; *Res Polonicae Iacobo I Angliae Regnante, Conscriptae ex Archivis Publicis Londiniarum* (1603-29), Rome, 1962, Pp. xi + 396.

1317 JANTA, ALEXANDER, 'Letters by Charles the First to the Polish Commons and by Charles the Second to John III of Poland', *P.R.*, vol. 18, no. 3, 1973, pp. 52-7.

1318 JASNOWSKI, J., 'England and Poland in the XVI and XVII Century, Political Relations', (Reprinted from *Polish Science and Learning*), Newtown, 1948, Pp. 54.

1319 PRZEŹDZIECKI, R., *Diplomatic Ventures and Adventures: Some Experiences of British Envoys at the Court of Poland*, London, 1953, Pp. 262.

1320 SCHOFIELD, A.N.E.D., 'Anglo-Polish Relations in the Seventeenth Century - a Contemporary Memorandum', *B.I.H.R.*, vol. 42, 1969, pp. 234-9.

1321 TALBOT, C.H., ed., *Relation on the State of Polonia and the United Provinces of that Crown, anno 1598*, Rome, 1965, Pp. xvi + 176.

1322 ŻANTUAN, K., 'Olbracht Laski in Elizabethan England', *P.R.*, vol. 8, 1968, pp. 3-22.

SEE ALSO: SECTION Q (3e); HINDS, (0021).

e) POLAND - MUSCOVY

1323   BARBOUR, P.L., *Dimitry, called the Pretender, Tsar and Great Prince of all Russia, 1605-6*, Boston, 1966, Pp. 387.

1324   KRUPNYTSKY, BORYS, 'The Treaty of Pereyaslav and the Political Orientations of B. Khmelnytsky', *Ukrainian Quarterly*, vol. 10, 1954, pp. 32-40.

1325   LEWITTER, L. R., 'Poland, the Ukraine and Russia in the XVIIth Century', *S.E.E.R.*, vol. 27, 1948-9, part 1, pp. 157-71, part 2, pp. 414-29.

1326   LEWITTER, L.R., 'The Russo-Polish Treaty of 1686 and its Antecedents', *P.R.*, vol. 9, (nos. 3-4), 1964, pp. 5-29 and 21-37.

1327   LOEWENSON, L., 'Sir Roger Manley's History of Muscovy: The Russian Imposter (1674)', *S.E.E.R.*, vol. 31, 1952, pp. 232-41.

1328   MACISZEWSKI, J., 'La noblesse polonaise et la guerre contre Moscou, 1604-18', *A.P.H.*, vol. 17, 1968, pp. 23-48.

1329   O'BRIEN, C.B., *Muscovy and the Ukraine. From the Pereiaslav Agreement to the Truce of Andrusovo, 1654-1667*, Berkeley, 1963, Pp. 138.

1330   OHLOBLYN, O., 'The Pereyaslav Treaty and Eastern Europe', *Ukrainian Quarterly*, vol. 10, 1954, pp. 41-50.

1331   PRZEŹDZIECKI, R., 'Les ambassades moscovites en Pologne au XVI et XVII siècles', *R.H.D.*, vol. 43, 1929, pp. 312-49.

1332   THOMPSON, A.H., 'The Legend of the Tsarevich Dimitriy: Some Evidence of an Oral Tradition', *S.E.E.R.*, vol. 46, 1968, pp. 48-60.

1333   ŻÓŁKIEWSKI, S., *Expedition to Moscow - a Memoir*, London, 1959, Pp. 167.

SEE ALSO:

PIERLING, **(0871)**, **(0872)**; KUKIEL, **(1034)**; LEITSCH, **(1308)**.

f) PETER THE GREAT AND POLAND

1334   LEWITTER, L.R., 'Peter the Great and the Polish Election of 1697', *C.H.J.*, vol. 12, 1956, pp. 126-43.

1335   LEWITTER, L.R., 'The Apocryphal Testament of Peter the Great', *P.R.*, vol. 6 (3), 1961, pp. 27-44.

1336   LEWITTER, L.R., 'Peter the Great and the Polish Dissenters', *S.E.E.R.*, vol. 33, 1954, pp. 75-101.

1337   ROBERTS, L.B., 'Peter the Great in Poland', *S.E.E.R.*, vol. 5, 1927, pp. 537-51.

SEE ALSO: SECTION Q (6); LEWITTER, (1326).

g) POLAND - SWEDEN AND THE BALTIC

1338 BIAUDET, HENRY, *Le Saint-Siège et la Suède durant la seconde moitié du XVI siècle, Etudes politiques, 1570-1576*, Paris, 1907, Pp. 580.

1339 CZAPLIŃSKI, W., 'Polish-Danish Diplomatic Relations, 1598-1648' in *Poland at the XI International Congress of Historical Sciences, Stockholm*, Warsaw, 1960, pp. 179-204.

1340 KARTTUNEN, K.I., *Jean III et Stefan Batory, 1576-83*, Helsinki, 1912, Pp. 186.

1341 KONOPCZYŃSKI, W., *Poland and Sweden*, Toruń, 1935, Pp. 60.

1342 KUJAWSKI, M., 'The Battle of Kircholm, 1605', *P.R.*, vol. 11, no. 1, 1966, pp. 40-61.

1343 LEPSZY, K., 'The union of the Crown between Poland and Sweden in 1587', in *Poland at the XI Congress of Historical Science: Stockholm*, Warsaw, 1960, pp. 155-78.

1344 REDDAWAY, W., 'The Vasa in Sweden and Poland, 1560-1630', *C.M.H.*, vol. 4, ch. 5, pp. 158-89.

1345 VON TORNE, P.O., 'Poland and the Baltic in the First Half of the Seventeenth Century', *C.H.P.*, vol. 1, ch. 22 (A), pp. 475-87.

SEE ALSO:

WEDKIEWICZ, (0127); BIAUDET, (0587-0588); PÄRNÄNEN, (0591); MARCINOWSKI, (0597); BAGIŃSKI, (1228); LEPSZY, (1300).

h) POLAND - TURKEY

1346 SCHÜTZ, E., ed., *An Armeno-Kipchak Chronicle of the Polish-Turkish Wars, 1620-1*, Budapest, 1968, Pp. 216.

1347 SZCZEŚNIAK, B., 'A Turkish Chapter in the Thirty Years' War: the Partnership of Polish and Imperial forces as Documented in a Unique Pamphlet of 1621,' *S.R.*, vol. 12, 1967-8, pp. 226-31.

1348 WOLIŃSKI, J., 'Les guerres polono-turques dans la seconde moitié du XVII siècle et la situation internationale, *Revue Int. d'Histoire Militaire*, no. 28, 1969, pp. 458-67.

SEE ALSO:

STURMINGER, (0052); GARBACIK, (0955).

6) GREAT NORTHERN WAR

1349 GIEROWSKI, J., 'From Radoszkowice to Opatów: the History of the Decomposition of the Stanisław Leszczyński Camp: an Aspect of the Great Northern War', in *Poland at the XI Congress of Historical Sciences, Stockholm*, Warsaw, 1960, pp. 217-37.

1350 GIEROWSKI, J., *W cieniu Ligi Pólnocnej, (A l'ombre de la Ligue du Nord)*, Wrocław, 1971, Pp. 211, (French summary).

1351 GIEROWSKI, J.,'La Pologne et Venise au dernier siècle des deux républiques nobiliaires', in *Venezia e la Polonia nei secoli dal XVII al XIX'*, Cini, L., ed., (Civiltà Veneziana, Studii 19), Venice-Rome, 1965, pp. 133-50.

1352 HASSINGER, E., *Brandenburg-Preussen, Schweden und Russland, 1700-13*, Munich, 1953, Pp. 319.

1353 HATTON, R., *Charles XII of Sweden*, London, 1968, Pp. 656.

1354 KURAT, A.N., 'Letters of Poniatowski on the Pruth Campaign, 1711', *S.E.E.R.*, vol. 26, 1947-9, pp. 239-58.

1355 LEWITTER, L.R., 'Russia, Poland and the Baltic, 1697-1721', *Hist.J.*, vol. 11, 1968, pp. 3-34.

1356 LEWITTER, L.R., 'Poland, Russia and the Treaty of Vienna of 5 Jan. 1719', *Hist. J.*, vol. 13, 1970, pp. 3-30.

1357 KALISCH, JOHANNES; GIEROWSKI, J., ed.,*Um die Polnische Krone: Sachsen und Polen während des Nordischen Krieges, 1700-21*, (East) Berlin, 1962, Pp. 307.

1358 ZIEKURSCH, J., 'Die polnische Politik der Wettiner im 18 Jahrhundert', *Neues Archiv für sächsische Geschichte*, vol. 26, 1905, pp. 107-120.

SEE ALSO: GIEROWSKI, (0606).

7) 1721 - 1772

1359 BOYÉ, P., *La cour Polonaise de Lunéville, 1737-66*, Paris, 1926, Pp. 352.

1360 BOYÉ, P., S. *Leszczynski et la cour d'Espagne, 1722-33*, Nancy, 1938.

1361 DÉFOURNEAUX, M., 'L'ambassade du Comte d'Aranda en Pologne, 1760-1', *R.H.D.*, vol. 83 (1), 1969, pp. 20-45.

1362 DESPREAUX, E., 'Le cabinet de Versailles et le conflit entre le Russie et la Pologne en Courlande, 1726-7', *R.H.D.*, vol. 53, 1939, pp. 368-88 and 518-34.

1363 DESPREAUX, E., 'Memoires inédits du baron Heyking, 1764-77', *R.H.D.*, vol. 45, 1931, pp. 47-67.

1364 KONOPCZYŃSKI, W., 'Le deuxième mission de duc de Broglie en Pologne, 1755-6', *R.H.D.*, vol. 21, 1907, pp. 495-508.

1365 LANGROD-VAUGHAN, M.,'Le mariage polonais de Louis XV', *Rev. Int. d'Hist. Pol. et Const.*, vol. 5, 1955, pp. 244-52.

1366 LODGE, R., 'English Neutrality and the War of the Polish Succession', *T.R.H.S.*, vol. 14 (4th series), 1931, pp. 141-73.

1367 OLIVA, L., 'France, Russia and the Abandonment of Poland: The Seven Years' War', *P.R.*, vol. 7, No. 2, 1962, pp. 65-79.

1368 PADOVER, S.K., 'Prince Kaunitz's Resumé of his Eastern Policy', 1763-71, *J.M.H.*, vol. 5, 1933, pp. 352-65.

1369 REDDAWAY, W.F., 'Great Britain and Poland, 1762-72', *C.H.J.*, vol. 4, 1934, pp. 223-62.

1370 SPENCER, F., ed., *The Fourth Earl of Sandwich, Diplomatic Correspondence 1763-1765*, Manchester, 1961, Pp. 334.

1371 WOLOSZYŃSKI, R.W., 'La Pologne vue par l'Europe au XVIII siècle', *A.P.H.*, vol. 11, 1965, pp. 22-42.

8) THE PARTITIONS OF POLAND

The classic study of 'The Partitions' is undoubtedly Lord (**1399**). Lewitter (**1379**) (**1380**) provides shorter introductions, scholarly and popular. Halecki (**1377**) tries to answer the question why, whilst Serejski (**1383**) comments on both history and historians in a fascinating way.

On the First Partition, Kaplan (**1388**) provides a modern evaluation. Carlyle (**1386**) is listed to exemplify hero-worship of the Partitioners.

On the Second Partition, Bain (**1394**) and Reddaway (**1400**) are still worth reading to supplement Lord.

On the Third Partition, Lord's article (**1404**) acts as a guide to the wider problem of Kosciuszko's Rising.

a) GENERAL

1372 BELOFF, M., *The Age of Absolutism, 1660-1815*, London, 1954, Pp. 191, (Chapter 4).

1373 BEREDAY, GEORGE Z.F.,'A Japanese View on the Partitions of Poland', *P.R.*, vol. 19, no. 2, 1974, pp. 89-91.

1374 EVERSLEY, G.J.S. LORD, *The Partitions of Poland*, London, 1915. (Republished, 1973).

1375 FRILLI, O., 'Il matirio della Polonia e le colpe dei grandi', *Nuova Rivista Storica*, vol. 47, 1963, pp. 282-306.

1376 GROSSBART, H., 'La presse polonaise et la Révolution, 1789-94',

A.H.R.F., vol. 14, 1937, pp. 127-50, pp. 241-56.

1377 HALECKI, OSCAR, 'Why Was Poland Partitioned?', *S.R.*, vol. 22, 1963, no. 3, pp. 432-41.

1378 LEHTONEN, U.L., *Die polnischen Provinzen Russlands unter Katharina II in die Jahren 1772-1782*, (Translated from the Finnish), Berlin, 1907, Pp. 634.

1379 LEWITTER, L. R., 'The Partitions of Poland', *N.C.M.H.*, vol. 8, ch. 12, pp. 333-59.

1380 LEWITTER, L. R., 'The Partitions of Poland', *H.T.*, vol. 8, 1958, pp. 873-82, 1959, vol. 9, pp. 30-9.

1381 LODGE, R., 'The Extinction of Poland, 1788-97', *C.M.H.*, vol. 8, ch. 17, pp. 521-52.

1382 LUTOSŁAWSKI, K., *Les partages de la Pologne et la lutte pour l'indépendence. Documents*, Paris, 1918, Pp. xix + 712.

1383 SEREJSKI, M.H., *Europa a Rozbiory Polski*, (with summary in French), Warsaw, 1970, Pp. 515.

1384 THOMSON, G.S., *Catherine the Great and the Expansion of Russia*, London, 1947, Pp. x + 294. (Chapter 5).

SEE ALSO:

BAIN, (**0614**); FORST BATTAGLIA, (**0616**); KIENIEWICZ, (**0618**); RECUEIL, (**1241**); GROSSBART, (**1416**); *Peace Handbook*, (**1639**).

b) THE FIRST PARTITION, 1772

1385 ANDERSON, M.S., 'Great Britain and the Russo-Turkish War of 1768-74', *E.H.R.*, vol. 69, 1954, pp. 38-58.

1386 CARLYLE, T., *History of Frederick II of Prussia, Called Frederick the Great*, London, 1858-65, 6 vols.

1387 HORN, D.B., *British Public Opinion and the First Partition of Poland*, Edinburgh, 1945, Pp. vii + 98.

1388 KAPLAN, H.H., *The First Partition of Poland*, New York, 1962, Pp. xvi + 215.

1389 KONOPCZYŃSKI, W., 'England and the First Partition of Poland', *J.C.E.A.*, vol. 8, no. 1, 1948, pp. 1-23.

1390 PADOVER, S.K., 'Prince Kaunitz and the First Partition of Poland', *S.E.E.R.*, vol. 13, 1935, pp. 384-98.

1391 PADOVER, S.K., 'The First Partition: Selected Austrian Documents', *S.E.E.R.*, vol. 14, 1936, pp. 682-87.

1392 TOPOLSKI, J., 'Reflections on the First Partition, (1772), *A.P.H.*, vol. 27, 1973, pp. 89-104.

1393 WHITE, J.A., *The Occupation of West Russia after the First Partition of Poland*, New York, 1940.

SEE ALSO:

ZATKO, **(0896)**; OLIVA, **(1367)**; PADOVER, **(1368)**; REDDAWAY, **(1369)**.

c) THE SECOND PARTITION, 1793

1394 BAIN, R.N., 'The Second Partition of Poland, 1793' *E.H.R.*, vol. 6, 1891, pp. 331-401.

1395 BOZZOLATO, G., *Polonia e Russia alla fine del XVIII secolo - un avventuriero onorato, Scipione Piattoli*, Padua, 1964, Pp. 513.

1396 DE MONTFORT, H., 'La politique de la Prusse en Pologne de 1780-92', *R.H.D.*, vol. 60, 1946, pp. 47-70.

1397 DOYON, P., 'La Mission de Descorches en Pologne, 1791-2', *R.H.D.*, vol. 39, 1925, pp. 168-201, pp. 302-33.

1398 KIRALY, B.K., 'A Prussian Diplomatic Adventure with Poland and the Hungarian Revolt of 1790', *P.R.*, vol. 12, 1967, pp. 3-11.

1399 LORD, R.H., *The Second Partition of Poland, a Study in Diplomatic History*, Cambridge (Mass), 1915, Pp. xxx + 586.

1400 REDDAWAY, W., 'The Second Partition', *C.H.P.*, vol. 2, ch. 7, pp. 137-56.

1401 ROSTWOROWSKI, E., 'Scipione Piattoli e la Dieta di Quattro Anni, 1788-92', *Riv. Stor. Ital.*, vol. 78, 1966, pp. 922-31.

1402 STRUVE, GLEB, 'A Chapter in Russo-Polish Relations, 1785-93', *Russian Review*, vol. 6, no. 1, 1946, pp. 56-68. [on Count Semyon Vorontsov].

1403 STRUVE, G., 'Vorontsov et le Deuxième Partage, 1792-3', *R.H.D.*, vol. 61, 1947, pp. 199-214.

SEE ALSO: HANDELSMAN, **(0451)**.

d) THE THIRD PARTITION

1404 LORD, R.H., 'The Third Partition of Poland' *S.E.E.R.*, vol. 3, 1924, pp. 481-98.

SEE ALSO: JOHNS, **(0147)**; KUKIEL, **(0619)**.

9) THE POLISH QUESTION, 1795 - 1914

On the subject as a whole, neither Chowaniec (**1406**) nor Frankel (**1408**) nor Leslie (**1232**) is adequate. Kukiel deals soundly with the first half only (**1410**). Askenazy (**1413**) is a standard work on the Napoleonic era, as is Namier's brilliant essay on 1848, (**1442**). The November Rising (**Q 9e**) is less accessible than the January Rising (**Q 9h**), though both can be followed in the political sections (**J 18, 20**). On the later phase, Dmowski's political tract (**1454**) can still be read with profit.

Throughout, the interrelations of Polish and Russian opposition to Tsardom are well worth tracing. See **Section Q** (3).

a) GENERAL

1405 CARR, E.H., *The Romantic Exiles*, Harmondsworth, 1949, Pp. 448.

1406 CHOWANIEC, C., 'La Question Polonaise, 1796-1921', in *L'Europe du XIX et du XX Siècles*, ed. Beloff, Max, etc., Milan, 1968, vol. 7, pp. 179-231.

1407 DZIEWANOWSKI, M.K., 'Czartoryski and his 'Essai sur la diplomatie', *S.R.*, vol. 19, 1970, pp. 589-605.

1408 FRANKEL, HENRYK, *Poland: the Struggle for Power, 1772-1939*, London, 1946, Pp. 191.

1409 KIENIEWICZ, S., *La Polonia e il risorgimento italiano*, Rome, 1961, Pp. 35.

1410 KUKIEL, M., *Czartoryski and European Unity, 1770-1861*, Princeton, 1955, Pp. xvii + 354.

1411 ROOS, H., 'Die polnische Nationalgesellschaft und die Staatsgewalt der Teilungsmächte in der europäischen Geschichte, 1795-1863', *J.G.O.*, vol. 14, 1966, pp. 388-99.

1412 ZYZNIEWSKI, S.J., 'Miljutin and the Polish Question', *H.S.S.*, vol. 4, 1957, pp. 237-49.

SEE ALSO: LESLIE, (**1232**); BARRATT, (**1775**)

b) THE NAPOLEONIC PERIOD 1795 - 1815

1413 ASKENAZY, S., *Napoléon et la Pologne* (Translated by H. Grégoire), Brussels, 1925, 3 vols.

1414 DARD, E., 'Le passage de Napoléon à Varsovie, 10.XII.1812', *R.H.D.*, vol. 48, 1934, pp. 321-9.

1415 DRIAULT, E., 'La question de Pologne', *Napoléon et l'Europe*, Paris, 1917, 3 vols. Pp. viii + 491.

1416 GROSSBART, J., 'La politique polonaise de la Revolution française jusqu'aux traités de Bâle', *A.H.R.F.*, vol. 6, 1929, pp. 34-55; vol. 7, 1930, pp. 129-51, pp. 242-55, pp. 476-85.

1417 HANDELSMAN, M., *Napoléon et la Pologne, 1806-7*, Paris, 1909, Pp. iv + 208.

1418 KRAKOWSKI, E., 'Pologne et Lithuanie en 1812', *R.H.D.*, vol. 51, 1937, pp. 467-89.

1419 MANSUY, ABEL, *Jérome Napoléon et la Pologne en 1812*, Paris, 1931, Pp. 704.

1420 MORLEY, C., 'Alexander I and Czartoryski - The Polish Question, 1801-13', *S.E.E.R.*, vol. 25, 1947, pp. 405-26.

1421 MORLEY, C., 'Czartoryski's Attempts at a New Foreign Policy under Alexander I', *S.R.*, vol. 12, 1953, pp. 475-85.

1422 ROSE, W.J., 'Napoleon and Poland', *C.H.P.*, vol. 2, ch. 10(A), pp. 208-19.

1423 ZAMOYSKI, A., 'Napoleon's Polish Aide-de-Camp', *H. Today*, vol. 23, no. 7, 1973, pp. 479-85.

SEE ALSO:

SECTION J (16); KUKIEL, (1034); PACHONSKI, (1037); SKOWRONEK, (1753); ZAWADZKI, (1771).

c) CONGRESS OF VIENNA

1424 MONTGOMERY HYDE, H., 'The Congress of Vienna', *C.H.P.*, vol. 2, ch. 12, pp. 257-74.

1425 WEBSTER, C.K., 'England and the Polish-Saxon Problem at the Congress of Vienna', *T.R.H.S.*, vol. 7 (2nd Series), 1913, pp. 49-101.

SEE ALSO: *Peace Handbooks*, (1639), (1643), (1644).

d) 1815 - 1830

1426 BLECKWELL, W.L., 'Russian Decembrist Views of Poland', *P.R.*, vol. 3, no. 4, 1958, pp. 30-54.

1427 KUKIEL, MARIAN, 'Lelewel, Mickiewicz and the underground movement of European Revolution, 1816-33', *P.R.*, vol. 5, no. 3, 1960, pp. 59-76.

SEE ALSO: SECTIONS J (17), (18); TAMBORRA, (0895); LEDNICKI, (0998); WEINTRAUB, (1004).

e) 1830 - 1831 THE NOVEMBER RISING

1428 BETLEY, J.A., *Belgium and Poland in International Relations, 1830-31*, The Hague, 1960, Pp. 298.

1429 BLOCH, C., 'Aid of the English People to Poland, 1831', *A.P.H.*, vol. 16, 1966, pp. 117-23.

1430 PERELMAN-LIWER, F., *La Belgique et la revolution polonaise de 1830*, Brussels, 1948, Pp. 69.

SEE ALSO: KUKIEL, **(1033)**.

f) 1831 - 1864

1431 GÖMÖRI, GEORGE, 'East-European Federation - Worcell's Forgotten Plan', *P.R.*, vol. 12, 1967, pp. 37-43.

1432 HANDELSMAN, M., *Czartoryski, Nicolas I et la question du Proche Orient*, Paris, 1934, Pp. 151.

1433 ROSE, W.J., 'Wielopolski to Metternich, April 1846', *S.E.E.R.*, vol. 26, 1947, pp. 90-106.

1434 SKWARCZYNSKA, S., *Mickiewicz et la Revolution de Francfort en 1833*, Centre Scientifique, Paris, 1962, Pp. 20.

1435 TESLAR, J.A., 'English Correspondence of A. Czartoryski and W. Zamoyski, 1832-1861', *S.E.E.R.*, vol. 29, 1950, pp. 153-76.

1436 WEBSTER, C., 'Britain, the Liberal Movement and the Eastern Question', in *The Foreign Policy of Palmerston, 1830-41*, London, 1951, 2 vols.

1437 WEISSER, H.G., 'Polonophilism and the British Working Class, 1830-45', *P.R.*, vol. 12, 1967, pp. 78-96.

SEE ALSO: SECTION J (19).

g) 1848 THE SPRINGTIME OF NATIONS

1438 BATOWSKI, HENRYK, 'The Poles and their Fellow Slavs in 1848', *S.E.E.R.*, vol. 27, pp. 404-13.

1439 HAWGOOD, J.A., '1848 in Central Europe', *S.E.E.R.*, vol. 26, 1948, pp. 314-28.

1440 KNAPOWSKA, W., 'La France, la Prusse et la question polonaise en 1848', in *La Pologne au VI Congrès International des Sciences Historiques à Oslo*, Warsaw, 1930, pp. 147-66.

1441 KUCHARZEWSKI, J., 'The Polish Cause in the Frankfort Parliament of 1848', *Bul. Pol. Inst.* , vol. 1, 1942-43, pp. 11-73.

1442 NAMIER, L.B., *The Revolution of the Intellectuals 1848*, London, 1946, Pp. 124.

1443 SIGMANN, J., *1848: the Romantic and Democratic Revolutions in Europe*, (Translated from French by L.F. Edwards), London, 1973, Pp. 352.

SEE ALSO:

BLACK, (0664); FELDMAN, (0667); POPIOLEK, (0679), (0702); DZIEWANOWSKI, (1185).

h) 1863 - 1864: THE JANUARY RISING

1444 BOBR-TYLINGO, S., 'Napoléon III, l'Europe et la Pologne, 1863-4', *Antemurale*, vol. 8, 1963, pp. 1-362.

1445 GLEASON, J.H., *The Genesis of Russophobia in Great Britain - a Study of the Interaction of Policy and Opinion*, Cambridge, Mass., 1950, Pp. ix + 314.

1446 GRZEBIENIOWSKI, T., 'Lord Durham at St. Petersburg and the Polish Insurrection', *S.E.E.R.*, vol. 13, 1935, pp. 627-32.

1447 GRZEBIENIOWSKI, T., 'The Polish Cause in England a Century Ago', *S.E.E.R.*, vol. 11, 1932, pp. 81-7.

1448 HARLEY, J.H., 'Great Britain and the Polish Insurrection of 1863', *S.E.E.R.*, vol. 16, 1937, pp. 155-67, pp. 425-38.

1449 LORD, R.H., 'Bismarck and Russia in 1863', *A.H.R.*, vol. 29, 1923-4, pp. 24-48.

1450 MOSSE, W.E., 'England and the Polish Insurrection of 1863', *E.H.R.*, vol. 71, 1956, pp. 28-55.

1451 WERESZYCKI, H., 'Great Britain and the Polish Question in 1863', *E.H.R.*, 1935, vol. 50, pp. 78-108.

1452 WIECZERAK, J.W., *A Polish Chapter in Civil War America: the Effects of the January Insurrection on American Opinion and Diplomacy*, New York, 1967, Pp. 264.

SEE ALSO: SECTION J (20); PASIEKA, (0654); GENTZEN, (0668); KUKIEL, (1033).

i) 1864-1914

1453 CHMIELEWSKI, E., *The Polish Question in the Russian State Duma*, Knoxville, Tenn., 1970, Pp. 187.

1454 DMOWSKI, R., *La Question Polonaise*, Paris, 1909, Pp. xxiv + 336.

1455   MICHAELS, A.J., *Neoslavism and its Attempt at Russo-Polish Rapprochement, 1908-10.*, Washington, 1956, Pp. x + 163.

SEE ALSO: KIMBALL, (0995); BOREJSZA,, (1776).

10) THE REBIRTH OF INDEPENDENT POLAND, 1914-19

The period of independence is not well digested despite a mass of primary and secondary material. Komarnicki (1459) in particular is unreliable.

On World War One, recent work by Basler (1460), Conze (1462) and Geiss (1468) has made German policies clearer than Russian or Allied ones.

The Peace Conference, **Section Q (10c)**, and the consequent Territorial Settlements, **Section Q (11b)**, are rarely treated with sympathy.

a) GENERAL

1456   BLOCISZEWSKI, J., *La restauration de la Pologne et la diplomatie européenne*, Paris, 1927, Pp. 234.

1457   GĄSIOROWSKI, Z.J., 'Dmowski's Overture to Masaryk', *P.R.*, vol. 19, no. 1, 1974, pp. 90-2.

1458   GERSON, LOUIS, *Woodrow Wilson and the rebirth of Poland, 1914-10*, New Haven, 1953, Pp. xi + 166. Reprinted, 1972.

1459   KOMARNICKI, T., *The Rebirth of the Polish Republic - a Study in the Diplomatic History of Europe, 1914-20*, London, 1957, Pp. xiii + 776.

SEE ALSO:

WUNDERLICH, (0076); MILYUKOV, (0156); NAMIER, (0157); PIŁSUDSKI, (0162); POMIAN, (0164); GROVE, (0294); DAVIES, (1222); SENN, (1751); SMOGORZEWSKI, (1754).

b) WORLD WAR ONE, 1914 - 1918

1460   BASLER, WERNER, *Deutschlands Annexionspolitik in Polen und Baltikum, 1914-18*, Berlin, 1962, Pp. 457.

1461   BURKE, E.R., *The Polish Policy of the Central Powers during the World War*, Chicago, 1936, Pp. 115.

1462   CONZE, W., *Polnische Nation und deutsche Politik im Ersten Weltkrieg*, Cologne, 1958, Pp. xxii + 415.

1463   DALLIN, A., 'The Future of Poland', in *Russian Diplomacy and Eastern Europe, 1914-17*, New York, 1963, Pp. xviii + 305.

1464   DMOWSKI, R., *Problems of East and Central Europe*, London, 1916.

1465   DYBOSKI, R., 'The Polish Question during the World War', 'Military Efforts and Political Activities of the Poles', *C.H.P.*,vol. 2, ch. 20, pp. 461-80.

1466   DZIEWANOWSKI, M.K., 'Piłsudski, the Bolshevik Revolution and East Europe', *P.R.*, vol. 14, no. 4, 1969, pp. 14-30.

1467   DZIEWANOWSKI, M.K., 'World War One and the Marxist Movement in Poland', *S.R.*, vol. 12, 1953, pp. 72-92.

1468   GEISS, I., *Der Polnische Grenzstreifen, 1914-18: ein Beitrag zur deutschen Kreigspolitik im Ersten Weltkreig*, Lübeck and Hamburg, 1960, Pp. 187.

1469   GROSFELD, LEON, 'La Pologne dans les plans impérialistes allemands, 1914-18', in *La Pologne au X Congrès International des Sciences Historiques à Rome*, Warsaw 1955, pp. 327-55.

1470   GROSFELD, LEON, ' "Mitteleuropa" und die Polnische Frage im Jahre 1915', *La Pologne au XII Congrès International des Sciences Historiques à Vienne*, Warsaw, 1965, pp. 115-32.

1471   GRZYBOWSKI, A., 'The Jakhontov Papers - Russo-Polish Relations, 1914-16', *J.C.E.A.*, vol. 18, 1958, pp. 3-24.

1472   GRZYBOWSKI, A.; SENN, A.E., *The Russian Revolution in Switzerland, 1914-17*, Madison, Wisconsin, 1971, Pp. xvi + 250.

1473   HARLEY, J.H., ed., *Poland's Case for Independence, Polish Information Committee*, London, 1916, Pp. 352.

1474   MAMATEY, V., *The United States and East Central Europe, 1914-1918: a study in Wilsonian Diplomacy and Propaganda*, Princeton, 1959, Pp. 431. republished, London, 1972.

1475   SLADKOWSKI, WIESLAW, 'L'opinion occidentale et la cause de l'indépendence de la Pologne pendant la Première Guerre Mondiale: l'activité d'Edmond Privat', *A.P.H.*, vol. 27, 1973, pp. 105-33.

1476   STANDING, P.C., *The Campaign in Russian Poland*, London, 1914, Pp. vi + 185.

1477   TAMBORRA, ANGELO, *Benedetto XV d i problemi nazionali e religiosi dell'Europa Orientale*, Rome, 1963, Pp. 32.

1478   WHEELER-BENNETT, J.W., *Brest-Litovsk, the Forgotten Peace - March 1918*, London, 1938, Pp. 478.

SEE ALSO:

PIKHAINI, (**1162**); SENN, (**1751**); SWEET, (**1759**).

c) THE PEACE CONFERENCE

1479 KUSIELEWICZ, E., 'Wilson and the Polish Cause', *P.R.*, vol. 1, no. 1, 1956, pp. 64-79.

1480 REDDAWAY, W., 'The Peace Conference, 1919', *C.H.P.*, vol. 2, ch. 21, pp. 490-511.

SEE ALSO:

PADEREWSKI, (**0159**); GERSON, (**1458**); *Peace Handbooks*, (**1632-45**).

11) FOREIGN RELATIONS, 1918-39

Dębicki (**1483**) together with Horak (**1488**) can be used to establish the outlines.

On the territorial settlements, comment tends to be as confused as the subject itself. Przybylski (**1505**) is a simple military chronicle. Wambaugh (**1509**) describes the various plebiscites dispassionately.

On the Polish-Soviet War, Davies (**1513**) must be matched against personal accounts by D'Abernon (**1511**), Piłsudski (**1523**) and Sikorski (**1524**), and against Wandycz's diplomatic monograph (**1526**).

The 1920s are well-illumined by Wandycz (**1495**), Korbel (**1536**) and Riekhoff (**1539**).

The crisis of the 1930s can most vividly be approached through contemporary diplomatic accounts: Laroche (**1537**), Beck (**1542**), Noël (**1558**), Szembek (**1565**). Polish policy is evaluated negatively by Namier (**1557**) and Roberts (**1559**), and more sympathetically by Cienciala (**1545**), (**1547**).

a) GENERAL

1481 AUGUR, R., 'Foreign Policy of Poland', *S.E.E.R.*, vol. 15, 1937, pp. 350-6.

1482 CARR, E.H., *German-Soviet Relations between the Two World Wars*, Oxford, 1952, Pp. ix + 146.

1483 DĘBICKI, R., *Foreign Policy of Poland*, 1919-1939, New York, 1962, Pp. 192.

1484 DZIEWANOWSKI, M.K., *Joseph Piłsudski - a European Federalist, 1918-22*, Stanford, 1969, Pp. 369.

1485 FISHER, H.H., *America and the New Poland*, New York, 1938, Pp. 403.

1486 GATSKE, M.W., ed., *European Diplomacy Between Two Wars, 1919-1939*, New York, 1972.

1487 GROMADA, THADDEUS., ed., *Essays on Poland's Foreign Policy*, 1918-39, New York, 1970, Pp. 71.

1488 HORAK, S., *Polish International Affairs, 1919-60: a Calendar of Treaties and Agreements*, Bloomington, 1964, Pp. 248.

1489 JANTA, A., 'Conrad's "Famous Cablegram" in Support of a Polish Loan, 1920', *P.R.*, 1972, vol. 17, pp. 69-77.

1490 PIWARSKI, K., 'Gdańsk and Poland (1919-1939)', *Poland at the XI Congress of Historical Sciences in Stockholm*, Warsaw, 1960, pp. 265-99.

1491 ROSE, A.C., *La politique polonaise entre les deux guerres. Un aspect du problème européen*, Neuchâtel, 1945, Pp. 201.

1492 ROTHSCHILD, J., 'Poland between Germany and USSR, 1926-39: The Theory of Two Enemies' (Piłsudski Institute Symposium), *P.R.*, vol. 20, no. 1, 1975, pp. 3-63.

1493 SYMMONS-SYMONOLEWICZ, K., 'Polish Political Thought and the Problem of the Eastern Borderlands of Poland, 1918-39', *P.R.*, vol. 4, (1), 1959, pp. 65-81.

1494 UMIASTOWSKI, R., *Russia and the Polish Republic, 1918-41*, London, Undated (1945?), Pp. 319.

1495 WANDYCZ, P., *France and her Eastern Allies, 1919-25*, Minneapolis, 1962, Pp. 454.

1496 WISKEMANN, E., *Germany's Eastern Neighbours. Problems relating to the Oder-Neisse Line and the Czech Frontier Regions*, London, 1956, Pp. 309.

SEE ALSO: RAIN, (0719).

b) TERRITORIAL SETTLEMENTS

1497 CAMPBELL, F.G., 'The Struggle for Upper Silesia, 1919-22', *J.M.H.*, vol. 42, 1970, pp. 361-85.

1498 CECIL, R., 'The Question of Upper Silesia', *Nineteenth Century and After*, 1921, pp. 961-70.

1499 *Conflit Polono-Lithuanien, Question de Vilna, 1918-24*, Lithuanian Ministry of Foreign Affairs, Kaunas, 1924.

1500 ELCOCK, H.J., 'Britain and the Russo-Polish frontier, 1919-21', *Hist.J.*, vol. 12, 1969, pp. 137-54.

1501 KUTRZEBA, S., 'The Struggle for the Frontiers, 1919-23', *C.H.P.*, vol. 2, ch. 22, pp. 512-34.

1502 LAROCHE, J., 'La Question de Teschen devant la Conférence de La Paix en 1919-20', *R.H.D.*, vol. 62, 1948, pp. 8-27.

1503 MORROW, I.F.D., *The Settlement in the German-Polish Borderlands*, London, 1936, Pp. 558.

1504   PERMAN, D., *The Shaping of the Czechoslovak State: the Diplomatic History of the Boundaries of Czechoslovakia, 1914-20*, Leyden, 1962.

1505   PRZYBYLSKI, A., *La Pologne en lutte pour ses frontières - 1918-20*, Paris, 1929, Pp. 172.

1506   SENN, A.E., *The Great Powers, Lithuania and Vilna Question, 1920-28*, Leiden, 1966, Pp. 239.

1507   SKRZYPEK, S., *The Problem of East Galicia*, London, 1948, Pp. vii + 94.

1508   TAPIÉ, V., *Le Pays de Teschen et les rapports entre la Pologne et la Tchécoslovaquie*, Paris, 1936.

1509   WAMBAUGH, SARAH, *Plebiscites since the World War*, Washington, 1933, 2 vols.

1510   WITT, K., *Die Teschener Frage*, Berlin, 1935, Pp. 291.

SEE ALSO:

ROSE, (**0171**); ROSE, (**0682**); SIKORSKI, (**1041**); KAECKENBEECK, (**1149**); MACHRAY, (**1150**); ZIELIŃSKI, (**1153**); RESHETAR, (**1163**); STACHIW, (**1167**); BAILLY, (**1177**).

c) POLISH-SOVIET WAR, 1919 - 1920

1511   D'ABERNON, VISCOUNT, VINCENT, E., *The Eighteenth Decisive Battle of the World, Warsaw, 1920*, London, 1931, Pp. 178.

1512   DĄBROWSKI, S., 'The Peace Treaty of Riga', *P.R.*, vol. 5, 1960, pp. 3-34.

1513   DAVIES, NORMAN, *White Eagle, Red Star - The Polish-Soviet War*, 1919-20, London, 1972, Pp. 318.

1514   DAVIES, NORMAN, 'The Soviet Command and the Battle of Warsaw, 1920', *Soviet Studies*, vol. 23, 1972, pp. 573-85.

1515   DAVIES, NORMAN, 'Izaak Babel's "Konarmiya" Stories and the Polish-Soviet War, 1919-20', *M.L.R.*, vol. 23, 1972, pp. 845-57.

1516   DAVIES, NORMAN, 'Lloyd George and Poland, 1919-20', *J.Cont.H.*, vol. 6, 1971, pp. 132-54.

1517   DAVIES, NORMAN, 'August 1920', *Eur St. R.*, vol. 3, No. 3, 1973, pp. 269-81.

1518   DAVIES, NORMAN, 'The Genesis of the Polish-Soviet War; 1919-20, *Eur.St.R.*, vol. 5, 1975, pp. 47-68.

1519   DZIEWANOWSKI, M.K., 'Piłsudski's Foreign Policy, 1919-21', *J.C.E.A.*, vol. 10, 1950-1, pp. 113-28.

1520 HUNCZAK, TARAS, 'Operation Winter and the Struggle for the Baltic', *E.E.Q.*, vol. 4, 1970, pp. 40-57.

1521 KUKIEL, M., 'Polish-Soviet Campaign of 1920', *S.E.E.R.*, vol. 8, 1929-30, pp. 48-65.

1522 MACFARLANE, H.J., 'Hands Off Russia. British Labour and the Russo-Polish War, 1920', *P.R.*, vol. 38, 1967, pp. 126-52.

1523 PIŁSUDSKI, J., *Year 1920*, London, 1972, Pp. 283. (including TUKHACHEVSKY, M., *Advance to the Vistula*).

1524 SIKORSKI, W., *La campagne polono-russe de 1920*, (Translated by M. Larcher), Paris, 1928, Pp. 320.

1525 SWORAKOWSKI, W., 'An Error Regarding Eastern Galicia in Curzon's Note to the Soviet Government', *J.C.E.A.*, vol. 4, 1944, pp. 3-26.

1526 WANDYCZ, P., *Soviet-Polish Relations, 1917-21*, Cambridge, Mass., 1969, Pp. 403.

1527 WANDYCZ, P., 'Polish Federalism 1919-20 and its Historical Antecedents', *E.E.Q.*, vol. 4, 1970, pp. 25-39.

1528 WANDYCZ, P., 'General Weygand and the Battle of Warsaw, 1920', *J.C.E.A.*, vol. 19, 1960, pp. 357-65.

1529 WANDYCZ, P., 'Secret Soviet-Polish Peace Talks in 1919', *S.R.*, vol. 25, 1965, pp. 425-49.

SEE ALSO:

RESHETAR, (**1163**); STACHIW, (**1167**); KOMARNICKI, (**1459**); DZIEWANOWSKI, (**1466**), (**1484**); JANTA, (**1489**); SYMMONS, (**1493**); ELCOCK, (**1500**); PRZYBYLSKI, (**1505**); DAVIES, (**1678**); *Laboratoire de Slavistique*, (**1718**).

d) 1921 - 1932

1530 GĄSIOROWSKI, Z.J., 'Polish-Czechoslovak Relations, 1918-26,' *S.E.E.R.*, vol. 35, 1956-7, pp. 172-94, 473-505.

1531 GĄSIOROWSKI, Z.J., 'Stresemann and Poland before Locarno', *J.C.E.A.*, vol. 18, 1958, pp. 25-47.

1532 GĄSIOROWSKI, Z.J., 'Joseph Piłsudski in the Light of American Reports, 1919-22', *S.E.E.R.*, vol. 49, 1971, pp. 425-36.

1533 GROMADA, T.V., 'Piłsudski and the Slovak Autonomists', *S.R.*, vol. 28, 1969, pp. 445-62.

1534 JACKSON, G.D., *Comintern and Peasant in Eastern Europe, 1919-30*, New York, 1966, pp. 340.

1535   KELLERMAN, V., *Schwarzer Adler, weisser Adler: die Polenpoltik der Weimarer Republic*, Cologne, 1970, Pp. 196.

1536   KORBEL, J., *Poland between East and West, 1919-33. Soviet and German Diplomacy toward Poland 1919-33*, New York, 1963, Pp. 321.

1537   LAROCHE, J., *La Pologne de Piłsudski. Souvenir d'une ambassade 1926-35*, Paris, 1953, Pp. 233.

1538   RIEKHOFF, H. von, 'Piłsudski's Overtures to Stresemann', *C.S.P.*, vol. 9, 1967, pp. 74-85.

1539   RIEKHOFF, H., *German-Polish Relations, 1918-33*, Baltimore, 1970, Pp. 421.

1540   WANDYCZ, PIOTR, 'French Diplomats in Poland, 1919-26', *J.C.E.A.*, vol. 23, 1964, pp. 440-50.

SEE ALSO:

KIMMICH, (**1142**); MAMEL, (**1143**); MASON, (**1144**); WILDER, (**1145**).

e) BECK'S FOREIGN POLICY, 1932-1939

1541   BATOWSKI, H., 'Polnische Diplomatische Akten aus den Jahren 1938-9', *Jb. f G. d UdSSR*, vol. 8, 1964, pp. 424-45.

1542   BECK, J., *Final Report*, New York, 1957, Pp. 278.

1543   BREYER, RICHARD, *Das Deutsche Reich und Polen, 1932-7: Aussenpolitik und Volksgruppenfragen*, Würzburg, 1955, Pp. 372.

1544   BUDUROWYCZ, B., *Polish-Soviet Relations, 1932-9*, New York, 1963, Pp. 229.

1545   CIENCIALA, ANNA, *Poland and the Western Powers, 1938-9*, London, 1968, Pp. 310.

1546   CIENCIALA, ANNA, 'The Significance of the Declaration of Non-aggression of 26 January 1934 in Polish-German and International Relations - A Reappraisal', *E.E.Q.*, vol. 1, 1967, pp. 1-30.

1547   CIENCIALA, ANNA, 'Poland and the Munich Crisis, 1938 - A Reappraisal', *E.E.Q.*, vol. 3, 1969, pp. 201-19.

1548   DALLIN, ALEXANDER, 'The Month of Decision: German-Soviet Diplomacy, 22 July - 22 August, 1939', *J.C.E.A.*, vol. 9, 1949-50, pp. 1-31.

1549   DOPIERALA, B., 'Beck and the Gdańsk Question (1930-35)', *A.P.H.*, vol. 17, 1968, pp. 71-104.

1550   GASIOROWSKI, Z.J., 'Did Piłsudski Attempt to Initiate a Preventative War in 1933?', *J.M.H.*, vol. 27, 1955, pp. 135-51.

1551 GĄSIOROWSKI, Z.J., 'The German-Polish Non-Aggression Pact of 1934', *J.C.E.A.*, vol. 15, 1955, pp. 4-29.

1552 GROMADA, THADDEUS, V., 'Poland and Slovakia during the September-October Crisis of 1938', in *Studies in Polish Civilisation*, ed., Wandycz, D., New York, 1966, pp. 117-28.

1553 JEDRUSZCZAK, TADEUSZ, *La genèse de la deuxième guerre mondiale*, Warsaw, 1967, Pp. 119.

1554 JĘDRZEJEWICZ, W., ed., *Diplomat in Berlin, 1933-39. Papers and Memoirs of Józef Lipski, Ambassador of Poland.*, New York, London, 1968, Pp. xxxvi + 679.

1555 JĘDRZEJEWICZ, W., ed., *Diplomat in Paris, 1936-39, Papers and Memoirs of J. Lukasiewicz, Ambassador of Poland*, New York, 1970, Pp. 408.

1556 JĘDRZEJEWICZ, W., 'The Polish Plan for a Preventative War against Germany, 1933', *P.R.*, vol. 11, no. 1, 1966, pp. 62-91.

1557 NAMIER, L.B., *Diplomatic Prelude, 1938-39*, London, 1948, Pp. 502.

1558 NOEL, LÉON, *Une Ambassade à Varsovie, 1935-1939: L'agression allemande contre la Pologne*, Paris, 1946, Pp. 509.

1559 ROBERTS, H.L., 'The Diplomacy of Colonel Beck', in *The Diplomats*, ed., Craig, G., Gilbert, F., Princeton, 1953, pp. 579-614.

1560 RYSZKA, FRANCISZEK, *La genèse de la seconde guerre mondiale: Problèmes historiographiques*, (PAN), Warsaw, 1967, Pp. 58.

1561 SAKWA, G., 'The "Renewal" of the Franco-Polish Alliance in 1936 and the Rambouillet Agreement', *P.R.*, vol. 16, 1971, pp. 45-66.

1562 SAKWA, G., 'The Franco-Polish Alliance and the Remilitarization of the Rhineland', *Hist. J.*, vol. 16, no. 1, 1973, pp. 125-46.

1563 SMOGORZEWSKI, K., 'Poland's Foreign Relations', *S.E.E.R.*, vol. 16, 1938, pp. 558-71; 1938, vol. 17, pp. 105-21.

1564 STANISLAWSKA, S., 'Poland's Attitude towards the London Conference of April 29th-30th, 1938', *A.P.H.*, vol. 4, 1961, pp. 58-84.

1565 SZEMBEK, J., *Journal 1933-39*, Paris, 1952, Pp. 504.

SEE ALSO:

FRANCE, (**1628**); *GREAT BRITAIN*, (**1630**); *POLAND*, (**1646**); CANNISTRA, (**1669**).

12) Second World War, 1939-45.

On the September Campaign, the military aspect is treated by Kennedy (**1573**) and Neugebauer (**1578**). Bethell (**1567**) is mainly concerned with British reactions.

The diplomacy of the Polish Question during the war is still under intensive study, but an introduction is provided by Reddaway (**1579**), Rozek (**1580**), Keplicz (**1574**), Wagner (**1585**), Yakemtchouk (**1600**) and Gati (**1694**).

On the Polish Government-in-Exile, Anders (**1589-1590**) describes military experiences, and Raczynski (**1592**) political ones.

Polish-Soviet Relations can best be approached in the Sikorski Institute's documents (**1593**). Kot (**1595**) contributes some vivid insights. Kusnierz (**1596**) chronicles Polish grievances in detail.

All aspects of the war as relevant to Poland are documented in Jędrzejewicz (**1571**).

Problems of Occupation and Resistance are treated in **Section J (26)**.

a) GENERAL

1566 ARCT, BOHDAN, *Polish Wings in the West: After the September Disaster, the Battle of Britain, Air Offensives, and Final Victory*, Warsaw, 1971, Pp. 145.

1567 BETHELL, N., *The War Hitler Won*, London, 1972, Pp. 472.

1568 GARLINSKI, J., *Poland, SOE and the Allies*, (Translated by P. Stevenson), London, 1969, Pp. 248.

1569 HAMMERSMITH, JACK L., 'The U.S. Office of War Information (OWI) and the Polish Question, 1943-45', *P.R.*, vol. 19, no. 1, 1974, pp. 67-76.

1570 HEYDON, P., 'Protecting Polish Interests in the USSR, 1943-4: an Episode in Australian Representation', *Australian Journal of Politics*, vol. 18, 1972, pp. 189-213.

1571 JĘDRZEJEWICZ, W., ed., *Poland in the British Parliament, 1939-45*, New York, 1946-62, 3 vols..

1572 JURGA, T., 'La guerre défensive de la Pologne en 1939', *Revue Int. d'Histoire Militaire*, no. 28, 1969, pp. 482-500.

1573 KENNEDY, R.M., *The German Campaign in Poland, 1939*, Washington, 1956, Pp. 141.

1574 KEPLICZ, KLEMENS, *Potsdam: Twenty Years After*, Warsaw, 1965, Pp. 130.

1575 KUKIEL, M., *Six ans de guerre pour l'indépendance*, Paris, 1948, Pp. 48.

1576 LUKACS, J.A., *The Great Powers and Eastern Europe*, New York, 1953, Pp. 878.

1577 MACHRAY, R., *The Polish-German Problem*, London, 1941, Pp. 56.

1578 NEUGEBAUER, M.N., *The Defense of Poland (September 1939)*, London, 1942, Pp. 228.

1579 REDDAWAY, W.F., 'The Polish Question in November 1939', *History*, vol. 24, 1939, pp. 220-35.

1580 ROZEK, E.J., *Allied Wartime Diplomacy - a Pattern in Poland*, New York, 1958, Pp. xvii + 481.

1581 SONTAG, R.J.; BEDDIE, J.S., ed., *Nazi-Soviet Relations, 1939-41: Documents from the Archives of the German Foreign Office*, Dept. of State, Washington, 1948, Pp. 362.

1582 TABORSKY, E., 'A Polish-Czechoslovak Confederation: The Story of the First Soviet Veto', *J.C.E.A.*, vol. 9, 1949-50, pp. 379-85.

1583 VIERHELLER, V., *Polen und die Deutschland Frage, 1939-45*, Cologne, 1970, Pp. 184.

1584 VOIGT, F.A., *Pax Britannica*, London, 1949, Pp. viii + 575.

1585 WAGNER, W., *The Genesis of the Oder-Neisse Line: A Study in Diplomatic Negotiations during World War Two*, Stuttgart, 1957, Pp. 168.

1586 WANDYCZ, P.S., 'The Beneš-Sikorski Agreement' in *The Central European Federalist*, vol. 1, 1953.

1587 WEINBERG, G.L., *Germany and the Soviet Union, 1939-41*, Leiden, 1954, Pp. 218.

1588 ZAŁUSKI, Z., *Poles on the Fronts of World War Two*, Warsaw, 1969, Pp. 93.

SEE ALSO:

(ANON), (**0131**); LEDNICKI, (**0153**); POMIAN, (**0164**); RZEPNIEWSKI, (**1039**); STAPOR, (**1042**); WISKEMANN, (**1496**); JĘDRUSZCZAK, (**1553**); NOEL, (**1558**); RYSZKA, (**1560**).

b) GOVERNMENT-IN-EXILE

1589 ANDERS, W., *Mémoires, 1939-46*, (Translated by J. Rzewuska), Paris, 1948, Pp. 478.

1590 ANDERS, W., *An Army in Exile - the Story of the Second Polish Corps*, London, 1949, Pp. xvi + 319.

1591 IRVING, D., *Accident - the Death of General Sikorski*, London, 1967, Pp. 231.

1592 RACZYŃSKI, EDWARD, *In Allied London*, London, 1963, Pp. xiv + 381.

SEE ALSO:

CAZALET, (**0138**); POMIAN, (**0164**); ROSE, (**0170**); KLECZKOWSKI, (**1031**); REDLICH, (**1746**).

c) POLAND-USSR

1593   *Documents on Polish-Soviet Relations, 1939-45*, London, 1961, (Sikorski Institute, vols. 1 and 2).

1594   KEETON, G.W.; SCHLESINGER, R., *Russia and her Western Neighbours*, London, 1942, Pp. 160.

1595   KOT, S., *Conversations with the Kremlin and Despatches from Russia*, (Translated by H. Stevens), London, 1963, Pp. xxx + 285.

1596   KUŚNIERZ, B., *Stalin and the Poles - an Indictment of the Soviet Leaders*, London, 1949, Pp. xx + 317.

1597   POLONSKY, A., ed., *The Great Powers and the Polish Question, 1941-1945: A Documentary Study in Cold War Origins*, London, 1976, Pp. 282.

1598   SHOTWELL, J.T.; LASERSON, M.M., *Poland and Russia, 1939-45*, London, 1946, Pp. 114.

1599   UMIASTOWSKI, R., *Poland, Russia and Great Britain, 1941-45*, London, 1946, Pp. 554.

1600   YAKEMTCHOUK, R., *La Ligne Curzon et la IIème Guerre Mondiale*, Paris, 1957, Pp. 135.

SEE ALSO:

KORBONSKI, (**0543**); SZPORLUK, (**1762**).

13) FOREIGN RELATIONS SINCE 1945

Although most studies treat Poland within the context of the Soviet bloc, notably Brzezinski (**1604**), Korbonski (**1612**) and Remington (**1621**); Horak (**1609**) puts post-war policy into longer perspective.

The continuing complications of the Polish Western Territories are outlined in Bierzanek (**1601**), Bluhm (**1602**), Jordan (**1610**), Wiewora (**1626**) and Zdiechowski (**1627**).

1601   BIERZANEK, REMIGIUSZ, *et al.*, *"Heimatrecht": Instrument of Revisionism*, Warsaw, 1963.

1602   BLUHM, GEORG, *Die Oder-Neisse Frage*, Hanover, 1967, Pp. xiii +.541.

1603 BROMKE, ADAM, 'Polish Foreign Policy in the 1970s', *C.S.P.*, vol. 15, 1973, pp. 192-204.

1604 BRZEZINSKI, Z.K., *The Soviet Bloc - Unity and Conflict*, Cambridge, Mass., 1960, Pp. xxii + 470.

1605 BYRNES, R.F., *The United States and Eastern Europe*, (Report of the 31st American Assembly), Englewood Cliffs, New Jersey, 1967.

1606 DOBROSIELSKI, MARIAN, 'The Polish Institute of International Affairs', *Polish Perspectives*, vol. 16, No. 7/8, 1973, pp. 18-23.

1607 GIERTYCH, J., *Poland and Germany*, London, 1958, Pp. 158.

1608 GRIFFITH, W.E., ed., *Communism in Europe: Continuity, Change and the Sino-Soviet Dispute*, Cambridge, Mass., 1964-6, 2 vols.

1609 HORAK, S., *Poland's International Affairs, 1919-60*, Bloomington, 1964, Pp. 248.

1610 JORDAN, Z., *The Oder-Neisse Line: a Study of the Political, Economic and European Significance of Poland's Western Frontier*, London, 1952, Pp. 133.

1611 KERTESZ, S.D., ed., *The Fate of East Central Europe: Hopes and Failures of American Foreign Policy*, Notre Dame (Indiana), 1956, Pp. xii + 463.

1612 KORBONSKI, ANDRZEJ, *The Warsaw Pact*, New York, 1969, Pp. 74.

1613 KOLARZ, W., *Russia and her Colonies*, London, 1952, Pp. xiv + 334.

1614 KOKOT, J., *The Logic of the Oder-Neisse Line*, Poznań, 1959, Pp. 289.

1615 LEMBERG, E., *Osteuropa und die Sowjet-Union: Geschichte und Probleme der Welt hinter dem Eiseren Vorhang*, Stuttgart, 1956, Pp. 301.

1616 MEISSNER, B., *Der Warschauer Pakt - Dokumentensammlung*, Cologne, 1963, Pp. 622.

1617 MICEWSKI, ANDRZEJ, 'Polish Foreign Policy: Historical Perspectives', *C.S.P.*, vol. 15, 1973, pp. 184-91.

1618 MIKOŁAJCZYK, S., 'Poland in the New Europe', *S.E.E.R.*, vol. 23, 1945, pp. 41-46.

1619 OLSZOWSKI, STEFAN, 'Polish Foreign Policy in an Age of Détente', *Polish Perspectives*, vol. 17, no. 3, 1973, pp. 3-12.

1620 OSTASZEWSKI, J., ed., *Modern Poland between East and West*, Warsaw, 1971, Pp. 144.

1621 REMINGTON, R.A., *The Warsaw Pact: Case Studies in*

Communist Conflict Resolution, M.I.T., Cambridge, Mass., 1971, Pp. xix + 268.

1622 ROBERTS, H.L., *Eastern Europe - Politics, Revolution and Diplomacy*, New York, 1970, Pp. 324.

1623 TREPCZYŃSKI, S., 'Poland and European Security', *C.S.P.*, vol. 15, 1973, pp. 205-12.

1624 WANDYCZ, PIOTR, 'The Soviet System of Alliances in Eastern Europe', *J.C.E.A.*, vol. 16, 1956, pp. 117-84.

1625 WASSERMANN, CHARLES, *Europe's Forgotten Territories*, Copenhagen, 1960, Pp. 272.

1626 WIEWIORA, B., *The Polish-German Frontier from the Standpoint of International Law*, Poznań, 1964, Pp. xxxii + 224.

1627 ZDZIECHOWSKI, J., *Le problème clef de la réconstruction européenne: la Pologne sur l'Oder*, Paris, 1965, Pp. 228.

SEE ALSO:

IONESCU, (**0227**); BANASIAK, (**0301**); SCHECHTMAN, (**0316**); SPEAJGHT, (**1015**); WALICHNOWSKI, (**1116**); ASCHERSON, (**1227**); GOETTINGEN RESEARCH COMMITTEE, (**1656**); GATI, (**1694**); OLSZOWSKI, (**1738**); WOJCIK, (**1769**).

R. GOVERNMENT PUBLICATIONS

Vigor (**0058**) lists all United Kingdom and Commonwealth, and United States Government Publications from 1946-1967. A comprehensive up-to-date list of the latter is found in the invaluable *Monthly Catalogue* (**0040**). American governmental publications frequently contain information and figures not found elsewhere.

The following items have all been issued by various government ministries and departments mainly in connection with the Peace Settlement of 1918-19 and the outbreak of the Second World War in 1939.

1628   FRANCE: MINISTÈRE DES AFFAIRES ETRANGÈRES, (Paris) *The French Yellow Book - Diplomatic Documents concerning the Events and Negotiations which Preceded the Outbreak of Hostilities . . . 1938-9*, London, 1940, Pp. xxxvi + 368.

1629   GERMANY: FOREIGN OFFICE, *Polish Acts of Atrocity against the German Minority in Poland*, Berlin - New York, 1940, Pp. 260.

1630   GREAT BRITAIN: H.M.S.O., Misc. No. 9 (1939) *Documents concerning German-Polish Relations and the Outbreak of Hostilities between Great Britain and Germany on 3rd Sept. 1939*, London, 1939, Pp. xxviii + 195.

1631   PEACE HANDBOOKS: (Handbooks Prepared Under the Direction of the Historical Section of the Foreign Office), Nos. 1, 2, 3, *Foreign Policy of Austria - Hungary*, London, March 1919, Pp. 126.

1632   PEACE HANDBOOK: No. 4a. *Austrian Silesia*, London, January 1919, Pp. 36.

1633   PEACE HANDBOOK: No. 34, *East and West Prussia*, London, July 1919, Pp. 65.

1634   PEACE HANDBOOK: no. 34a, *Prussian Silesia, (Oppeln)*, London, May 1919, Pp. 43.

1635   PEACE HANDBOOK: No. 51, *Russian Poland, Lithuania and White Russia*, London, April 1919, Pp. 149.

1636   PEACE HANDBOOK: No. 57, *Courland, Livonia, and Esthonia*, London, February 1919, Pp. 88.

1637   PEACE HANDBOOK: No. 49, *Poland - General Sketch of History, 1569-1772*, London, March 1919, Pp. 22.

1638   PEACE HANDBOOK: No. 49°, *Maps of Poland: 1. Berlin, 2. Varshava, 3. Minsk, 4. Wien, 5. Krakau, 6. Jitomir, 8. Partitions of Poland*, London, April 1919.

1639 PEACE HANDBOOK: No. 50, *Poland - the Three Partitions: the Settlement of 1815, London,* March 1919, Pp. 11.

1640 PEACE HANDBOOK: No. 52, *Prussian Poland,* London, March 1919, Pp. 58.

1641 PEACE HANDBOOK: No. 53, *Galicia, (Austrian Poland),* London, March 1919, Pp. 79.

1642 PEACE HANDBOOK: No. 164, *Zionism,* London, February 1919, Pp. 52.

1643 PEACE HANDBOOK: No. 165, *The Congress of Vienna, 1814-15,* London, December 1918, Pp. 189.

1644 PEACE HANDBOOK: No. 165a, *The Congress of Vienna,* (Maps), London, 1918.

1645 PEACE HANDBOOKS: No. O°, *Ethnographical Maps of Central and South Eastern Europe and Western Asia*; No. 2, *Poland,* London, April 1919.

1646 POLAND: MINISTRY OF FOREIGN AFFAIRS, *The Polish White Book: Official Documents concerning Polish-German and Polish-Soviet Relations, 1933-39,* London, 1940, Pp. xvii + 222.

1647 POLAND: MINISTRY OF FOREIGN AFFAIRS, *The German Occupation of Poland,* New York, Undated, (1940?), Pp. 240.

1648 POLAND: MINISTRY OF INFORMATION, *The German Fifth Column in Poland,* London, 1941, Pp. 157.

1649 POLAND: MINISTRY OF INFORMATION, *The German Invasion of Poland (The Polish Black Book),* London, 1940, Pp. 128.

1650 POLAND: MINISTRY OF INFORMATION, *The Polish Black Book,* New York, 1942, Pp. xiv + 615.

1651 POLAND: MINISTRY OF INFORMATION, *The German New Order in Poland,* London, 1942, Pp. xiv + 585.

1652 POLAND: MINISTRY OF PREPARATION CONCERNING THE PEACE CONFERENCE: *The Eastern Provinces of Poland,* London, 1944.

1653 POLAND: MINISTRY OF PREPARATION CONCERNING THE PEACE CONFERENCE: *Lwów and the Lwów Region,* London, 1945.

1654 U.S.A.: HOUSE OF REPRESENTATIVES SELECT COMMITTEE ON COMMUNIST AGGRESSION: Special Report No. 1, *Communist Takeover and Occupation of Poland,* (House Report No. 2684, Part 3), Washington, 1954, Pp. 37; *Appendix: Polish Documents Report,* Washington 1954, Pp. 176.

1655 U.S.A.: HOUSE OF REPRESENTATIVES, SELECT COMMITTEE ON COMMUNIST AGGRESSION: Hearings: Fourth Interim Report, (*Communist Aggression Investigation, Part*

2), Washington 1954, Pp. 1448; Sixth Interim Report, Washington 1954, Pp. 214; Tenth Interim Report, Washington 1954, Pp. 174.

1656   U.S.S.R.: PEOPLE'S COMMISSARIAT OF JUSTICE, *Trial of the Organisers, Leaders and Members of the Polish Diversionist Organisations* . . . June 18-21, 1945, Moscow-London, 1945, Pp. 240.

ADDENDA

[Many of these works have been cross-referenced in the preceding sections]

1657   AINSZTEIN, R., *Jewish Resistance in Nazi - Occupied Eastern Europe*, London, 1974, Pp. 970.

1658   AUFRICHT, HANS, *Guide to League of Nations Publications, 1920-47*, New York, 1966, Pp. 682.

1659   BACKUS, OSWALD, *The Motives of West Russian Nobles for deserting Lithuania, 1377-1514*, Lawrence, 1957, Pp. 174.

1660   BIRKOS, A.S.; LEWIS, A.T., *East European and Soviet Economic Affairs, A Bibliography, 1965-1973*, Littleton, Colorado, 1975, Pp. 170.

1661   BLEJWAS, STANISLAUS B., 'The Origins and Practice of 'Organic Work' in Poland, 1795-1863', *P.R.*, vol. 15, no. 4, 1970, pp. 23-54.

1662   BOCHNAK, ADAM; BUCZKOWSKI, K., *Decorative Arts in Poland*, Warsaw, 1972, Pp. 39 + 325 plates.

1663   BOGUCKA, MARIA, "The Monetary Crisis of the XVIIth Century and its Social and Psychological Consequences in Poland", *Journal of European Economic History*, IV, 1, Spring, 1975.

1664   BOREJSZA, JERZY B., 'Portrait du revolutionnaire polonais', *A.P.H.*, vol. 30, 1974, pp. 119-62.

1665   BORKOWSKI, J., 'Les paysans polonais aux XIX-XX siècles', *E.C.E.*, vol. 1, 1974, pp. 132-52.

1666   BRATKOVSKI, J., *Poland on the Road to Revolutionary Crisis*, London, 1933, Pp. 218.

1667   BROCK, PETER, 'The Political Program of the Polish Democratic Society', *P.R.*, vol. 14, no. 1, pp. 89-105, no. 2, pp. 5-24.

1668   BUIST, M., *At Spes non Fracta: Hope and Co. 1770-1815*, The Hague, 1974, Pp. 716.

1669   CANNISTRA, P.V.; WYNOT, E.D., 'Polish Foreign Policy in 1934: an Unpublished Document from the Italian Archives', *E.C.E.*, vol. 1, 1974, pp. 71-81.

1670   [CHECINSKI, MICHAEL] ANON., 'The USSR and the Politics of Polish Antisemitism 1956-8', *S.J.A.*, no. 1, 1971, pp. 19-44.

1671   CHECINSKI, MICHAEL, 'An Intended Polish Explanation, December 1956, (Such was Reality . . . *Nowe Drogi*)', *S.J.A.*, no. 3, 1972, pp. 82-93.

1672   CHECINSKI, MICHAEL, 'The Kielce Pogrom: (1946) Some

Unanswered Problems', *S.J.A.*, vol. 5, no. 1, 1975, pp. 57-72.

1673   CHELMINSKI, JAN, MALIBRAN, A., *L'armèe du Duché de Varsovie*, Paris, 1913.

1674   CHMIELEWSKI, E., ed., *The Fall of the Russian Empire*, (Major Issues in History Series), New York, 1973.

1675   COHEN, I, *Vilna*, Philadelphia, 1943, Pp. 531.

1676   CZARNECKI, JAN, *The Goths in Ancient Poland*, Miami, 1975.

1677   DASZYNSKA-GOLINSKA, ZOFIA, 'L'accroissement de la population en Pologne a l'époque des partages, 1816-1914', *La Pologne au VII Congrès des Sciences Historiques*, Warsaw, 1930, vol. 1, pp. 115-25.

1678   DAVIES, NORMAN, 'The Missing Revolutionary War: The Polish Campaigns and the Retreat from Revolution in Soviet Russia, 1919-21', *Sov. Stud.*, vol. 27, 1975, pp. 178-95.

1679   DOROSHENKO, DMYTRO, 'Mykhailo Dragomanov and the Ukrainian National Movement', *S.E.E.R.*, vol. 16, 1937-8, pp. 654-66.

1680   DZIEWANOWSKI, M.K., 'Joseph Pilsudski, 1867-1967', *E.E.Q.*, vol. 2, 1969, pp. 359-83.

1681   EVANS, GEOFFREY, *Tannenberg, 1410-1914*, London, 1970, Pp. 182.

1682   FABER, B.L., ed., *The Social Structure of Eastern Europe. Transition and Process in Czechoslovakia, Hungary, Poland, Romania and Yugoslavia*, New York, 1975, Pp. 450.

1683   FALLENBUCHL, Z.M., ed., *Economic Development in the Soviet Union and Eastern Europe*, New York, 1975, 2 vols., Pp. 360, 400.

1684   FEDYSHYN, OLEH S., *Germany's Drive to the East and the Ukrainian Revolution, 1917-18*, New Brunswick, N.J., 1971.

1685   FISHMAN, JOSHUA A., ed., *Studies on Polish Jewry, 1919-39*, New York, 1974, Pp. 294 + 538.

1686   FLORINSKY, M.T., *The End of the Russian Empire*, London, 1961.

1687   FOREIGN SCIENTIFIC PUBLICATIONS DEPARTMENT, NATIONAL CENTER FOR SCIENTIFIC, TECHNICAL AND ECONOMIC INFORMATION, WARSAW, ed., *Polish Research Guide*, Warsaw, 1974, Pp. 638.

1688   GARLIŃSKI, JÓZEF, *Fighting Auschwitz*, London, 1975.

1689   GARLIŃSKI, JÓZEF, 'The Polish Underground State, 1939-45', *J.C.H.*, vol. 10, 1975, pp. 219-59.

1690   GĄSIOROWSKA, NATALIA, 'Les origines de la grande industrie polonaise au XIX siècle', in *La Pologne au VI Congrès International des Sciences Historiques*, Warsaw-Lwów, 1930.

1691 FLAKIERSKI, H., 'Polish Post-war Economic Growth', *Sov. Stud.*, vol. 17, 1975, pp. 460-76.

1692 GĄSIOROWSKA, NATALIA, 'Commercialisation, concentration et mécanisation de l'industrie minière et metallurgique d'Etat dans le Royaume de Pologne pendant la période de l'administration de la Banque de Pologne', *La Pologne au VII Congrès International des Sciences Historiques*, Warsaw, 1933.

1693 GĄSIOROWSKI, ZYGMUNT, J., 'Poland's Policy towards Soviet Russia, 1921-22', *S.E.E.R.*, vol. 53, 1975, pp. 230-47.

1694 GATI, CHARLES, *The International Politics of Eastern Europe*, New York, 1976, Pp. 400.

1695 'General History in Polish Historiography, 1945-74', *A.P.H.*, vol. 32, 1975, pp. 7-224, (A Symposium).

1696 GOETTINGEN RESEARCH COMMITTEE, ed., *The Eastern Part of Germany beyond Oder and Neisse in the Polish Press, 1958-1961*, Wurzburg, 1964, Pp. 155.

1697 GOŁĘBIOWSKI, JANUSZ W., 'General Regularities and Specific Features of the Building of Socialism in Poland, 1944-8', *A.P.H.*, vol. 30, 1975, pp. 59-86.

1698 GRUDZIŃSKI, TADEUSZ, 'The Beginnings of Feudal Disintegration in Poland', *A.P.H.*, vol. 30, 1974, pp. 5-32.

1699 GRYNWASER, HIPOLIT, 'Le Code Napoléon dans le Duché de Varsovie', *Revue des Études Napoléoniennes*, vol. 12, 1917, pp. 129-70.

1700 GUNTHER, JOHN, *Inside Europe*, New York, 1938, Pp. 532.

1701 HALECKI, OSCAR, 'Jadwiga of Anjou and the Rise of East Central Europe', *P.R.*, vol. 19, no. 4, pp. 157-69.

1702 HANDELSMAN, MARCELI, *Les idées francaises et la mentalité politique de la Pologne au XIX siècle*, , Paris, 1927.

1703 HANDELSMAN, MARCELI, *La Pologne, sa vie économique et sociale pendant la guerre*, Paris, 1933.

1704 HARASYMIW, B., ed., *Education and the Mass Media in the Soviet Union and Eastern Europe*, New York, 1975, Pp. 200.

1705 HOWE, IRVING, *World of our Fathers. The Journey of the East European Jews to America and the Life They Found and Made*, New York, 1976, Pp. 714.

1706 JAKOBCZYK, WITOLD, *Die Hakatisten: der deutsche Ostmarkverein 1894-1934*, Berlin, 1966.

1707 JEDLICKI, JERZY, 'Bilan social du Duché de Varsovie', *A.P.H.*, vol. 14, 1966, pp. 93-104.

1708 KAMIŃSKI, ANDRZEJ, 'Neo-serfdom in Poland-Lithuania', *S.R.*, vol. 34, 1975, pp. 253-68.

1709 KATZ, B., 'Polish Post-war Economic Growth', *Sov. Stud.*, vol. 27, Oct. 1975, pp. 639-42.

1710 KATZ, ALFRED, *Poland's Ghettoes at War*, New York, 1970, Pp. xiii + 175.

1711 KEEFE, E., *et al.*, *Area Handbook for Poland*, Washington, 1973, Pp. 335.

1712 KERSTEN, KRYSTYNA, 'The New Territorial Shape of the Polish State and the Evolution of the Political Attitudes of Polish Society, 1944-48', *A.P.H.*, vol. 30, 1975, pp. 119-50.

1713 KIENIEWICZ, STEFAN, 'Le développement de la conscience nationale polonaise au XIXème siècle', *A.P.H.*, vol. 19, 1968, pp. 37-48.

1714 KORTH, RUDOLF, *Die preussische Schulpolitik und die polnischen Schulstreiks; ein Beitrag zur preussischen Polenpolitik der Ära Bulow*, Würzburg, 1963, Pp. xvi + 184.

1715 KOSINSKI, L., *Demographic Developments in the Soviet Union and Eastern Europe*, New York, 1976, Pp. 302.

1716 KRAMER, H.M., *Eastern European Economics*, White Plains, New York, 1974, Pp. 90.

1717 KRZYWICKI-HERBURT, GEORGE, 'Polish Philosophy', *The Encyclopedia of Philosophy*, ed. Edwards, P., New York, 1967.

1718 LABORATOIRE DE SLAVISTIQUE, ed., *La guerre polono-soviétique de 1919-20:* [Actes du Colloque, organisé par le Laboratoire de Slavistique à Paris, le 4 Mai 1973] (Institut d'Etudes Salves, no. 32,) Paris, 1975, Pp. 151.

1719 LAUTER, G.P.; DICKIE, P.M., *Multinational Corporations and East European Socialist Economies*, New York, 1975, Pp. 154.

1720 LAVIGNE, MARIE, *The Socialist Economics of the Soviet Union and Europe* (Translated by T.G. Waywell), London, 1974, Pp. 396.

1721 LESCOVER, LOUIS, *L'Église Catholique en Pologne sous le gouvernement russe, 1772-1875*, Paris, 1875.

1722 LEWANSKI, R., comp., *Guide to Polish Libraries*, New York, 1975.

1723 LINCOLN, W. BRUCE, 'Milyutin and the Polish Question 1861-3', *P.R.*, vol. 15, no. 4, 1970, pp. 54-66.

1724 LOJEK, JERZY, 'International French Newspapers and Their Role in Polish Affairs during the Second Half of the Eighteenth Century', *E.C.E.*, vol. 1, 1974, pp. 54-64.

1725 ŁEPKOWSKI, TADEUSZ, 'La formation de la nation polonaise moderne dans les conditions d'un pays démembré', *A.P.H.*, vol. 19, 1968, pp. 18-36.

1726 MARER, PAUL, U.S. *Financing of East-West Trade: The Political Economy of Government Credits and the National Interest,* Bloomington, Indiana, 1975, Pp. 442.

1727 MATEJKO, ALEXANDER, *Social Change and Stratification in Eastern Europe: An Interpretive Analysis of Poland and her Neighbours,* New York, 1974, Pp. 302.

1728 MATERNICKI, JERZY, 'L'enseignement de L'histoire en Pologne au XVIII siècle', *A.P.H.*, vol. 29, 1974, pp. 161-79.

1729 MENDELSOHN, EZRA, 'The Politics of *Agudas Yisroel* in Interwar Poland', *S.J.A.*, vol. 2, no. 2, pp. 47-60.

1730 MICHALSKI, JERZY, 'L'opposition capitale - province et ville-campagne dans la mentalité des polonais de la seconde moitié du XVIII siècle', *A.P.H.*, vol. 30, 1974, pp. 53-70.

1731 MICHAOWSKI, K., *Faras (Wall Paintings in the Collection of the National Museum in Warsaw),* Warsaw, 1974, Pp. 332.

1732 MIECZKOWSKI, B., *Personal and Social Consumption in Eastern Europe,* New York, 1975, Pp. 368.

1733 MIZWA, STEFAN, ed., *Great Men and Women of Poland,* (Kosciuszko Foundation), New York, 1942, Pp. 397.

1734 MURZYNOWSKI, A., REZLER, J., 'Les codifications du droit judiciaire', *A.P.H.*, vol. 30, 1975, pp. 151-85.

1735 MYERS, P.F., 'Demographic Trends in Eastern Europe', in U.S. Congress Joint Economic Committee, *Economic Developments in Countries of Eastern Europe,* Washington, D.C., 1973.

1736 NEUBACH, HELMUT, *Die Ausweisungen von Polen und Juden aus Preussen, 1885-6,* Wiesbaden, 1967.

1737 NUSSBAUM, KLEMENS, 'Jews in the Polish Army in the USSR, 1943-4', *S.J.A.*, no. 3, 1972, pp. 94-104.

1738 OLSZOWSKI, STEFAN, 'The Foreign Policy of People's Poland in the Last Thirty Years', *A.P.H.*, vol. 30, 1975, pp. 33-58.

1739 PAULU, BURTON, *Radio and Television Broadcasting in Eastern Europe,* Minneapolis, 1975, Pp. 592.

1740 PIEKALKIEWICZ, J., *Communist Local Government. A Study of Poland,* Ohio, 1975, Pp. 282.

1741 PIENKOS, DONALD E., 'Education and Emigration as Factors in Rural Societal Development: the Russian and Polish Peasantries' Responses to Collectivisation', *E.E.Q.*, vol. 9, 1975, pp. 75-95.

1742 PIESOWICZ, KAZIMIERZ, 'Les facteurs sociaux dans l'évolution démographique de la Pologne dans les années, 1945-70', *A.P.H.*, vol. 30, 1975, pp. 87-118.

1743 POUNDS, N.J.G., *The Upper Silesian Industrial Region*, Indiana, 1958, Pp. 260.

1744 RAJANA, CECIL, *Chemical and Petro-chemical Industries of Russia and Eastern Europe, 1960-1980*, New York, 1975, Pp. 950.

1745 REDLICH, SHIMON, 'The Jews in the Soviet Annexed Territories, 1939-41', *S.J.A.*, no. 1, 1971, pp. 81-90.

1746 REDLICH, SHIMON, 'Jews in General Anders' Army in the Soviet Union, 1939-42', *S.J.A.*, no. 1, 1971, pp. 81-90, no. 2, 1971, pp. 90-8.

1747 ROSEVEARE, IRENA M., 'Wielopolski's Reforms and their Failure before the Uprising of 1863', *Antemurale*, vol. 15, 1971, pp. 87-214.

1748 ROTHSCHILD, J., *East Central Europe between the Two World Wars*, Seattle, 1975, Pp. 420.

1749 SABALIUÑAS, LEONAS, 'Social Democracy in Tsarist Lithuania, 1893-1904', *S.R.*, vol. 31, 1972, pp. 323-42.

1750 SCOTT, H.M., 'France and the Polish Throne, 1763-4', *S.E.E.R.*, vol. 53, 1975, pp. 370-88.

1751 SENN, ALFRED ERICH, 'A Russian Voice on the Polish Question, 1916', *P.R.*, vol. 19, no. 2, 1974, pp. 83-87.

1752 SERENY, G., *Into that Darkness: From Mercy Killing to Mass Murder*, London, 1974, Pp. 380. (On Nazi concentration camps in Poland.)

1753 SKOWRONEK, JERZY, 'Le programme européen du Prince Adam Jerzy Czartoryski en 1803-1805', *A.P.H.*, vol. 17, 1968, pp. 137-59.

1754 SMOGORZEWSKI, CASIMIR, *Joseph Pilsudski et les activistes polonais pendant la guerre*, Paris, 1931.

1755 SOBOCIŃSKI, WLADYSLAW, 'Quelques observations sur le bilan social de la Pologne en 1815', *A.P.H.*, vol. 15, 1966, pp. 105-16.

1756 STARR, ROBERT, ed., *East-West Business Transactions*, New York, 1974, Pp. 596.

1757 STILES, W.H., *Austria in 1848-9*, London, 1852, 2 vols..

1758 STUKAS, JACK J., *Awakening Lithuania: a Study on the Rise of Modern Lithuanian Nationalism*, Madison, N.J., 1966.

1759 SWEET, P.R., 'Germany, Austria and Mitteleuropa, August 1915-April 1916', *Festschrift für Heinrich Benedikt*, ed., H.Hansch, A. Novotny, Vienna, 1957.

1760 SZCZEŚNIAK, BOLESLAW B., 'The Dependency of Kievan Rus on King Bolesław the Great: Numismatic Evidence', *P.R.*, vol. 18, no. 3, 1973, pp. 31-43.

1761 SZERMER, BOHDAN, *Gdansk - Past and Present*, Warsaw, 1971, Pp. 215.

1762 SZPORLUK, ROMAN, *The Influence of East Europe and the Soviet West on the USSR*, New York, 1975, Pp. 280.

1763 TOPOLSKI, JERZY, 'Creative Processes of the Formation of Socialist Society in Poland, 1944-74', *A.P.H.*, vol. 31, 1975, pp. 5-32.

1764 VAKAR, NICHOLAS P., *Belorussia: The Making of a Nation*, Cambridge, Mass., 1956, Pp. 297.

1765 VOLGYES, IVAN, *Political Socialization in Eastern Europe. A Comparative Framework*, New York, 1975, Pp. 220.

1766 WASSERMAN, PAUL, ed., *Statistics Sources. A Subject Guide*, Detroit, 1971, Pp. 647, "Poland", pp. 458-462.

1767 WHITE, STEPHEN, 'Labour's Council of Action', *J.C.H.*, vol. 10, 1975, pp. 99-122.

1768 WILCZYNSKI, L., *Technology in COMECON*, London, 1971, Pp. 375.

1769 WOJCIK, A., *The War Settlement in Eastern Europe*, New York, 1967, Pp. 124.

1770 ZAWADZKI, W.H., 'Prince Adam Czartoryski and Napoleonic France, 1801-5: A Study in Political Attitudes', *Hist. J.*, vol. 18, 1975, pp. 145-77.

1771 ZIOMEK, HENRYK, 'Historic Implications and the Dramatic Influences in Calderon's 'Life is a Dream', *P.R.*, vol. 20, no. 1, 1975, pp. 111-28.

1772 ZWASS, ADAM, *Monetary Cooperation Between East and West*, New York, 1973, Pp. 265.

1773 ANCKER - JOHNSON, B., ed., *Proceedings of the East-West Technological Trade Symposium* [19 Nov. 1975], Washington, 1976, Pp. 127.

1774 ATTMAN, A., *The Russian and Polish Markets in International Trade, 1500-1650*, Götenborg, 1973, Pp. 232.

1775 BARRATT, G.R., 'M.S. Lunin and Polish Sovereignty', *E.E.Q.*, vol. 5, 1971, no. 1, pp. 1-12.

1776 BOREJSZA, J., 'De Sedan à Versailles: esquisse des relations franco-polonaises, 1870-1919', *A.P.H.*, vol. 24, 1972, pp. 78-99.

1777 BROMKE, A., 'Catholic Social Thought in Communist Poland', *Problems of Communism*, July-August 1975, pp. 67-72.

1778 BROMKE, A., et al., eds., 'Poland in the Last Quarter of the Twentieth Century: A Panel Discussion', *S.R.*, December, 1975, pp. 769-789.

1779 CARBONE, M., *La questione agraria in Polonia, 1918-1939*, Naples 1976, Pp. 295.

1780 CARLEY, M.J., 'The Politics of Anti-Bolshevism: The French

Government and the Russo-Polish War, December 1919 to May 1920', *Historical Journal*, XIX, 1, 1976, pp. 163-190.

1781   DEAN, R.W., 'Gierek's Three Years: Retrenchment and Reform', *Survey*, vol. 20, nos 2-3, 1974, pp. 59-75.

1782   DREZGA, T., 'Włodkowic's "Epistola ad Sbigneum Episcopum Cracoviensem" ', *P.R.*, vol. 20, no. 4, 1975, pp. 43-64.

1783   FEIWEL, G.R., 'Causes and Consequences of Disguised Industrial Unemployment in a Socialist Economy', *Sov Stud*, vol. 26, no. 3, 1974, pp. 344-62.

1784   GREAT BRITAIN: CABINET OFFICE, *Principal War Telegrams and Memoranda, 1940-1943*, London and Nendeln, 1976, 7 vols. .

1785   GREAT BRITAIN: FOREIGN OFFICE, *Index to Foreign Office Correspondence, 1920-1945*, London and Nendeln, 1969-72, 107 vols. .

1786   GROSFELD, J., 'Les coopératives industrielles en Pologne. Quelques problèmes économiques de propriété, '*Rev. d'Etudes Comp. Est-Ouest*, vol. 7, no. 2, 1976, pp. 79-128.

1787   GUTKIND, E.A., *Urban Development in East-Central Europe: Poland, Czechoslovakia, and Hungary*, New York, 1972, Pp. 475.

1788   HÖHMANN, H.H., KASER, M., THALHEIM, K., eds., *The New Economic Systems of Eastern Europe*, Berkeley, 1975, Pp. 585.

1789   JAMPEL, W., 'L'evolution de la consommation en Pologne', *Le Courrier des Pays de l'Est*, June 1974, No. 175, pp. 9-20.

1790   KOMOROWSKI, E.A., GILMORE, J.L., *Night Never Ending*, London, 1974, Pp. xi + 285, (On the Katyn Massacre.)

1791   KOSIŃSKI, L., 'Secret German War-Sources for Population Study of East Central Europe and the Soviet Union', *EEQ*, vol. 10, no. 1, 1976, pp. 21-34.

1792   LAVIGNE, M., 'Some Studies of Comecon Trade, Pricing and Integration', *Sov. Stud.*, vol. 27, no. 4, 1975, pp. 648-654.

1793   LOJEK, J., 'The International Crisis of 1791: Poland between the Triple Alliance and Russia', *East Central Europe*, vol. 2, fasc. 1, 1975, pp. 1-63.

1794   LUKAS, R., 'Russia, the Warsaw Rising and the Cold War', *PR* vol. 20, no. 4, 1975, pp. 13-26.

1795   McMILLAN, C., *Changing Perspectives in East-West Trade*, New York 1974, Pp. 198.

1796   MARCZEWSKI, J., *Crisis in Socialist Planning: Eastern Europe and the USSR* (translated by N. Lindsay), New York, London, 1974, Pp. 245.

1797   MASON, J.B., *Research Resources: Annotated Guide to the Social*

Sciences, Santa Barbara, California, 1968-71, 2 vols.

1798 NATO ECONOMIC DIRECTORATE: ed., *Banking, Money and Credit in Eastern Europe: Essays given at the 24-26 January Colloquium, 1973*, Brussels, 1973, Pp. 166.

1799 NATO ECONOMIC DIRECTORATE: ed., *East-West Technological Co-operation: Essays given at the 17-19 March 1976 Colloquium*, Brussels, 1976, Pp. 280.

1800 OPPMAN, R., 'The Archives of Immigrant Communities in Great Britain: the Archives of the Polish Institute', *Archives*, vol. 11, 1974, pp. 157-60.

1801 PACZKOWSKI, A., 'La loi de la presse en Pologne (1918-1939), *Rev. d'Etudes Comp. Est-Ouest*, vol. 7, no. 2, 1976, pp. 211-48. (Summary in English).

1802 PIENKOS, D., 'Party Elites and Society: the Shape of the Polish Party Central Committee since 1945', *PR*, vol. 20, no. 4, 1975, pp. 43-64.

1803 RAČKAUSKAS, J.A., 'Education in Lithuania prior to the Dissolution of the Jesuit Order (1773)', *Lituanus*, vol. 22, no. 1, 1976, pp. 5-41.

1804 ROSE, W.J., *The Polish Memoirs of William John Rose*, DANIEL STONE, ed., Toronto, 1975, Pp. 248.

1805 RYBICKI, M., 'Le front d'Unité Nationale dans le système politique de la République Populaire de Pologne', *East Central Europe*, vol. 2, fasc. 1, 1975, pp. 64-77.

1806 SCOTT, H.M., 'Great Britain, Poland and the Russian Alliance, 1763-1767', *Historical Journal*, XIX, 1, 1976, pp. 53-75.

1807 SERANNE, C., 'L'intégration economique à l'Est: le CAEM (Comecon)', *Notes et Etudes Documentaires*, 8 May 1976, pp. 1-115 + tables.

1808 SKUBISZEWSKA, M., 'Death as Birth: a Symbol on the Tomb of a Polish King', *British Archaeological Association Journal*, vol. 36, 1973, pp. 43-51.

1809 SOKOLEWICZ, W., 'Changes in the Structure and Functions of the Polish Sejm', *East Central Europe*, vol. 2, facs. 1, 1975, pp. 78-91.

1810 SOLCHANYK, R., 'Revolutionary Marxism in Galicia before 1918', *EEQ*, vol. 10, no. 1, 1976, pp. 35-41.

1811 SOWINSKI, A., *Les musiciens polonais et slaves*, Paris, 1857 (Reprinted 1971).

1812 SPIELMANN, K.F., et al., *Security Implications of Alternate Soviet Energy Policies toward Europe, 1976-81*, (Institute of Defense Analyses) Arlington, 1975, Pp. 218.

ADDENDA

1813   STONE, D., 'The Cultural Life of Conservative Polish Nobles in the late Eighteenth Century', *EEQ*, vol. 9, 1975, no. 3, pp. 271-7.

1814   SZRETER, R., 'Education for Nation-Saving: Poland between the Partitions', in *The History of Education in Europe*, COOK, T.G., ed., London, 1974, pp. 53-66.

1815   TURSKI, R., *Les transformations de la campagne polonaise*, Wrocław, 1970, Pp. 578.

1816   United States Congress, Joint Economic Committee Report. *Economic Developments in Countries of Eastern Europe: A Compendium of Papers*, Washington, 1970, Pp. 634.

1817   van BRABANT, J.M., *A Reconstruction of the Composition of Intra-CMEA Trade Relations*, Berlin, 1975, Pp. 305.

1818   VAUGHAN, M., 'A Multidimensional Approach to Contemporary Polish Stratification', *Survey*, vol. 20, no. 1, 1974, pp. 62-74.

1819   VOLGYES, I., ed., *Environmental Deterioration in the Soviet Union and Eastern Europe*, New York, 1974, Pp. 168.

1820   WOJCIK, A., 'Eastern Europe in the Year 2000: the Case of Poland', *EEQ*, vol. 9, no. 3, 1975, pp. 365-72.

1821   WYNAR, L. R., ed., *Habsburgs and Zaporozhian Cossacks: the Diary of Erich Lassota von Steblau, 1594*, (Translated by Orest Subtelny), Littleton, Colorado, 1975, Pp. 144.

1822   ZDZIECHOWSKI, G., ed., 'L'evolution economique et culturelle des "Territoires du Nord et de l'Ouest de la Pologne" ', *Notes et Etudes Documentaires*, 29 mars 1968, pp. 3-20.

APPENDIX I

PERIODICALS

This handlist contains details of some two hundred periodicals relevant to the study of Polish history. It is intended as an aid to quick reference, and is by no means exhaustive. But it includes most of the periodicals which deal exclusively with the subject, and a large proportion of those which show something more than occasional interest. In the main it is confined to titles, dates and place of publication, and frequency. In some instances it also includes the name of the editorial institution and a note on areas of specialist concern. Fuller information, if required can be obtained by consulting Ullrich's PERIODICALS DIRECTORY. (New York), the BRITISH UNION-CATALOGUE OF PERIODICALS and Supplements (London), or, for publications in Poland, the Polish Academy of Science's POLISH SCIENTIFIC PUBLICATIONS. It is worth remembering that foreign language periodicals usually embellish their articles with summaries in English, French or German. This practice certainly applies to the leading journals in Poland, such as *Kwartalnik Historyczny* or *Przegląd Historyczny*, and enables scholars to jump the language barrier without too much difficulty.

ABBREVIATIONS USED: (A) = Annual; (Bi-A) = Bi-annual; (Bi-m) = Bi-monthly; (F) = Fortnightly; (Irr) = Irregular; (M) = Monthly; (Q) = Quarterly; (Tri-A) = Tri-annual; (W) = Weekly.

ABN CORRESPONDENCE, Munich, 1949-; (Irr); (Bulletin of the Anti-Bolshevik Block of Nations).
ABSEES, Glasgow, 1970-; (Q); University of Glasgow; (Soviet and East European Abstract Series).
ACTA BALTICO-SLAVONICA, Białystok, 1963-; (Baltic History).
ACTA POLONIAE HISTORICA, Warsaw, 1959-; (Q); (Historical Research in Poland in Translation).
ADVANCE BIBLIOGRAPHY OF CONTENTS: POLITICAL SCIENCE AND GOVERNMENT. American Bibliographical Center, Santa Barbara, Cal. (M).
ALLIANCE JOURNAL, Cambridge Springs, Pennsylvania, 1951-60; (Polish American Themes).
AMERICAN HISTORICAL REVIEW, New York, 1895-; (Q); (American Historical Association).
AMERICAN POLITICAL SCIENCE REVIEW, Baltimore, 1906-; (Q); (American Political Science Association).
AMERICAN REVIEW OF EAST-WEST TRADE, New York (M).
ANEKS, KWARTALNIK POLITYCZNY, Uppsala, 1973-; (Q).
ANNALES-ECONOMIES, SOCIÉTÉS, CIVILISATIONS, Paris, 1929-; (Bi-m).

ANNALES HISTORIQUES DE LA RÉVOLUTION FRANÇAISE, Rheims, 1908-; (Q); (Société des Etudes).

ANNALES SILESIAE, Wrocław, 1960-; (Irr); (Silesian History in Polish and English).

ANNALS OF THE UKRAINIAN ACADEMY OF ARTS AND SCIENCES IN THE UNITED STATES, New York, 1951-; (Irr).

ANNUAIRE DE L'INSTITUT DE PHILOLOGIE ET D'HISTOIRE ORIENTALES ET SLAVES, Brussels, (A).

ANTEMURALE, Rome, 1954-; (A); (Polish Historical Institute, Rome).

ARCHEOLOGIA POLSKI, Wrocław, 1957-; (Bi-A); (Institute for the History of Material Culture, Polish Academy of Sciences).

ARCHEION, Warsaw, 1927-; (Irr); (Archivalia).

AUSTRIAN HISTORY YEARBOOK, Houston, Texas, 1965-; (A).

BALTIC COUNTRIES, Toruń, 1935-9; Baltic Institute.

BELLONA, Warsaw, 1921-39; (Military History).

BELLONA, London, 1942-64; (Q); General Sikorski Historical Institute, (Military History).

BIBLIOTHÈQUE D'HUMANISME ET RENAISSANCE, Paris/Geneva, 1941; (Tri-A); (Association d'Humanisme et Rennaissance).

BULLETIN INTERNATIONAL DE L'ACADEMIE DES SCIENCES DE CRACOVIE, Cracow, 1902-1920; (Classe de philologie, d'histoire, et de philosophie).

BIULETYN HISTORII SZTUKI, Warsaw, 1938-9; 1949-; (Q); Polish Academy of Sciences, Institute of Fine Art.

BIULETYN ŻYDOWSKIEGO INSTYTUTU HISTORYCZNEGO, Warsaw, 1951-; (History of Polish Jewry).

BULLETIN OF THE ASSOCIATION FOR THE ADVANCEMENT OF POLISH STUDIES, Alliance College, Alliance Springs, Pennsylvania, 1975-; (Q).

BULLETIN OF THE POLISH INSTITUTE OF ARTS AND SCIENCES IN AMERICA, New York.

BULLETIN OF THE INSTITUTE OF HISTORICAL RESEARCH, London, 1923-; London University.

CAHIERS DU MONDE RUSSE ET SOVIÉTIQUE, Paris, 1960-; (Q); (École Pratique des Hautes Études).

CAHIERS POLOGNE-ALLEMAGNE, Paris, 1959-1964.

CALIFORNIA SLAVIC STUDIES, Berkeley, 1960-7.

CANADIAN SLAVIC STUDIES, (Loyola College), Montreal, 1967-; (Q); (Revue Canadienne d'Études Slaves); now CANADIAN-AMERICAN SLAVIC STUDIES - University of Pittsburgh.

CANADIAN SLAVONIC PAPERS, Ottawa, 1957-69 (Q).

CATHOLIC HISTORICAL REVIEW, Washington, 1915-; (Q); (American Catholic Historical Association).

CENTRAL EUROPEAN FEDERALIST, New York, 1953-; (Bi-A); (Czechoslovak-Hungarian-Polish Research Committee).

CENTRAL EUROPEAN HISTORY, Atlanta, 1968-; (Q); (Conference Group for Central European History, American Historical Association).

CURRENT HISTORY, New York, 1941-; (M).

CZASOPISMO PRAWO-HISTORYCZNE, Warsaw, 1948; (Irr); (Legal and Constitutional History).

DZIEJE NAJNOWSZE, Warsaw, 1969-; (Twentieth Century History).

EAST CENTRAL EUROPE, Pittsburgh, 1974-; (Irr); (University Centre for International Studies).

EAST EUROPE, New York, 1952-; (M); (Formerly 'News From Behind the Iron Curtain', 1952-57).

EASTERN EUROPE, London, 1970-; (Bi-w) (London Chamber of Commerce and Industry).

EASTERN EUROPE REPORT, Geneva, 1971-; (Bi-w).

EAST EUROPEAN QUARTERLY, Boulder, 1967-; (Q); (University of Colorado).

EAST-WEST COMMERCE, London; (M).

EASTWEST MARKETS, Vienna; (Bi-w).

EAST-WEST TRADE INFORMATION BULLETIN, U.S. East-West Trade Centre, Prinz Eugen Strasse 8-10, Vienna; (M).

ECONOMIC HISTORY REVIEW, London, 1927-; 1971- (Q); Economic History Society.

ENGLISH HISTORICAL REVIEW, London/Oxford, 1886-; (Q).

EST EUROPÉEN, Paris, 1962-; (M); (Union of Ukrainians in France).

ETNOGRAFIA POLSKA, Wrocław, 1958-; (Irr); (Ethnography).

DER EUROPÄISCHE OSTEN, Munich, 1954.

EUROPEAN STUDIES REVIEW, Lancaster, 1971-; (Q).

L'EUROPA ORIENTALE, Rome, 1921-39.

FONTES ARCHEOLOGICI POSNANSIENSIS, Poznań, 1951-; (A); (Archeology).

FORSCHUNGEN ZUR OSTEUROPÄISCHES GESCHICHTE, Berlin, 1956-; (Irr).

GEOGRAFIA POLONICA, Warsaw, 1962-; (Geography).

GEOGRAPHICAL MAGAZINE, London, 1935-; (M).

HARVARD SLAVIC STUDIES, Cambridge (Mass.), 1952-; (Irr); (Department of Slavic Languages and Literatures, Harvard University).

HISTORY, London, 1912-; (Tri-A); (Historical Association).

HISTORICAL JOURNAL, Cambridge, 1958-; (Q); (Cambridge Historical Society).

HISTORISCHE ZEITSCHRIFT, Munich, 1859-; (Bi-A).

HISTORY TODAY, London, 1951; (M).

JAHRBUCH FÜR GESCHICHTE DER UdSSR UND DER VOLKS-DEMOKRATISCHEN LÄNDER EUROPAS, Halle, 1956-.

JAHRBÜCHER FÜR GESCHICHTE OSTEUROPAS, (formerly *Jahresberichte für Kultur und Geschichte der Slaven*, Breslau, 1926-), Wiesbaden, 1952; Munich 1953-; (Q); (East European historical studies published in German and English).

JEWISH SOCIAL STUDIES, New York, 1939-; (Q).

JEWS IN EASTERN EUROPE, London, 1959-g (Bi-M).

JOURNAL OF BALTIC STUDIES, Muhlenburg, Pa., 1969-; (Q).

JOURNAL OF CENTRAL EUROPEAN AFFAIRS, Boulder, Colorado, 1941-1964.

JOURNAL OF CONTEMPORARY HISTORY, London, 1966-; (Irr).

JOURNAL OF MODERN HISTORY, Chicago, 1929-.

KOMUNIKATY MAZURSKO-WARMINSKIE, Olszłyn, 1959-; (Mazuria).

KULTURA, Paris, 1947-; (Polish political and literary review).

KWARTALNIK HISTORII KULTURY MATERIALNES, Warsaw, 1953-; (Q); (History of Material Culture).

KWARTALNIK HISTORII NAUKI I TECHNIKI, Warsaw, 1956-; (Q); (History of Science and Technology).

KWARTALNIK HISTORYCZNY, Warsaw, 1889-; (Q); (The senior Polish historical journal).

KWARTALNIK OPOLSKI, Opole, 1955-; (Q); (Silesian Affairs).

KYRIOS [: VIERTELJAHRESSCHRIFT FÜR KIRCHEN-UND GEISTESGESCHICHTE OSTEUROPAS], Königsberg, 1910; Berlin, 1936-; (East European Religious History).

LE MOCI (Moniteur du Commerce International), Paris, (W) [good for East-West trade].

LE MONDE SLAVE, Paris, 1917-1938.

LE MOYEN AGE, Paris, 1888-; (M); (Mediaeval History).

LITUANUS - the Lithuanian Quarterly, Chicago, New York, 1954-; (Q).

MAŁOPOLSKIE STUDIA HISTORYCZNE, Kraków, 1956-; (History of Galicia and Malopolska).

MATERIAŁY ZACHODNIO-POMORSKIE, Gdańsk, 1954-; (Pomeranian Affairs).

MEANDER, Warsaw, 1945-g (Antiquity).

MEDIAEVALIA PHILOSOPHICA POLONORUM, Warsaw, 1957-; (Irr); (Mediaeval Philosophy).

MUZEALNICTWO, Poznań, 1951-; (Museums).

NAJNOWSZE DZIEJE POLSKI, Warsaw, 1957-; (Irr); (Polish History from 1918).

(NEUES) ARCHIV FÜR SACHSISCHE GESCHICHTE, Leipzig, 1863-80, Dresden, 1880-; (History of Saxony).

THE NEW EUROPE: A WEEKLY REVIEW OF FOREIGN POLITICS, Vols. I-XVII, London, October 1916-October 1920; (Independence Movements in Eastern Europe).

THE NEW POLAND, London, 1919-20; (Organ of the Polish Republic).

NINETEENTH CENTURY AND AFTER, London, 1877-1950; thereafter the TWENTIETH CENTURY, (Contemporary History).

NOTATKI PŁOCKIE, Płock, 1945-; (Local History - Płock).

NOWE DROGI, Warsaw, 1947-; (M); (Communist Ideology).

NUOVA RIVISTA STORICA, Milan, 1917-; (Modern History).

ODRODZENIE I REFORMACJA W POLSCE, Kraków, Warsaw, 1955-; (Irr); (Renaissance and Reformation Studies).

ORGANON, Warsaw, 1970-; (A); (History of Science).

OSTEUROPA: ZEITSCHRIFT FÜR GEGENWARTSFRAGEN DES

OSTENS, Königsberg-Berlin, 1925-39; Stuttgart, 1952-; (M), (Russian and East European Affairs). Has numerous translations of Polish articles of current interest; bibliography.

OXFORD SLAVONIC PAPERS, Oxford, 1950-; (A); (Literary and historical studies on Russia and Eastern Europe).

PAST AND PRESENT, Oxford, 1952-; (A Journal of scientific history).

POLAND: OUR ALLY IN PEACE, London, 1945-6; later 'The New Poland'.

POLAND (POLAND-AMERICA), New York, 1928-33; (American-Polish Chamber of Commerce and Industry).

POLAND, Warsaw, 1957-; (M); (Interpress Agency).

POLAND AND GERMANY, London, 1957-67; (Q); (Studies Centre on Polish-German Affairs).

POLES ABROAD: YEARBOOK AND DIRECTORY, London/New York, 1950-; (A).

POLISH AFFAIRS, London, 1952-; (Executive of the Polish Political Council).

POLISH-AMERICAN STUDIES, Orchard Lake, 1944-70.

POLISH-AMERICAN HISTORICAL ASSOCIATION BULLETIN, Orchard Lake, Michigan, 1946-; (M).

POLISH ARCHAEOLOGICAL ABSTRACTS, Poznań, 1972-; (A).

POLISH FORTNIGHTLY REVIEW, London, 1941-5; (Polish Ministry of Information).

POLISH NEWS, London, 1915-16; (Polish Information Committee).

POLISH PERSPECTIVES, Warsaw, 1957-; (M); (Interpress Agency).

POLISH PRESS SUMMARY, Munich, 1956-; (Radio Free Europe).

POLISH REVIEW, London, 1917-18; (Polish Information Committee).

POLISH REVIEW, New York, 1941-; (Quarterly from 1956).

POLISH SCIENTIFIC PERIODICALS, Warsaw, 1962-; (M); (Polish Academy of Sciences, Documentation Centre).

POLISH SOCIOLOGICAL BULLETIN, Warsaw, 1961-; (Irr).

POLISH WESTERN AFFAIRS, Poznań, 1959-; (M); (Instytut Zachodni, Poznań).

PROBLEMS OF COMMUNISM, Washington, 1949-; (Bi-M).

PRZEGLĄD HISTORYCZNY, Warsaw, 1905-; (M); (The leading journal of General History).

PRZEGLĄD KAWALERII I BRONI PANCERNEJ, London, 1963-; (Polish Military History).

PRZEGLĄD NAUK HISTORYCZNYCH I SPOŁECZNYCH, Lodz, 1951-; (Review of Historical and Social Sciences).

PRZEGLĄD ZACHODNI, Poznań, 1945-; (Western Territories).

LES QUESTIONS MINORITAIRES, Warsaw, 1928-34; (Institute for Research into National Minorities).

RADIO FREE EUROPE RESEARCH, Munich, (W).

REFERENCE SERVICES REVIEW, Ann Arbor, 1930-;.

REFORMACJA W POLSCE, Warsaw, 1921-39, 1951-; (Reformation Studies).

PERIODICALS

REVUE D'HISTOIRE DIPLOMATIQUE, Paris, 1889-;.
REVUE HISTORIQUE DE DROIT FRANÇAIS ET ÉTRANGER, Paris, 1855-; (Comparative Constitutional History).
REVUE D'HISTOIRE MODERNE ET CONTEMPORAINE, Paris, 1898-;.
REVUE DU NORD, Lille, 1910-3, 1951-; (North European Affairs).
REVUE HISTORIQUE, Paris, 1876-.
REVUE DES ÉTUDES SLAVES, Paris, 1921, 1951-; (Q); Institut d'Etudes Slaves de L'Universite de Paris.
REVUE BELGE DE PHILOLOGIE ET D'HISTOIRE, Brussels, 1922-; (Belgian University Foundation).
REVUE DES ETUDES JUIVES, Paris, 1880-1945; (Jewish Studies).
REVUE D'HISTOIRE ÉCONOMIQUE ET SOCIALE, Paris, 1908-.
RICERCHE SLAVISTICHE, Rome, 1952-; (Slavic Research).
RIGHT REVIEW, London, 1936-47; (Official Organ of the Royal House of Poland).
RIVISTA STORICA ITALIANA, Turin, 1884-; (Italian History Review).
ROCZNIK BIAŁOSTOCKI, Bialystok Museum, 1961-; (A); (Local History Society - Białystok).
ROCZNIK BIBLIOTEKI GDAŃSKIEJ, Gdańsk, 1967-; (A); (Gdansk Library Annual).
ROCZNIK DZIEJÓW RUCHU LUDOWEGO, Warsaw, 1961-; (A); (Gdańsk Library Annual).
ROCZNIK DZIEJÓW RUCHU LUDOWEGO, Warsaw, 1961-; (A); (Peasant History).
ROCZNIK GDAŃSKI, Gdańsk, 1927-39, 1954-; (A); (Local History Society - Gdańsk).
ROCZNIK ELBLĄSKI, Elbląg, 1957-; (A); (Local History Society - Elbing).
ROCZNIK GRUDZIĄDZKI, Grudziądz, 1959-; (A); (Local History Society - Grudziądz).
ROCZNIK HISTORII CZASOPISMIENNICTWA POLSKIEGO, Warsaw, 1962-; (A); (Press History).
ROCZNIK HISTORII SZTUKI, Wrocław-Warsaw, 1956-; (A); (Polish Academy of Sciences), (History of Art).
ROCZNIK JELENIOGORSKI, Jelenia Góra, 1959-; (A); (Local History Society - Jelenia Góra).
ROCZNIK KALISKI, Kalisz, 1959-; (A); (Local History Society - Kalisz).
ROCZNIK KOMISJI HISTORYCZNO-LITERACKIEJ, (PAN), Kraków, 1963-; (A); (History of Literature).
ROCZNIK KRAKOWSKI, Kraków, 1957-; (A); (Local History Society - Cracow).
ROCZNIK ŁÓDZKI, Łódź, 1958-; (A); (Local History - Lódź).
ROCZNIK LUBUSKI, Zielona Góra, 1959-; (A); (Local History Society - Zielona Góra).
ROCZNIK OLSZTYNSKI, Olsztyn, 1958; (A); (Local History Society - Olsztyn).

ROCZNIK PRZEMYSKI, Przemyśl, 1958-; (A); (Local History Society - Przemyśl).

ROCZNIK SĄDECKI, Nowy Sącz, 1957-; (A); (Local History Society - Nowy Sącz).

ROCZNIK WARSZAWSKI, Warsaw, 1960-; (A); (Local History Society - Warsaw).

ROCZNIK WROCŁAWSKI, Wrocław, 1957-; (A); (Local History Society - Wrocław).

ROCZNIKI DZIEJÓW SPOLECZNYCH I GOSPODARCZYCH, Poznań, 1965-; (A); (Social and Economic History).

ROCZNIKI HISTORYCZNE, Poznań, 1925-49; (A).

RUSSIAN REVIEW, New York, 1941-; (Q); (Russia Past and Present).

SCANDINAVIAN ECONOMIC HISTORY REVIEW, Copenhagen, 1953-;

SCANDOSLAVICA, Copenhagen, 1954-; (Association of Scandinavian Slavicists).

SLAVIA ANTIQUA, Poznań, 1948-; (Mediaevalia).

SLAVIA ORIENTALIS, Warsaw, 1951-; (Polish-Soviet relations).

SLAVIC AND EAST EUROPEAN JOURNAL, Bloomington, Indiana, 1957-.

SLAVIC AND EAST EUROPEAN STUDIES, (Etudes Slaves et Est-Européennes), Montreal, 1956-.

SLAVIC REVIEW, Washington, 1941-; (Q); (formerly American Slavic Review).

SLAVONICA, Nottingham, 1968-; (Irr.); Department of Slavonic Studies, University of Nottingham.

SLAVONIC AND EAST EUROPEAN REVIEW, London, 1922-; (Bi-A); (S.S.E.E.S., University of London).

SOBÓTKA, Wrocław, 1946-; (Q); (Silesian History).

SOVIET AND EASTERN EUROPEAN FOREIGN TRADE. A JOURNAL OF TRANSLATIONS, White Plains, N.Y., 1965; (Q).

SOVIET JEWISH AFFAIRS, London, 1971-; (Irr.).

SOVIET STUDIES, Oxford-Glasgow, 1949-; (Q); (Social and economic affairs of U.S.S.R.).

SPRAWOZDANIE ARCHEOLOGICZNE, Warsaw, 1948-; (Archaeology Abstracts).

SPRAWY MIĘDZYNARODOWE, Warsaw, 1948-; (International Affairs).

STUDIA HISTORIAE OECONOMICAE, Poznań, 1966-; (Economic History).

STUDIA HISTORICA SLAVO-GERMANICA, Poznań, 1973-; (Slav-German Relations).

STUDIA HISTORYCZNE, Cracow, 1967-; (Q); (Polish Academy of Science, Historical Institute).

STUDIA: MATERIAŁY DO DZIEJÓW WIELKOPOLSKI I POMORZA, Poznań, 1955-; (History of Wielkopolska and Pomerania).

STUDIA I MATERIAŁY Z DZIEJÓW ŚLĄSKA, Katowice, 1958-;

(Upper Silesian History).
STUDIA I MATERIAŁY DO HISTORII SZTUKI WOJENNEJ, Warsaw, 1954-; (Q); (Ministry of Defence), (Military History).
STUDIA MEDIEWISTYCZNE, Warsaw, 1958-; (Irr.); (Mediaeval Studies).
STUDIA Z DZIEJÓW Z.S.R.R. I ŚRODKOWEJ EUROPY, Warsaw, 1962-; (Polish Academy of Sciences), (Soviet and Central European History).
STUDIA I MATERIAŁY Z HISTORII KULTURY MATERIALNEJ, Wrocław-Warsaw, 1957-; (Polish Academy of Sciences), (History of Material Culture and Technology).
STUDIA SLĄSKIE, Opole, 1958-; (Irr.); (Silesian Studies).
STUDIA ŹRODŁOZNAWCZE, Warsaw, 1957-; (Historical Source Materials).
SUMMARY OF WORLD BROADCAST [EAST EUROPE], London, 1953-; (W); Polish radio translations.
SURVEY: A JOURNAL OF SOVIET AND EAST EUROPEAN STUDIES, London, 1961-; (Q); (Soviet, East European and Communist Affairs).
TEKI ARCHIWALNE, Warsaw, 1953-; (State Archives).
TEKI HISTORYCZNE, London, 1947-; (Q); (Polish Historical Society in Great Britain).
LES TEMPS MODERNES, Paris, 1945-; (M).
TRANSACTIONS OF THE ROYAL HISTORICAL SOCIETY, London, 1884-.
TRYBUNA, London, 1953-; (Q); (Kwartalnyk Polityczny)
UKRAINIAN QUARTERLY, New York, 1944-; (Q); (Ukrainian Congress Committee of America).
UKRAINIAN REVIEW, London, 1957-; (Association of Ukrainians in Great Britain).
UKRAINIAN REVIEW, Munich, 1955-; (Institute for Study of U.S.S.R.).
WIADOMOŚCI ARCHEOLOGICZNE, Warsaw, 1873-82, 1919-; (Archaeological News).
WIADOMOŚCI HISTORYCZNE, Warsaw, 1953-; (History Teaching).
WIADOMOŚCI NUMIZMATYCZNE, Cracow, 1892-1937; Warsaw, 1966-; (Numismatics).
WIENER ARCHIV FÜR GESCHICHTE DES SLAWENTUMS UND OSTEUROPAS, Graz, 1955-; (University of Vienna),(Slavonic and East European History).
WOJSKOWY PRZEGLĄD HISTORYCZNY, Warsaw, 1956-; (Q); (Institute of Military History.).
WORLD TODAY, London, 1935-; (Association for International Understanding).
ZAPISKI HISTORYCZNE, Toruń, 1945; (Pomerania).
ZARANIE ŚLĄSKIE, Katowice, 1908-; (Irr.); (Silesian Prehistory).
ZEITSCHRIFT FÜR OSTFORSCHUNG, Marburg, 1952-; (Eastern European Affairs).

ZESZYTY HISTORYCZNE, Paris, 1962-; (Kultura, Polish Literary Institute).
ZESZYTY NAUKOWE. (PRACE HISTORYCZNE), Series published by the Historical Institutes of each of the main universities in Poland - Łódź, Lublin, Kraków, Poznań, Toruń, Warsaw, Lublin (Maria Sktodowska-Curie).
Z POLA WALKI, Warsaw, 1947; (Communist Party Affairs).

APPENDIX II

GLOSSARY

(The following list contains some 50 terms frequently encountered in works on Polish History. As technical terms, they are essentially untranslatable and have to be used even in texts written in English or other foreign languages.)

AKCYZA: Purchase Tax (excise)
First imposed 1459 on alcohol, and from 1658 on all traded goods.

ARTYKUŁY HENRYKOWSKIE: Henrician Articles
A constitutional contract drawn up by the Sejm of 1573 for Henry Valois, and subsequently exacted from all kings of the **RZECZPOSPOLITA**. The various articles guaranteed the elective, constitutional and limited nature of the monarchy, and specifically enjoined the nobility to deny obedience to any king who disregarded their provisions.
See also: **ELEKCJA, KONFEDERACJA, PACTA CONVENTA**

ATAMAN: Cossack Chief
Leader of a small military detachment; sometimes applied to the **HETMAN** of the Registered Cossacks.
See also: **KOZAK, HETMAN**

CYRKUŁ: Circle, (Kreis (G))
Administrative areas established in Galicia from 1792.

DANINA: Contribution
Early medieval tax in kind; later, the rent in kind which serfs paid to their landlords.

DEPUTAT: Judicial Deputy
Officials elected by the dietines to supervise the work of the judges at the **TRYBUNAL**. Not to be confused with **POSEL**.

DYSUNITA: Orthodox
Name given to the Orthodox after the Union of Brest, 1596, to distinguish them from the 'Uniate' Greek Catholics united with Rome.
See also: **DYSYDENT**

DYSYDENT: Religious Dissident
Originally applied to Lutheran non-conformists, but eventually to all non-Catholic Christians, both Protestant and Orthodox, whose refusal to conform was both religious and political.
See also: **DYSUNITA**

EGZEKUCYA: 'Implementation of the laws' (Execution movement)
Programme of the nobility of the 16th century, demanding the return of crown lands leased to the magnates and the observance of laws restricting

the rights of office holders.
See also: **KRÓLEWSZCZYZNA**

ELEKCJA: Royal Election
A constitutional practice originating in mediaeval times and abolished by
the Constitution of 3 May 1791
(1) **ELEKCJA VIVENTE REGE:**   election of the King's successor
during his own lifetime, as in 1529;
(2) **ELEKCJA WOLNA** or **ELEKCJA VIRITIM** (General Election)
1573-1764, royal election conducted by the entire nobility of the
Rzeczpospolita, assembled on horseback at the Wola Field near Warsaw.

FOLWARK: Manorial Plantation/Estate
A landed estate specially organised for the production of a cash crop,
usually corn for export; a typical agrarian feature of the 16C and after,
closely connected with the growth of serf labour.
See also: **PAŃSZCZYZNA**

GILDIA: Merchants' Guild
14-19C, the commercial equivalent of artisans' **CECHA**. (Guild).

GRÓD: Fortified town
From 11C, administrative centres and bases for frontier defence, under
authority of a **KASZTELAN**.

GUBERNIA: Province
1837-1917, Administrative areas, each under a Governor, adopted in
Russian Poland.

HETMAN: Commander-in-Chief
Commander of royal troops. 1569-1795, there were two such
commanders: one **HETMAN WIELKI KORONNY**, (Grand Hetman of
the Crown) for the 'Korona', the other, **HETMAN WIELKI LITEWSKI**
(Grand Lithuanian Hetman), for the Grand Duchy, each with his own
deputy or **HETMAN POLNY**, (Field Hetman). From 1598, there also
existed a Hetman of the registered Zaporozhian Cossacks.
See also: **ATAMAN, KOZAK**

KANCLERZ: Chancellor
Head of the royal secretariat, responsible for foreign affairs and keeper of
the state seal and **METRYKA**.

KASZTELAN: Castellan
Until 13C, the royal official administering the **GRÓD** and the surrounding
territory; later, an honorary position with ex-officio membership of the
Senate.
See also: **GRÓD, SENAT, WOJEWODA**

KONFEDERACJA: Confederation
An established constitutional device invoked in times of crisis when
regular institutions proved incapable of maintaining the laws and
privileges of the state. The Right of Confederation, confirmed in 1573,
was invested in every citizen, and was invoked by towns seeking to

protect municipal rights, by nobles seeking to preserve their privileges, by soldiers trying to recover back pay, by the King, seeking to repel a foreign invader, or even by the entire **SEYM**, seeking to resist an attack on established procedures. Confederates formed an armed league, sworn to make decisions by majority voting and to fight together until its ends were achieved; provided that their aims were constitutional, they were not rebels in any sense, even if they opposed the King.
See also: **LIBERUM VETO, SEJM, ROKOSZ**

KONGRESÓWKA: Congress Kingdom of Poland
1815-31(64), a constitutional kingdom created by the Congress of Vienna, with the Tsar of Russia as hereditary monarch. After 1831, it declined into an administrative unit of the Russian Empire in all but name. After 1864 it lost even its name, being officially referred to as 'Privislinskiy Kray' (Vistulaland). In Russian terminology, it was popularly known as the 'Tsarstvo Pol'skoe'.
See also: **KRÓLEWSTWO.**

KONSTITUCJA: Statute
Name given to laws passed by the Sejm. From 1791, it referred to the basic law passed on 3 May 1791.

KORONA: Kingdom of Poland
The lands of the Crown of Poland, as distinct from those of the Grand Duchy of Lithuania, forming the larger part of the united **RZECZPOSPOLITA**, 1569-1792, and retaining its own laws, army and administration; Derived from the concept of 'Corona Regni' (L). **KRÓLEWSTWO** (P) means both 'Kingdom' and 'Kingship', but was not used in the same sense as Korona until the time of the **KONGRESÓWKA**
See also: **KRÓLEWSZCZYZA.**

KOZAK: Cossack
(i) in the **RZECZPOSPOLITA**, a free community of largely Tartar and Ruthenian origin, inhabiting the Lower Dnieper from the 15C onwards and providing paid infantry in time of war;
(ii) Registered Cossacks; as from 1578, Cossacks whose names appeared on the Cossack Register of full-time, indentured soldiers in the royal service;
(iii) A name given to Cossack-style light cavalry regiments 16-17C.

KRÓLEWSZCZYZNA: Crown Land/Royal Demesne
Landed properties of the Crown, in the 15-16C, frequently leased to magnates in lieu of services rendered; after 1590 under state control.
See also: **EGZEKUCJA, EKONOMIE**

LATYFUNDIUM: A large complex of landed properties, consisting of numerous separate estates administered centrally, often on an autarchic economic basis, in the interests of the magnatial proprietor; 17-18C, it frequently possessed the attributes of a state-within-the-state, (**PAŃSTEWKO**) including chancelry, bureaucracy and private army.
See also: **FOLWARK**

LIBERUM VETO:
An extreme application of the theory of unanimity, whereby any deputy could end the proceedings of the **SEYM** by a simple expression of dissent, (Veto = I deny), thereby invalidating all measures passed hitherto during the session; First invoked 1652, abandoned after 1764, and formally abolished in 1791.

ŁAN: Hide, 'Manse' (F)
A measure of land, varying between 16.7 and 25.8 hectares (40-60 acres) forming the basis of peasant labour dues and noble land tax; originally the 'holding' (or fief) of one household; cf. Lehn (G). In Poland, the 'Flemish łan' equalled c 17 hectares or 30 morgs, the 'Teutonic łan' c 25 hectares or 43 morgs.
See also: **MORGA**

MAGNATERIA: Magnates
A small but distinct class of pre-eminent families, possessing no formal or constitutional privileges, but whose immense landed wealth, patronage and control of hereditary offices set them apart from the rest of the nobility.
See also: **SZLACHTA, LATYFUNDIA**

MANDATARIUSZ:
18-19C, Galician land official, appointed by the **CYRKUŁ** to supervise functions previously directly exercised by landlords over peasants.

METRYKA: Statute-Book
The official register of royal decrees and Sejm constitutions as recorded by the Chancellor, kept separately in Lithuania, and in Mazovia to 1526.

MIECZNIK: Sword Bearer
A royal official originally charged with the King's arsenal, after 15C a court sinecure.

MORGA: (L), jutrzyna (P), morgen (G), 'ploughland'
A measure of land originally representing the area ploughed in 1 day by an ox-pair; roughly half a hectare.
See: **ŁAN**.

NEMINEM CAPTIVABIMUS: "We shall arrest no-one..."
Basic law of 1433, whereby the king undertook not to deprive the nobility of their freedom or property without previous trial and sentence.

NIHIL NOVI: "Nothing New"
Basic law of 1505, whereby the king undertook to promulgate no new laws without the agreement of the nobility in the Sejm.

OBRONA POTOCZNA: Continuous Defence
A standing army on the S.E. frontiers, fixed in 1527 at 2,000 men, and regularly expanded in time of war.

OLEDRZY: Hollanders
In origin, mediaeval Dutch peasant colonists who took over waste or devastated land, especially in Vistula Valley; from 17C, the name applied

to all tenant farmers owing rent as distinct from peasants owing labour services.

ORDYNACJA: Ordination, Majorat (F).
A legal institution ensuring that family estates would be inherited intact according to the principle of primogeniture; first applied in 1589 to the Zamoyski estates.

PACTA CONVENTA: Royal Covenant
A variable list of financial and political conditions added to the Henrician Articles to form the contract between the Sejm and the King-Elect.
See also: **ARTYKUŁY HENRYKOWSKIE, ELEKCJA**

PAŃSZCZYZNA: Labour Dues
The peasant's obligation to work for his lord, fixed in 1505 at 1 day per week, but rising in 18C to as much as 6 days.

POGLÓWNA: Poll Tax
A fixed, personal tax originally imposed in 14C on Jews and landless nobility, and in 16C on peasants.

PORADLNE: Corn tax, assessed on the **ŁAN.**

POSPOLITE RUSZENIE: Levée-en-masse
The feudal host, raised by a call-to-arms to all the nobility; after 15C, increasingly replaced by paid troops, but retained as a last line of defence. In 1794, the national forces applied it to peasants as well as nobles. Raised also 1806-7, 1830, 1863.

POSEŁ: Envoy, Representative
(i) Until 1792, and 1807-1830, a member of the Lower House of the Sejm, elected by the provincial noble assemblies, whose instructions he carried out; since 1921, elected by universal suffrage.
(ii) Diplomatic Minister below ambassadorial rank.
See also: **SEJM, SEJMIK, SZLACHTA**

ROKOSZ:
A sworn league, resembling the **KONFEDERACJA**, in which the entire nobility of the Rzeczpospolita was called together to resist the encroachment of King and magnates; its name was derived from the Rakos Field in Hungary where similar assemblies met.

RZECZPOSPOLITA: Commonwealth/Republic
Official title of the Polish-Lithuanian state as established in 1569; also used for the 'Rzeczpospolita Polska' (Polish Republic) 1918-39, and for the Polska Rzeczpospolita Ludowa, (Polish People's Republic) since 1944; always essentially republican in character, supposedly modelled on ancient Roman Republic as opposed to the Empire, where the king was more of a manager than a monarch.
See also: **ELEKCJA, ARTYKULY HENRYKOWSKIE, KORONA**

SANACJA: Clean government "Ablutionism"
Popular name for the movement of national unity as launched after 1926 to eliminate the corruption and graft of parliamentary government. Adapted

from the name of the Austrian reform movement of the 1920's.

SEJM [SEYM]:   Diet, Assembly
The legislative assembly of the Polish Kingdom and, after 1569, of the united **RZECZPOSPOLITA**; 15C, grew out of the practice of summoning noble representatives to royal council; 16C developed two chambers, Senate and Chamber of Deputies; 19-20C, name adopted for various parliamentary assemblies.
See also: **POSEL, SEJMIK, SENAT, LIBERUM VETO, ELEKCJA, SZLACHTA**

SEJMIK: Dietine
Assembly of nobles, meeting in each of the lands and provinces of the **RZECZPOSPOLITA**, and electing two envoys to the **SEJM**, and numerous local officials; 17-18C, assumed considerable financial and military functions, in response to the decline of the Sejm.
See also: **SEJM, POSEL, SZLACHTA, WOJEWODA**

SENAT: Senate
Upper House of the Sejm, consisting of King, Bishops and Chief Office-holders of the **RZECZPOSPOLITA**, successor to earlier Royal Council; exercised an executive function, including the appointment of 16 'RESIDENTS' from among its own members who assisted the King in day-to-day management of policy, especially in foreign affairs.
See also: **SEJM**

SOLTYS: Village Headman, Schultzheiss (G)
Often chosen from the peasantry, whose rents he collected and whose misdemeanours he punished; originally provided with land to support his independence; after 15C, at the disposition of the local magnate.
See also: **WÓJT**

STAROSTA: "Elder" (Sheriff)
Territorial administrators appointed by the King. From 14C, 3 types existed: 'Starosta Generalny, (Provincial Governor), Starosta Grodowy (Castle Governor) 'Starosta Niegrodowy', usually the lease-holder of Crown Lands; 1918-39, the chief official of a **STAROSTWO**, a sub-division of the **WOJEWÓDSTWO**.

SZLACHTA: (P) Nobility
(i) The hereditary political estate of old Polish society, deriving from the early 'nobiles' and 'milites', and from the mediaeval 'rycerstwo' (knighthood); from 1374, it enjoyed equal rights and privileges, and from 1569, provided the only 'citizens' of the Rzeczpospolita; dominated by the landowning interest, its sole qualification remained the possession of a motto and coat-of-arms; by 18C, it included over 10 percent of population, and embraced the magnat (magnate): the szlachta zamozna possessing land and serfs: the szlachta zagrodowa or zaścianki possessing land but no serfs: and the gołota, 'the rabble', possessing neither land nor serfs. To 15C, and from 1669, there also existed a 'half-noble' class, the ścierciałek (P) or scartabellus (L), who could not hold public office for

three generations.

(ii) In common usage, 'the Gentry', meaning the lesser nobility as distinct from the magnates.

See also: **MAGNATERIA**

TRYBUNAŁ: Assessorial Court
Courts of highest instance created in 1578 in Piotrków and later Lublin for the 'Korona', and at Wilno for the Grand Duchy. The courts were attended by deputies from the noble dietines who supervised the work of the judges.

See also: **DEPUTAT, SEJMIK**

ZŁOTY: "Piece of gold"
Popular name for gold ducat, either foreign, or Polish issued in 1320 and again in 1528; from 1564, a separate silver coin equivalent to the German thaler, *talar* (P), known as *srebrny złoty* (silver zloty), as opposed to the *czerwony złoty* (red zloty) or ducat: 1 zl = *30 groszy*; from 1663, the devalued 'Tymf' zloty = ¼ thaler = 30 gr.; 19-20C, basis for successive Polish monetary systems; from 1924, 1 zl. = 100 groszy.

WOJEWODA: Palatine
From 13C, the highest military and judicail official of the provinces, convenor of the **SEJMIK**, leader of the contingent to the **POSPOLITE RUSZENIE** and ex-officio member of the **SENAT**; 1919-50, chief official of the **WOJEWÓDSTWO** (Department/Voivodship)

See also: **STAROSTA**

WÓJT: Town Headman
Hereditary official, presiding over town corporations, often vassal of the local magnate; Commonly confused in later centuries with **SOŁTYS**.

APPENDIX III

GAZETTEER
For subject index, see the detailed table of Contents

1) Provinces

(Polish provincial and territorial names are frequently presented in an adjectival form - *Ziemia Krakowska* (Territory of Kraków), *Województwo Warszawskie* (Voivodship of Warsaw), *Księstwo Zatorskie* (Duchy of Zator) etc. This list is confined by necessity to Proper Nouns.)

Aukštota : see Żmudź

Barcia : see Prusy

Białoruś/Byelorussia: see Ruś

Cassubia (L) Ziemie Kaszubskie (P)
Area W of Vistula estuary in Pomerania, inhabited by Kashub population - a remnant of the ancient Pomeranians. No administrative significance.

Chełm Kholm (R)
District SE of Lublin, forming a separate Russian gubernia 1912-18, outside the Congress Kingdom. Not to be confused with the district of Chełmno, Culmerland (G).

Courland : see Kurlandia

Cujavia : see Kujawy

Dzikie Pola (P) "The Wild Plains"
15-18C, Lands W of Zaporoze and N of Oczaków (Odessa) virtually unsettled and unadministered owing to Tartar raids; nominally part of Lithuania, and 1569-1686 of the 'Korona', colonised in 18C by the Tsarist authorities as 'New Servia' and 'New Russia'.

Galicia (L) Galizien (G)
Popular name for the 'Kingdom of Galicia and Lodomeria" forming the Austrian Partition of Poland, 1777(95)-1918; derived from 'Halicz' and 'Włodzimierz'. 'Eastern Galicia', centred on Lwów and variously known as '*Małopolska Wschodnia*' (Eastern Little Poland) and as '*Western Ukraine*', comprised that part of former Austrian Galicia east of the so-called Curzon Line; occupied in 1919 by Poland but until 1925 not recognised by the Allied Governments: since 1939 part of the Ukrainian S.S.R. . Western Galicia was a name applied a) to the Austrian share of the Third Partition, 1795-1803, and b) to that part of former Austrian Galicia west of the Curzon Line, 1919-39. See: Małopolska, Ruś Czerwona.

Galindia : see Prusy

Great Poland : Wielkopolska

Inflanty (P), Livonia (L), Livland (G).
Baltic territory on Gulf of Riga, N of R. Dvina; to 1561, under German

163

Order of the Sword; 1561-1660 disputed between Poland, Sweden and Muscovy. The southern province of Latgalia remained a fief of the Rzeczpospolita, 1660-1772.

Jaćwiez (P) : see Prusy

Krajna, Literally "The Edge";
Territory to W of R. Notec, after 13C forming part of Wielkopolska.

Kujawy (P). Cujavia (L)
Ancient Polish province adjoining L. bank of Vistula in area of Bydgoszcz - Inowrocław - Brześć Kujawski; Prussian, 1772-1918.

Kurlandia (P), Kurland (G), Courland (Eng) (F)
Baltic territory to S of Gulf of Riga, centred on Lipawa, (Liepaja); together with Semigalia, formed a ducal fief of the Rzeczpospolita, 1561-1764(95).

Latgalia 'Polish Livonia'
SE province of Livonia, centred on Dunaburg; Polish 1561-1772.

Little Poland : see Małopolska
Lithuania : Litwa

Litwa (P) Lieutva (Lit) Litauen (G) Lithuania (Eng)
From an ethnic heartland comprising Samogitia and Aukštota, the Grand Duchy expanded rapidly southwards till c 1400 it reached the Black Sea; thereafter progressively reduced; 1385-1569 in personal union with Kingdom of Poland; 1569-1791 formed the lesser, eastern part of the dual Rzeczpospolita; 1793-5, incorporated into Russia, and 1940 into USSR; Independent Republic, 1918-40.

Litwa Środkowa 'Middle Lithuania': name given to Wilno area 1920-3 between its occupation by Polish Army and its incorporation into the Polish Republic.

Livonia : see Inflanty, Latgalia
Lubusz (P)
Territory formerly on both banks of the Oder, centred on Lubusz, Leibus (G). In Brandenburg, 1252-1945; recently revived as a synonym for the Wojewódstwo of Zielona Góra.

Małopolska (P), 'Little Poland' (Eng.), Petite Pologne (F), Kleinepolen (G), Polonia Minor (L)
Name used since 15C to distinguish this southerly province from the more ancient Wielkopolska, 'Great Poland'; it included Kraków, Sandomierz, Lublin, Lwów and the Ruthenian wojewodstwo. In Austrian times, the name 'Galicia' was preferred. 'Małopolska' was revived in 1918, but since 1945 refers exclusively to former 'Western Galicia'. See: Galicia.

Masuria : see Mazury
Mazovia : see Mazowsze

Mazowsze (P), Mazovia (L)
Principality on middle Vistula, centred on Warsaw, until 1526 a separate fief of the Polish Kingdom.

Mazury (P) Mazurien (G), Masuria (L).
Lakeland region in southern part of former East Prussia, incorporated into Poland, 1945.

Middle Lithuania : see Litwa Środkowa
Natangia : see Prusy
Neumark : see Nowa Marchia

Nowa Marchia (P), Neumark (G), 'New March'
A 13C extension of Brandenburg, E of the Oder along lower Warta between Western Pomerania and Wielkopolska.

Orawa (P), Orava (Cz)
Carpathian territory on river of same name; 1920, divided between Poland and Czechoslovakia.

Podhale
Mountain region in Tatra foothills, centred on Zakopane and Nowy Targ.

Podlasie (P), Podlachien (G)
Ancient Polish province lying on either side of R. Bug, E of Mazowsze, including Drohiczyn - Mielnik - Brześć Litewski

Podole (P) Podolia (L)
Ruthenian province on middle Dniester, centred on Kamieniec and including Tarnopol in W and Bracław in E; Polish 1366-1772(95).

Pokucie
Territory on upper Pruth, centred on Kolomiya; Polish 1531-1772.

Poland : see Polska

Polesie (P)
Geographical area on R. Pripet, centred on Pinsk, commonly known as 'Pripet Marshes'.

Polska (P), Pol'sha (R), Polen (G), Poland (Eng.), Pologne (F)
A name of widely varying application, originally connected with the Polanie, a West Slavonic tribe, 'people of the plains' whose territory formed the basis of the first Polish state; to 14C, applied to the area later known as Wielkopolska; 14-16C, coterminous with the lands of the Polish Kingdom; 1569-1795, correctly applied to the Korona alone, but frequently applied also to the united Rzeczpospolita; 19C, applied to Tsarist kingdom of Poland; since 1918, refers to the territory of the Polish Republic.

Pogezania : see Prusy
Pomerania : see Pomorze
Pomerelia : see Pomorze
Pomezania : see Prusy
Pommerellen (G) : see Pomorze
Pommern (G) : see Pomorze

Pomorze (P), Pomerania (L), Pommern (G)
Ancient Slavonic province, literally "By the sea", stretching along the

Baltic shore from Oder estuary to the Vistula, later divided between 'Western Pomerania' (Szczecin) and 'Eastern Pomerania' (Danzig). In German usage, following the Prussian conquest in 14C, Pomerania (Pommern) was confined to the western part, whilst the eastern part received the name of *Pomerelia, (Pommerellen)*. At various times, Eastern Pomerania was also known as '*Pomorze Gdanskie*' (Danzig Pomerania), '*Pomorze Nadwislanskie*' (Pomerania-by-the-Vistula), '*Royal Prussia*' (1454-1772), *Upper Prussia, West Prussia* (1772-1918) and '*The Polish Corridor*' (1920-39). Since 1945, the ancient attribution has been revived. See Prusy.

Posnania
Popular name for the Duchy of Posen (Poznań), 1815-48, which, within the Kingdom of Prussia, was largely coterminous with the former province of Wielkopolska.

Prussia : see Prusy

Prusy (P), Preussen (G), Prussia (Eng.) Borussia (L) Prusse (F)
The country of the Bruzi or Pruthenians, lying between the Vistula and the Niemen, conquered in 13C by Teutonic knights, who extended the name of 'Prussia' to all their possessions. Apart from Galindia and Sasinia which disappeared earlier, Ancient Prussia had 9 districts each named after a corresponding Baltic tribe: namely *Sambia* (Koenigsberg), *Warmia* - Ermeland (G) (Braniewo, Frombork, Lidzbard), *Pomezania* (Kwidzyn), *Pogezania* (Elblag), *Natangia, Nadrowia, Barcia, Skalovia*, and *Sudovia*, (Jaćwiez) (P). After 1454, the western part of the Teutonic State, comprising Eastern Pomerania and now joined to Poland, took the name of *Prusy Królewskie* ('Royal Prussia'); in 1525, the remaining, eastern part, secularised as a ducal fief of Poland, was known as *Prusy Ksiązece* (Ducal Prussia). The Kingdom of Prussia, 1701-1918, was made up from the juncture of Ducal Prussia, independent since 1657, with the Electorate of Brandenburg; after 1772, when it also absorbed Royal Prussia from Poland, two provinces were created, respectively 'West-Preussen (West Prussia) and Ostpreussen (East Prussia), the former corresponding to Royal Prussia or Eastern Pomerania, the latter to Ducal Prussia. Since 1945, Prussia has ceased to exist. See also: Pomorze.

Ruś (Ruthenia)
An elusive term, variously indicating the whole or part of the lands of the East Slavs, i.e. the Great Russians, Byelorussians and Ukrainians; traditionally, to 13C, applied to the state of 'Kiev Ruś. In later Polish usage, it referred to the non-Lithuanian parts of the Grand Duchy and to the non-Polish parts of the *Korona*, but never to Muscovy. In Muscovite usage, it referred to all the East Slav lands, progressively united under the aegis of *Rossiya* (Russia). In Austrian usage, it referred to the non-Polish parts of Galicia, in Hungarian usage to the non-Slovakian part of Transcarpathia - *Podkarpacká Ruš*, (Subcarpathian Ruthenia) in pre-1939 Czechoslovakia. See also: Ukraina
Bialoruś (P), Byelorussia (R), 'White Ruthenia' or, since 1772 'White

Russia'. A name current since 16C, together with 'Ruś Czarna', to designate the non-Lithuanian areas of the Grand Duchy; included the wojewodstwa of Minsk, Polock, Witebsk and Mohylew.

Ruś Czarna (P), 'Black Ruthenia'
1569-1772, included wojewodstwa of Nowogródek, Troki, Brześć. After incorporation into Russia, the term merged with 'Byelorussia'.

Ruś Czerwona (P) 'Red Ruthenia'
SW lands of ancient Kiev Ruś between the San and the Zbrucz; 1340 incorporated into Poland; included territories of Lwów, Halicz, Przemysl, Chełm and Belz; largely coterminous with the modern term, Eastern Galicia: annexed by USSR, 1939.

Samogitia : see Zmudź

Semigalia
Eastern area of Courland, centred on Mitawa (Mitau (G)).

Silesia : see Śląsk

Spisz (P) Spiś (Cz) Zips (G)
Small Carpathian territory centred on Poprad, given in dowry to Hungary in 1108, recovered in part in 1412, taken by Austria in 1769, and divided in 1920 between Poland and Slovakia.

Śląsk (P) Schlesien (G) Silesia (L)
Ancient Polish duchy on upper and middle Oder, centred on Wrocław (Breslau), incorporated respectively by Bohemia from 1335, by Austria from 1526, and by Prussia from 1742. Under Prussia, two provinces were created *Niederschlesien*, Dolny Śląsk (P), 'Lower Silesia' round Breslau, and *Oberschlesien*, Górny Śląsk (P), 'Upper Silesia', round Oppeln. In 1921, the southern part of Upper Silesia, awarded to Poland, became the *Województwo Śląskie* centred on Katowice. In 1945, the whole of Silesia returned to Poland. In 19C Austrian usage, 'Silesia' referred to the Austrian Duchy of Teschen and Troppau, centred on Teschen (Cieszyn (P)).

Ukraina (Ukraine)
Literally "land at the edge", presumably of Kiev Ruś or of Christendom, later of the Rzeczpospolita, and eventually of Russia; In Polish usage 1569-1772, included the województwa of Kiev, Czernihów and Bracław, but not Red Ruthenia. Left-bank Ukraine E of Dnieper, with Kiev, was lost in 1667, the right-bank in 1772. In 18C, following annexation by Russia and the introduction of Muscovite terms such as 'Little Russia' and 'New Russia', the Ruthenian population adopted the name of 'Ukrainians' to distinguish themselves from the Great Russians. See *Ruś*.

Warmia, Ermeland (G) : see Prusy

Wielkopolska : see Polska

Wołyn Volhynia (L), Wolhynien (G)
Ruthenian Province, centred on Włodzimierz (Vladimir), lying between Polesie and Podolia; 1366, divided between the Grand Duchy and the Kingdom; 1569-1772 in the *Korona*.

GAZETTEER

Zaporoze (P)
Literally "Beyond the Rapids"; Lower valley of Dnieper, settled in 15C by Cossack communities; to 1569 in Grand-Duchy, 1569-1686 in Korona.

Żmudź (P) Žemaičia (Lit.) Samogitia (L)
literally "the lower land" of ethnic Lithuania, centred on Klajpeda (Memel), as distinct from Aukštota, "the upper land", centred on Vilnius (Wilno). See *Litwa*.

See also: Batowski (**0064**) which provides the most detailed analysis of the history of Polish place names.

2) PLACE NAMES

(The present-day form, usually Polish, is given in capitals.)

G - German Spelling; P - Polish; R - Russian

Adelnau (G) - ODOŁANÓW
Adlerhorst (G) - ORŁOWO
Agnetendorf (G) - JAGNIĄTKÓW
Allenstein (G) - OLSZTYN
Annaberg (G) - CHAŁUPKI
Auschwitz (G) - OŚWIĘCIM
AUGUSTÓW - Augustov (R)

BABIMOST - Bomst (G)
Bad Langenau (G) - DŁUGOPOLE ZDRÓJ
BAGRATIONOVSK (R) - Preussish-Eylau (G) - Iławka (P)
BALTIISK (R) - Pillau (G) - Piława (P)
BAUTZEN (G) - Budziszyn (P)
Belgard (G) - BIAŁOGARD
BIAŁYSTOK - Byelostok (R)
BIELSKO - Bielitz (G)
BRANIEWO - Braunsberg (G)
Breslau (G) - WROCŁAW
BREST - LITOVSK (R) - Brześć-Litewski (P)
Bromberg (G) - BYDGOSZCZ
BYTOM - Beuthen (G)

CHAŁUPKI - Annaberg (G)
CHEŁM - Kholm (R)
CHEŁMNO - Culm, Kulm (G)

CHORZÓW - Königshütte (G), Królewska Huta (P) 1921-34.
CIECHANÓW - Zichenau (G)
CIESZYN (P) - TEŠIN (Cz.) - Teschen (G) - Teshen (Eng.)
Cracow (Eng.) - KRAKÓW
CZĘSTOCHOWA - Tschenstochau (G)

Danzig (G) - GDAŃSK
DAUGAVPILS (Lat.) - Dvinsk (R) - Dzwińsk, Dyneburg (P) -
  Dunaburg (G)
DĘBLIN - Ivanogorod (R)
Dirschau (G) - TCHEW
DOBRODZIEŃ - Guttentag (G)
DZIAŁDOWO - Soldau (G)

EŁK - Lyk (G)

Falkenberg (G) - NEIMODLIN
Fellhammer (G) - KUŹNICE SLĄSKIE
Frankenstein (G) - ŻĄBKOWICE

GDAŃSK - Danzig (G)
GDYNIA - Gdingen (G), Gotenhafen, 1940-5
Glatz (G) - KŁODZKO
Gleiwitz (G) - GLIWICE
GNIEŹNO - Gnesen (G)
GOMEL (R) - Homel (P)
Graudenz (G) - GRUDZIĄDZ
GRUNWALD (P) - Tannenberg (G)
Grunberg (G) - ZIELONA GÓRA

Halicz (P) - GALICH (R)
Hindenburg (G) - ZABRZE
Hirschberg (G) - JELENIA GÓRA
Humań (P) - UMAN' (R)

IŁAWA - Deutsch-Eylau (G)
Iławka (P) - BAGRATIONOVSK (R)
INOWROCŁAW - Inowrozlaw (G) Hohensalza, 1940-45
Ivangorod (R) - DEBLIN
IVANOFRANKOVSK (R) - Stanisławów (P)

JELENIA GÓRA - Hirschberg (G)
JELGAVA (Lat) - Mitawa (P) - Mitau (G)
JĘDRZEJÓW - Andreyev (R)

KALININGRAD (R) - Koenigsberg (G) - Królewiec (P)
KAMIEŃ POMORSKI - Cammin-in-Pommern (G)

KARTUZY - Karthaus (G)
KATOWICE - Kattowitz (G) - Stalingród (P), 1953-8
KAUNAS (Lit.) - Kovno (R) - Kowno (P)
KĘTRZYN - Rastenburg (G)
KĘTY - Kenty, Liebenwerde (G)
KIEV (R) - Kijów (P)
KLUCZBORK - Dreuzberg (G)
KŁODZKO - Glatz (G)
KOŁOBRZEG - Kolberg (G)
KOSZALIN - Koslin (G)
Königshütte - CHORZÓW
KRAKÓW - Krakau (G) - Cracovia (L) - Cracow (Eng.) - Cracovie (F)
KROSNO - Crossen
Kulm (R) - CHEŁMNO
KWIDZYN - Marienwerder (G)

Lauenburg (G) - LĘBORK
Leslau (G) - WLOCLAWEK
LESZNO - Lissa (G)
LIDZBARK WARMIŃSKI - Heilsberg (G)
LIDZBARK WIELKOPOLSKI - Lautenberg (G)
L'VIV (Ukr.) - Lvov (R) - Lwów (P)
   Leopolis (L) - Lemberg (G) - Léopol (F)
Lyck (G) - ELK
ŁANCUT - Landshut (G)
ŁÓDŹ - Lodz (G), Litzmannstadt, 1940-45

MALBORK - Marienburg (G)
Marienwerder (G) - KWIDZYN
MIŃSK MAZOWIECKI - Novominsk (R)
MODLIN - Novogeorgiyevsk (R)

Neufahrwasser (G) - NOWY PORT
Neu-Sandez (G) - NOWY SĄCZ
NIEDZICA - Nedec (Hung) to 1918
NYSA - Neisse (G)

Oder (G) - ODRA
ODOŁANOW - Adelnau (G)
OLSZTYN - Allenstein (G)
OPOLE - Oppeln (G)
OŚWIECIM - Auschwitz (G)

PIOTRKÓW TRYBUNALSKI - Pyotrokov (R)
Pless (G) - PSZCZYNA
Posen (G) - POZNAŃ
PRZEMYSL - Peremysh' (R)

PUCK - Putzig (G)
PUŁAWY - Novaya Aleksandriya (R)

RACIBÓRZ - Ratibor (G)
RADOMSK - Novoradomsk (R)
Rastenberg (G) - KĘTRZYN (P) - Rastembork (P)
RZESZÓW - Reichshof (G)

SIEDLCE - Sedlets (R)
SIERADZ - Seradz (R)
SŁUPSK - Stolp (G)
Soldau (G) - DZIAŁDOWO
Stalinogród (1952-6) - KATOWICE
Stanisławów - IVANOFRANKOVSK (R)
Stettin (G) - SZCZECIN
ŚWINOUJŚCIE - Swinemünde (G)

TCHEW - Dirschau (G)
TERNOPOL' (R) - Tarnopol (P)
Teschen (G) - CIESZYN
Thorn (G) - TORUŃ
Tschenstoshau - CZESTOCHOWA

VENTSPILS (Lat.) - Windawa (P)
VILNIUS (Lit.) - Vilna (R) - Wilno (P) - Wilna (G)

WALBRZYCH - Waldenburg (G)
WARSZAWA - Warschau (G) - Varshava (R) - Warsaw (Eng.)-
  Varsovie (F)
Wilno (P) - VILNIUS (Lit.)
WISŁA - Visla (R) - Vistula (Eng.) (L) - Weichsel (G)
WŁOCŁAWEK - Leslau (G)
Włodzimierz (P) - VLADIMIR VOLYN'SKII (R)
WROCŁAW - Breslau (G) - Vratislav (pre-14 Century)

ZABRZE - Hindenburg (G) 1915-45
ZAMOŚĆ - Zamost'e (R)
ZGORZELEC (P) - GÖRLITZ (G)
Zichenau (G) - CIECHANÓW
Zwiahel (P) - Novograd Volyn'skii (R)
ŻYWIEC - Saybusch (G)
ZHITOMIR (R) - Żytomierz (P)
ZIELONA GÓRA - Grünberg (G)

INDEX

INDEX